D1145886

Martyrs & Mystics

Martyrs & Mystics

ED GLINERT

Collins

Dedication

For John Nicholson, Cecilia Boggis, and
Dave and Pauline Hammonds

Collins
A division of HarperCollins*Publishers*
77-85 Fulham Palace Road, London W6 8JB

www.bookarmy.com

1

A catalogue record for this book is available from the British Library

ISBN 978 000 728642 3

Set in Minion by M.A.T.S. Southend-on-Sea, Essex

Printed and bound in Great Britain by Clays Ltd, St Ives plc

Picture credits:

Moses and the Burning Bush – Blake © Stapleton Collection/Corbis; Execution of John Rogers at /Smithfield © City of London/Heritage Images; Fire of London © Hulton Archive/Getty Images; Fire of London © Hulton Archive/Getty Images; The Gunpowder plot © Bettmann/Corbis; Monument © Davidgarry, Dreamstime.com; The Gordon Riots © Mary Evans Picture Library; Hampton Court Palace © Aida Tanaka, Dreamstime.com; John Nichols Thom © Mary Evans Picture Library; Canterbury Cathedral © London Aerial Photo Library, Ian/London Aerial; Pope-burning ceremonies, Lewes © Luke Macgregor/Reuters/Corbis; Children of God © Bettmann/Corbis; Matthew Hopkins, witchfinder general © Mary Evans Picture Library; John Wesley © Mary Evans Picture Library; Mary Queen of Scots at Fotheringay Castle © Bettmann/Corbis; Clifford's Tower © Mikule, Dreamstime.com; Whitby abbey ruins © Ian Wilson, Dreamstime.com; Lichfield Cathedral © Geoff Pickering, Dreamstime.com; Mother Shipton © Mary Evans Picture Library; Glastonbury Tor © Stephen Inglis, Dreamstime.com; Rosslyn Chapel – apprentice pillar © EE Image Library/Heritage Images; Battle of Boyne © Bettmann/Corbis; Shankill Road, Belfast © Jeff J Mitchell/Reuters/Corbis

Contents

ACKNOWLEDGEMENTS

This book was conceived with the help of my former editor at HarperCollins, Ian Metcalfe, my current editor at the same publishers, Sam Richardson, and my agent, Faith Evans. Without their tireless enthusiasm the project would have been as stillborn as Joanna Southcott's Shiloh. Many thanks are also due to Ruth Roff and Elizabeth Munns at HarperCollins, John Nicholson, for use of his extensive library, Cecilia Boggis, Dave and Pauline Hammonds, Clive Bettington, Bela Cunha, Mark Gorman, Sue Grimditch, Graeme and Kathy McIver, Anne Orsi, Sheila Redclift, Tim Richard, Adele, Juliet and Simon Rose, David Stone, Esther Whyatt, and of course Katy Walsh Glinert who may now understand the difference between the Muggletonians and the Sandemanians.

INTRODUCTION

It all started to get confusing when God handed Moses the Ten Commandments on Mount Sinai. The commandments began: 'I am the Lord thy God . . . Thou shalt have no other gods before me.'

Did people generally concur with this? Not quite. John Wroe announced in 1825 in the grim mill town of Ashton-under-Lyne, to the east of Manchester, that he was god. Ashton would duly become a holy city, the New Jerusalem, and Wroe built four 'holy' gateways while awaiting the imminent return of Jesus Christ, God's chosen one, presumably through one of them. He was still waiting when he died in 1863. It is not known whether Jesus did ever appear in Ashton.

Then there was the Revd John Hugh Smyth-Pigott. He was a charming Dubliner who in 1902 proclaimed his own divinity from the Ark of the Covenant, an extravagant temple he built in Lower Clapton, London. The Church of England defrocked Smyth-Pigott but he retorted: 'I am God. It does not matter what they do.' He probably wasn't and it probably did.

But let's go back to the story of Moses, receiver of the Ten Commandments in biblical times. Barely had he received the tablets than he took them down from the mountain to the Children of Israel, only to find that while he was gone they had made themselves a new god – a Golden Calf no less – and were dancing about ecstatically in front of it.

He broke the tablets and had to go back up the mountain to receive a new set. Two tablets of stone, or possibly not. According to Kabbalah legend, the Ten Commandments were not presented on two gravestone-like slabs, as depicted in countless paintings and book illustrations, but on two tiny jewels, possibly sapphires, more likely diamonds, which glowed when placed on the Breastplate of Judgment. If so, how did Moses break them? Diamonds are the hardest substance known to man, and even sapphires are not easy to destroy. And what happened to those sapphires?

So where does reality triumph over myth here? *Martyrs and Mystics* offers no definite explanation but it does attempt to recount such bizarre stories and legends – in Britain if not the Holy Land. Not that Britain hasn't been seen as being holy in its own right down the ages – by William Blake, Christopher Wren, George Fox, John Wroe – but you'll have to dip inside to find out how and why.

Buildings or sites which no longer exist are denoted by a different font.

CHAPTER 1

LONDON

The capital has been host to all the major disputes and upheavals in the nation's religious past. Here the shifts and schisms that have changed the history of England have been played out: from the break with Rome in the 1530s to the Glorious Revolution of the 1680s, and from the expulsion of the Jews in 1290 to the anti-Catholic Gordon Riots of 1780.

Here too a myriad of sects and cults have taken shape – the Freemasons, the Rosicrucians, the Hermetic Order of the Golden Dawn, the Peculiar People of Plumstead – driven by a succession of mavericks and mystics, as colourful as they were obscure. There was Thomas Tany, who in 1654 claimed to be Theauraujohn, High Priest of the Jews, about to rebuild the Temple in Jerusalem with himself in charge. And John Robins, a mid-seventeenth-century mystic from Moorfields, who failed in his plan to take nearly 150,000 followers to the Holy Land, feeding them solely on dry bread, raw vegetables and water. In 1814, more farcically, there was Joanna Southcott, who claimed she would give birth to Shiloh, the biblical child who, according to the Book of Revelation, was to 'rule all the nations with a rod of iron'.

Such drama continues to take place in the capital. As recently as 1985 the world's press gathered at a Brick Lane curry house to meet the Lord Maitreya (or Christ, the Imam Mahdi or Krishna according to the different religions), who may or may not have appeared – depending as always on one's faith. In 2008, when a member of the congregation at St Mary's church, Putney, disrupted the service shouting out his views on the controversy over gay clergy, he was simply another manifestation of the age-old unsolvable conundrum of what to do when one's own views differ from those of the next person.

Key events

616 **A fisherman has a vision of St Peter on Thorney Island and founds what becomes Westminster Abbey.**

1382 **The Archbishop of Canterbury's council meets at Blackfriars monastery to denounce John Wycliffe's religious doctrines and his pioneering translation of the Bible into English.**

1401 **The first of many martyrs to meet his death at Smithfield is William Sawtrey, priest and follower of the Bible translator John Wycliffe.**

1534 **Henry VIII declares himself supreme head of the English Church and orders that all references to the Pope be removed from prayer books.**

1535 **Thomas More, one of Henry VIII's leading aides, is executed at Tower Hill for opposing the king's decision to make himself head of the Church.**

1604 **From the Hampton Court Conference comes the greatest of all Bible translations – the King James or Authorised Version.**

1666 **The Fire of London destroys the City. Catholics are blamed, and a Frenchman, supposedly an agent of the Pope, is hanged (wrongly) for starting the blaze.**

1678 **One of the most infamous religious conspiracies in London history, the Popish Plot, unfolds after the body of Sir Edmund Berry Godfrey, a well-known Protestant, is found on Primrose Hill impaled on his own sword.**

1688–9 **The Bill of Rights ends the Stuart notion of the 'Divine Right' of kings to rule. From now on no monarch can be or marry a Catholic.**

1738 **John Wesley experiences an epiphany in Aldersgate that leads to the birth of a new creed: Methodism.**

1780 **The worst mob violence ever to hit London – the Gordon Riots – erupts on 2 June as the capital demonstrates against parliamentary attempts to grant Catholics further civil rights.**

1791 **The latest Catholic Relief Act gives Catholics the right to worship in public again.**

1865 **William Booth founds the Salvation Army after hearing two missionaries preach at an open-air meeting in the East End.**

1858 **The Jewish Relief Act allows Jews full civil rights, including being able to sit as MPs without having to take the Christian oath.**

1976 **The Jamme Masjid opens in Spitalfields – the only building in the West to have been church, synagogue and mosque.**

The Gordon Riots

London's most violent religious disturbance was a week of mayhem in June 1780 which resulted in hundreds of deaths and the burning and looting of much of the capital in the wake of government plans to allow Catholics greater civil rights. The protest became known as the Gordon Riots because the mob was whipped into a frenzy by Lord George Gordon, head of the Protestant Association.

Two years previously, the Catholic Relief Act had been passed, banning any further persecution of Catholic priests. This followed negotiations by the government with a group of Catholic gentry who agreed to drop Stuart claims to the throne and to deny the civil jurisdiction of the Pope. Catholics were still, however, banned from holding important public posts in teaching and the army, though by 1780 the government, concerned at the depleted number of troops available to fight in the American War of Independence, considered changing the law to allow Catholics to join the army.

On Friday 2 June 1780 Parliament met to debate the proposals. When Lord Gordon failed to win approval for his anti-Catholic petition by 192 votes to 6, the mob went on the rampage. Spoiling for a fight, they headed for the only places in London where Catholics could worship openly – two chapels in Soho and Holborn. They ransacked the buildings, smashed the doors and windows, and burnt prayer books and religious artefacts in the street.

By noon the next day it appeared the disturbance was over, but at three in the afternoon soldiers escorting a group of thirteen men to Bow Street Magistrates Court were pelted with mud. In the slum district of Moorfields the houses of Irish immigrants (mostly Catholic) were attacked. As the violence continued on the Sunday, householders chalked up the warning 'No Popery' on their doors. The Italian parents of the clown Joseph Grimaldi daubed on their door 'No religion', while in the Jewish ghetto around Houndsditch houses were chalked with the words: 'This is the home of a true Protestant.'

The following day riot leaders marched on Lord Gordon's house in Welbeck Street, Marylebone, to bring him trophies of relics ransacked from the looted chapels. Tuesday 6 June was the worst day of mayhem. A hugh mob swarmed through Seven Dials heading for Newgate Prison. One who joined it en route was the painter-poet William Blake, who had seen the crowd from his studio window and had joined it out of curiosity. The rioters attacked the gaol with sledgehammers and pickaxes, and prisoners poured out, though some stayed put, at a loss of where to go, until the rioters set fire to the building.

Trouble continued for the rest of the week, at the end of which 285 people were dead and 200 wounded. Although Lord Gordon was charged with high treason and sent to the Tower, where he languished for eight months, he was cleared of blame. Remarkably he later forsook the Anglican Church for Judaism, changed his name to Israel Abraham George Gordon, and died at the age of forty-two in Newgate Prison where, ironically, he had been incarcerated for libelling Marie Antoinette.

Bermondsey

ST THOMAS A WATERING, Old Kent Road at Albany Road

John Penry was publicly hanged in 1593 at this ancient site, where streams cross the ancient London to Dover road, and which was mentioned by Chaucer in *The Canterbury Tales*, for campaigning too vigorously for Welsh religious independence and a Welsh Bible. When Penry acquired a printing press John Whitgift, the Archbishop of Canterbury, was most vexed and had Penry arrested and imprisoned. He escaped to Scotland but eventually chose to return to London to continue campaigning for religious teaching in Wales to be conducted in Welsh. He was arrested in Islington in March 1593 and sentenced to death, without being allowed to see his wife or four daughters – Deliverance, Comfort, Safety and Sure-Hope.

→ Canterbury Cathedral, p. 142

Blackheath

During the Peasants' Revolt of 1381 John Ball preached a sermon here on the main route from Kent into London in which he thundered:

What right do they have to rule over us? Why do they deserve to be in authority? If we all came from Adam and Eve what proof do they have that they are better than we? Therefore why should we labour for them while they live in luxury?

From his preaching came the rhyme that was soon upon the lips of many: 'When Adam delved and Eve span, who was the gentleman?' However, in the rampage which followed, the mob dragged Simon Sudbury, the Archbishop of Canterbury, from the Tower of London and killed him.

Bloomsbury

JAMES PIERREPONT GREAVESS ADDRESS, 49 Burton Street
Greaves was an early nineteenth-century educationalist and theologian who promoted piety among his followers while urging them to embrace the latest fashionable dietary and sexual fads

such as vegetarianism, water-drinking and celibacy. Greaves was later described by G. J. Holyoake, pioneer of the co-operative movement, as 'the most accomplished, pleasant and inscrutable mystic this country has produced'. In the 1830s he opened a school on Ham Common near Richmond, Surrey, based on the healthy notion that 'Pure air, simple food, exercise and cold water are more beneficial to man than any churches, chapels, or cathedrals.' Thomas Carlyle, the great essayist and historian, was not convinced and denounced Greaves as a 'humbug . . . few greater blockheads broke the world's breads in my day'.

TEMPLE OF THE OCCULT, 99 Gower Street

Frank Dutton Jackson, a fake cleric, and his wife, Editha, set up a Temple of the Occult in the heart of Georgian Bloomsbury in the early years of the twentieth century. Here Jackson, describing himself as Theo Horos, debauched hundreds of young girls in mock religious ceremonies conducted under low lights in a haze of incense smoke. He told one girl, Daisy Adams, he was Jesus Christ and that she would give birth to a divine child. He and Editha, who claimed to be the illegitimate daughter of Ludwig I of Bavaria, were eventually prosecuted. They were tried at the Old Bailey where Jackson pleaded: 'Did Solomon not have 300 legal wives and 600 others?' He was nevertheless convicted of raping and procuring girls for immoral purposes.

The *Spectator* magazine occupied the building from the 1920s to 1975, and it now belongs to the Catholic chaplaincy.

→ The Hermetic Order of the Golden Dawn, p. 71

UNIVERSITY CHURCH OF CHRIST THE KING, Byng Place

This superb Gothic revival church was built in 1851–4 in the medieval Early English architectural style for the Catholic Apostolic sect. Its first preacher, Edward Irving, was expelled from a nearby Presbyterian church for encouraging the congregation to 'speak in tongues' – talk spontaneously in ancient biblical languages. In the church basement is a room filled with ceremonial cloaks, including one reserved for the return of Jesus Christ.

Canonbury

CANONBURY TOWER, Canonbury Place

This ancient and unusual-looking brick tower, north London's oldest building, was where Thomas Cromwell, Henry VIII's chief minister and vicar-general, organised the dissolution of the monasteries in the 1530s.

In April 1535 the authorities ordered 'all supporters of the Pope's jurisdiction' were to be arrested. On 20 April they arrested the priors of Charterhouse, Beauvale and Axholme, and Dr Richard Reynolds of the Bridgettine monastery of Syon near Brentford. One of Cromwell's agents discovered that the abbot there had persuaded a nun, to whom he was confessor, to submit her body to his pleasure 'and thus persuaded her in confession, making her believe that whensoever and as oft as they should meddle together, if she were immediately after confessed by him, and took of him absolution, she should be clear forgiven of God'.

Those arrested were charged with denying that the king was the supreme head of the English Church and were sentenced to death. A month later they were hanged at Tyburn. Later that year came the more infamous executions of Bishop Fisher and Thomas More (→ p. 52) for refusing to accept the Oath of Supremacy. At the end of the decade, with the dissolution of the religious houses practically complete, the king handed the Canonbury Manor to Cromwell. Unfortunately, the vicar-general had only a year to live: he was executed on trumped-up charges of treason in 1540.

In the eighteenth century Canonbury Tower and the

surrounding estate were rebuilt in a restrained but elegant Palladian style to the exact dimensions of Solomon's Temple, for reasons unknown but possibly connected with the earlier sojourn of polymath Francis Bacon – philosopher, science pioneer, Lord Chancellor and Rosicrucian – who worked there at the end of the sixteenth century.

In 1795 Richard Brothers, the false messiah who prophesied that he would lead the Israelites back to Palestine from across the world, was imprisoned in the tower for eleven years for sedition.

Canonbury Tower is now a Masonic research centre.

→ Richard Brothers, Prince of the Hebrews, p. 75.

The Rosicrucians

An ultra-secret, international, quasi-religious body, the Rosicrucians claim to possess mystical wisdom handed down through the generations. They have strong connections with Canonbury Tower, which some believe to be the location of their secret international headquarters. The group may have been founded by Christian Rosenkreutz, a fifteenth-century mystic who supposedly travelled extensively in the East before returning to Europe armed with the entire body of knowledge that would be useful to the world, the knowledge handed by God to Noah before the Flood and then to Moses on Mount Sinai – 'the knowledge that was, the knowledge that is, the knowledge that will be'.

Rosenkreutz then handed this information to German alchemists based in Kassel, choosing that city as it was the most scientifically advanced in the world at that time, and they in turn cryptically outlined their findings in a series of pamphlets published early in the seventeenth century which spoke of a secret brotherhood working for the good of mankind.

In 1622 the Rosicrucians announced themselves to the world, when one morning the citizens of Paris awoke to find the walls of their city covered with posters bearing the following message:

We, the deputies of the principal College of the Brethren of the Rose Cross (Rosicrucians) are among you in this town, visibly and invisibly, through the grace of the Most High to whom the hearts of all just men are turned, in order to save our fellow-men from the error of death.

In England Francis Bacon, James I's Lord Chancellor and the foremost scholar of his day, worked on the sect's findings at Canonbury Tower, while all over Europe leading philosophers, scientists, mystics and scholars waited for an invitation to join the organisation. When none came – officially – they formed their own Rosicrucian societies, which have continued to the present day. But which are the real Rosicrucians and which are imposters no one is willing to assert.

The City

The ancient heart of London, just one square mile in size, is the setting for the country's main cathedral, St Paul's. During the 1666 Fire of London eighty-six churches were destroyed here. Although over the subsequent centuries the City's population has withered away the area still has the greatest concentration of religious buildings in England – thirty-nine churches and one synagogue, Bevis Marks, Britain's oldest. In 1847 Lionel de Rothschild was elected MP for the City of London but was unable to take his seat as new MPs were required to take the Christian oath, something which as a Jew he refused to do. A compromise wasn't reached until 1858.

ALDERSGATE, **Aldersgate Street at Gresham Street**

Aldersgate was one of twelve traditional gates of the City of London (along with Aldgate, Moorgate, Newgate and others). Each represented one of the tribes of Israel, as medieval leaders thought this would give the city divine legitimacy. In 1603 when James VI of Scotland journeyed to London for the first time to take the throne as James I of England he entered through Aldersgate. The king later had the structure rebuilt with statues of Old Testament prophets Samuel and Jeremiah, and accompanying biblical texts. These told his subjects he was God's anointed monarch, a direct descendant of King David, and that the British were the chosen people, descendants of the lost tribes of Israel and now holders of Christianity's mantle, who at the Lord's second appearance would gather together as one family from whom 'the elect' would be chosen.

→ Creation of the King James Bible, p. 59

Sacred City

As with many ancient cities, London's early town planners were guided by the 'sacred' measurements of the Bible, which supposedly give cities divine protection. They are based on the Old Testament unit of the cubit, the length from the tip of the fingers to the elbow, set, inevitably, by the individual in charge of the measuring and thus differing from person to person.

The key 'sacred' lengths are 1,600 cubits, as used in building Solomon's Temple, and 2,000 cubits. The latter distance features prominently in the Old Testament Book of Numbers, chapter 35 which instructs builders: 'Ye shall measure from without the city on the east side two thousand cubits, and on the south side two thousand cubits, and on the west side two thousand cubits, and on the north side two thousand cubits, and the city shall be in the midst.'

This measurement has special significance. In Hebrew 1,000 is denoted by the letter *aleph* (א). Two thousand is therefore two alephs, and these letters spliced together form the Star of David, the great icon of Jewish lore. Two thousand cubits is the distance from Jerusalem to the Mount of Olives. In the City of London the distance from Temple Bar, the historic boundary between the cities of London and Westminster to St Paul's is 2,000 cubits. Similarly, the ancient church of St Dunstan-in-the-East stands 2,000 cubits from St Paul's as the City's eastern boundary.

Those in charge of rebuilding London after the 1666 Fire – Christopher Wren, Robert Hooke, Nicholas Hawksmoor and his team – were in thrall to the idea of sacred geometry. Although they were scientists and men of reason, their agenda was rich with religious arcana. They were influenced by the notion that Christianity had arrived in England as early as the first century AD, long before it had reached Rome. They were inspired by the story in the Book of Zechariah of how the Israelite prophet of the same name meets the Lord Himself, who is disguised as an architect:

I lifted up mine eyes again, and looked, and behold there was a man with a measuring line in his hand. Then said I, 'Whither goest thou?' And he said unto me, 'To measure Jerusalem, to see what is the breadth thereof, and what is the length thereof.'

Consequently they wanted to reshape London as the New Jerusalem – the leading city of Christendom in a world free of papist rule. The idea of London as the New Jerusalem had long been envisaged by the enlightened. Even Charles I had promised it in a 1620 sermon: 'For Here hath the Lord ordained the thrones of David, for judgement: and the charre of Moyses, for instruction, this Church, your Son indeed, others are but Synagogues, this your Jerusalem, the mother to them all.' It was a theme later adopted by William Blake, among others, whose epic poem *Jerusalem* casts London as the holy city: 'We builded Jerusalem as a City & a Temple'.

Wren, Hawksmoor and the other architects created a chain of buildings and features set apart by 'sacred' measurements. Two thousand cubits east of Wren's favourite church, St Dunstan-in-the-East, they created a haven for intellectuals and free-thinkers on the site of an ancient well. This became Wellclose Square (→ p. 55), for centuries the most prosperous location in east London but now almost derelict. In the centre of the square was a Hawksmoor church which stood 2,000 cubits from his better-known (and still standing) Christ Church Spitalfields. And Christ Church is itself 2,000 cubits north-east of Hawksmoor's St Mary Woolnoth by what is now Bank station.

The pattern continues with other well-known buildings from that period. Hawksmoor's church of St George-in-the-East stands 2,000 cubits from the Roman wall. The site of the now partly demolished St Luke's on Old Street is 2,000 cubits north of St Paul's, and the site of another now demolished Hawksmoor church, St John Horselydown, just south of Tower Bridge, lies 2,000 cubits from the Monument, whose own setting is a masterpiece of maths and astronomy (→ p. 22).

ALL HALLOWS THE GREAT, 90 Upper Thames Street

One of England's most extreme millennial sects, the Fifth Monarchy Men, was founded at this now demolished church in 1651. Exploiting the political and religious turmoil in the aftermath of the Civil War and the execution of Charles I, the Fifth Monarchy Men believed the days of earthly kings were over and sought to prepare the country for the imminent appearance of Jesus Christ himself as king.

Christ would rule the fifth kingdom outlined in the Old Testament Book of Daniel. (The first four, so they claimed, were those of the Babylonian, Persian, Greek and Roman empires.) But before he could do so a godly kingdom on earth – the Rule of the

Saints – would violently replace the old order. The Fifth Monarchists consequently lauded the execution of King Charles and urged similar attacks on the rich as they stood in the way of the saintly kingdom.

In 1653 the Fifth Monarchists attained some influence in Oliver Cromwell's new parliamentary assembly, so when he dissolved it that December and appointed himself Lord Protector – *de facto* king – the group felt betrayed. Three Fifth Monarchy Men were imprisoned for denouncing Cromwell, and their leader Thomas Harrison was expelled from the army. A Fifth Monarchist plot to overthrow the Lord Protector was uncovered in 1657 when its instigator, Thomas Venner, previously a minister at a church on Coleman Street in the City, was briefly imprisoned for planning to blow up the Tower of London.

On the restoration of the monarchy in 1660 Thomas Harrison was arrested and put to death for participating in Charles I's execution. Now Venner took over. He led the Fifth Monarchy Men along a distinctly militant path. Infuriated by the torture and execution of Harrison and the popish leanings of the Church reformed around the new king, Charles II, Venner planned insurrection before Charles could be crowned. On New Year's Day 1661 he and around fifty Fifth Monarchy rebels staged a violent but unsuccessful uprising in London. Shouting their war cry of 'King Jesus and the heads upon the gates', they attacked the major buildings of the City, as Samuel Pepys noted in his diary:

A great rising in the city of the Fifth-monarchy men, which did very much disturb the peace and liberty of the people, so that all the train-bands arose in arms, both in London and Westminster, as likewise all the king's guards; and most of the noblemen mounted, and put all their servants on coach horses, for the defence of His Majesty, and the peace of his kingdom.

Around forty soldiers and civilians were killed. Venner was captured and executed outside his Coleman Street church. The Fifth

Monarchy movement carried on briefly but then declined.

All Hallows the Great was demolished in the late nineteenth century for road widening.

→Cromwell in Ireland, p. 297

BLACKFRIARS MONASTERY, **Ireland Yard**

It was in Blackfriars that the Archbishop of Canterbury's council met in May 1382 to denounce John Wycliffe's religious doctrines and his pioneering translation of the Bible into English.

As the hearing began, an earthquake, rare for London, rocked the City. Wycliffe, understandably, claimed the event as a sign of God's discontent with the council's hostile attitude to his reformist teachings. The council, with equal confidence, took the quake as proof of the Lord's displeasure with Wycliffe.

As William Courtenay, the Archbishop of Canterbury, explained:

This earthquake foretells the purging of this kingdom from heresies, for as there are shut up in the bowels of the earth many noxious spirits which are expelled in an earthquake, and so the earth is cleansed but not without great violence, so there are many heresies shut up in the hearts of reprobate men, but by the condemnation of them, the kingdom is to be cleansed; but not without trouble and great commotion.

The synod then found against Wycliffe on twenty-four counts of heresy.

A 1529 court held at Blackfriars heard the divorce proceedings between Catherine of Aragon and Henry VIII. The king had become increasingly frustrated at his wife's inability to provide him with a male heir, despite seven pregnancies, so he sought permission from the Pope, Clement VII, to annul the marriage. Henry made a number of ingenious claims. First he said that he had committed incest by marrying Catherine as she had been the wife of his late brother, Arthur. There was much confusion over the Bible's position on such a matter, but as Catherine swore that her marriage to Arthur had not been consummated the point was dropped. Henry then asked the Pope for an annulment on the grounds that the original papal dispensation to marry his late brother's widow was invalid. Clement may well have wanted to help the king but was in the unfortunate position of being a prisoner of the Holy Roman Emperor Charles V at the time and was unwilling to jeopardise his position any further.

Catherine was consequently brought before the court at Blackfriars on 18 June 1529. The king, the cardinals, the Archbishop of Canterbury and several other bishops attended the proceedings which ended inconclusively. Henry now exacted revenge on Wolsey, Archbishop of York and his leading minister, whom he blamed for the fiasco. Four years later Henry married Anne Boleyn and the Pope excommunicated him. Henry then broke England's ties with Rome, declared himself head of the English Church and dissolved the monasteries. Blackfriars closed in 1538. Excavations conducted in 1890 and 1925 uncovered some remnants of the building but only a tiny portion of stone remains above ground.

→ Wycliffe in Oxford, p. 171

BRIDEWELL PRISON, **Bridewell Place**

The false messiah Elizeus Hall was sent to Bridewell Prison in 1562 after claiming to be a messenger from God who had been taken on a two-day visit to heaven and hell. In 1589 it was to Bridewell that one George Nichols was sent for being a Catholic priest. He and his associates, who had been arrested in Oxford (→ p. 174), were hung by their hands to make them betray their faith, but they refused to recant. They were all eventually hanged, drawn and quartered. The two founders of the Muggletonian sect, Lodowick Muggleton and John Reeve, were sent to Bridewell

Prison in 1653 in an attempt to convince them to renounce their beliefs.

→ The Muggletonians, p. 23

CHEAPSIDE

In 1591 William Hacket paraded up and down Cheapside in a cart, claiming to be the messiah. His supporters believed Hacket was both the king of Europe and the angel who would appear at the Last Judgment. Hacket threatened to bring down a plague on England unless he was rightfully acknowledged, but when he announced that Queen Elizabeth had no right to the crown he was arrested for treason and executed. Hacket's followers expected that divine intervention would save him, and were most vexed when none was forthcoming.

CHURCH OF THE HOLY SEPULCHRE-WITHOUT-NEWGATE, Holborn Viaduct

The largest parish church in the City of London, designed in a style similar to that of the Church of the Holy Sepulchre in Jerusalem, was founded in 1137. Indeed the distance from the church to the now demolished north-west gate of the City corresponded almost exactly with the distance inside its Jerusalem namesake from the Holy Sepulchre to the Calvary on which Jesus' cross was placed. The London church became an appropriate starting point for the Crusaders on their journey to the Holy Land to rescue the Holy Sepulchre from the Saracens.

EMANUEL SWEDENBORG'S VISION, Salisbury Court

While lodging in Salisbury Court in 1745 Emanuel Swedenborg, the major Swedish scientist-turned-mystic in whose name the New Church was founded after his death, had a religious vision. He described it to Thomas Hartley, rector of Winwick, as 'the opening of his spiritual sight, the manifestation of the Lord to him in person', and to his friend Robsahm as a vision of the Lord appearing before him announcing: 'I am God the Lord, the Creator and Redeemer of the world. I have chosen thee to unfold the spiritual sense of the Holy Scripture. I will Myself dictate to thee what thou shalt write.'

In the vision Swedenborg met Jesus Christ who told him that humanity needed someone to explain the Scriptures properly and that he, Swedenborg, had been chosen for the task. He devoted the remaining twenty-eight years of his life to religion and wrote eighteen theological works, which were a major influence on William Blake. The New Church which his followers founded after his death continues to thrive.

→ Emanuel Swedenborg in the East End, p. 46

FIRE OF LONDON, Pudding Lane

The fire that destroyed much of the City in 1666 was connected to many of the religious controversies of the day. Indeed, to a number of religious commentators its outbreak on 2 September that year was no surprise. At the beginning of the year doom-mongers noted the worrying numerical conjunction of 1,000 (Christ's millennium) with 666, the number of the Beast of the Book of Revelation. They predicted that London would turn into the fiery lake which according to the same book 'burneth the fearful and unbelieving, the abominable, the murderers, the whoremongers, sorcerers, idolaters and liars'.

London would burn for being a city of sin, and two books published at the beginning of that year contained ominous predictions about the blaze. Daniel Baker in *A Certaine Warning for a Naked Heart* explained how London would be destroyed by a 'consuming fire', while Walter Gostelo in *The Coming of God in Mercy, in Vengeance, Beginning with Fire, to Convert or Consume all this so Sinful City* boasted: 'If fire make not ashes of the City, and thy bones also, conclude me a liar for ever.'

Sure enough, on 2 September 1666, exactly a year after the Lord Mayor had ordered Londoners to light fires to burn out the Plague, the Great Fire of London broke out. Although at first many thought there was no reason for concern and that it would soon be contained, the Fire spread fast and eventually destroyed much of the capital, including eighty-six churches such as St Benet Sherhog and St Mary Magdalen Milk Street.

Immediately after the Fire the recriminations started. A local Catholic priest called Carpenter told his congregation that the flames 'were come upon this land and people for the forsaking of the true Catholic religion'. Catholics pointed to at least a hundred years' worth of transgressions by Londoners dating back to Henry VIII, whose defiance of the Pope in 1530 over his marriage to Catherine of Aragon broke the ties that bound the English Church to Rome, and led to the dissolution of the monasteries and abbeys. They pointed to the sins of Oliver Cromwell and the Parliamentarians, who had ordered the execution of the 'holy' king, Charles I, he who had lived a life of devotion and had 'suffered martyrdom in defence of the most holy religion'. They also drew up a list of current sins – 'the prodigious ingratitude, burning lusts, dissolute court, profane and abominable lives', as John Evelyn detailed in his diary – in which the mostly Protestant population had indulged.

And for Protestants there was an alternative list of sins that a presumably different God had punished in the Fire of London, namely those of the corrupt Romish monasteries and abbeys which had perverted the ancient religion and accumulated excessive wealth while indulging in simony, fecundity and hypocrisy. They remembered the sins of the Catholic queen, Mary Tudor, who had sent some 300 Protestants to a violent death for heresy in the 1550s and blamed Catholic agitators for starting the Fire. Yet others believed that the Fire had been started by a Jew distraught that the supposed messiah, Shabbatai Zevi, who had claimed he would be crowned that month, had backed down when faced with the wrath of the Turkish Sultan (→ p. 69).

Soon after the Fire, rumours spread that Robert Hubert, a French silversmith, allegedly an agent of the French king, had started the blaze on the Pope's orders. Hubert was arrested in east London. He admitted that he had left Sweden for the English capital and gone to Pudding Lane where he had used a long pole to lob a fireball through the window of Farriner's bakery. Hubert boasted of twenty-three co-conspirators, but his confession was probably false: there was no window at Farriner's bakery and no ship had sailed into east London from Sweden on the day he claimed to have arrived. Nevertheless he was a convenient scapegoat and was hanged at Tyburn (→ p. 79).

GREAT SYNAGOGUE **(1690–1941), Duke's Place**

Used by Jews of north European descent (Ashkenazis) until it was destroyed in the Second World War, the Great Synagogue was the traditional seat of the chief rabbi, a post and office which do not exist in Jewish law. Consequently, some religious Jews claimed that the office of the Chief Rabbi had been created only to make Judaism more acceptable to the Church of England, and would mock the incumbent as the *heimische* Archbishop of Canterbury.

When a fire broke out in the Great Synagogue in the 1750s, Chaim Jacob Samuel Falk, the eighteenth-century mystic known as the Ba'al Shem of London (master of the secret names of God), is alleged to have extinguished it by inscribing on the jamb of the entrance the four Hebrew letters of God's most-used name (*Yahweh* in English), supposedly causing the wind to change direction and the blaze to die down.

→ Falk in the East End, p. 55

HOLY TRINITY PRIORY ALDGATE, **Mitre Square**

The priory which opened in 1109 and soon became the grandest religious house in London, was the scene of one of the first recorded murders in London history. In 1530 Brother Martin, a priory monk, stabbed to death a woman praying at the high altar and then killed himself. The body of Catherine Eddowes, one of Jack the Ripper's victims, was found on the same site more than 350 years later. Some Ripper experts believe Eddowes was killed elsewhere and the corpse placed there as part of a still unexplained ritualistic agenda.

After Henry VIII passed the Act of Supremacy in 1534 declaring himself head of the Church of England, he closed down establishments such as Holy Trinity. The priory surrendered its authority to the Crown by 'mutual agreement' and its incumbents were forced to embark on secular life. The buildings lay in ruins for some years and, even when the owners offered the stone free to any man who would take it down, there were no takers.

JEWRY STREET

The street was home in the sixteenth century to the first Jewish community allowed to live in the capital since Edward I expelled the Jews from Britain in 1291. Its number included Rodrigo Lopez, physician to Elizabeth I, who was once accused of participating in a plot to poison the queen and on whom Shakespeare partly based Shylock. Most of the new immigrant Jews came from Spain and Portugal, where they had been forced to convert to Christianity and were known by the insulting name *marranos* (Spanish for 'swine') due to their practice of hanging pigs outside their homes to show they had converted to Catholicism. After Oliver Cromwell officially allowed the Jews to return to the capital in 1656, this eastern edge of the City became the main centre of Jewish immigration into London. Their first new synagogue, on Creechurch Lane, has long been demolished.

JOHN WESLEY'S CONVERSION, Aldersgate Street by Ironmongers' Hall

John Wesley, the early eighteenth-century preacher who founded Methodism, experienced an epiphany at Hall House, Nettleton Court on 24 May 1738. He later wrote that:

In the evening I went very unwillingly to a society in Aldersgate Street, where one was reading Luther's preface to the Epistle to the Romans. About a quarter before nine, while he was describing the change which God works in the heart through faith in Christ, I felt my heart strangely warmed. I felt I did trust in Christ, Christ alone for salvation.

→ Wesley in Bolton, p. 220

THE MONUMENT, Fish Street Hill

The tall Doric column just north of London Bridge was built as a memorial to the 1666 Great Fire of London but has many religious connections. It was designed by Christopher Wren and Robert Hooke in 1671–7, and decorated by the artist Caius Gabriel Cibber during his daytime parole from debtors' prison. He designed a relief depicting a female figure (London) grieving in front of burning buildings to recall the fallen Jerusalem from the Book of Lamentations 'sitting solitary as a widow [that] weepeth sore in the night, her tears on her cheeks'.

Because so many people believed Catholics were responsible for the Fire, the Monument was given an inscription in 1681 (not removed until 1831) which blamed the disaster on the 'treachery and malice of the Popish faction, in order to the effecting their horrid plot for the extirpating the Protestant religion and English liberties, and to introduce Popery and Heresy'. And just in case there was anyone who hadn't fully received the message, another inscription by Farriner's bakery, where the blaze began, stated that 'here by permission of heaven hell broke loose upon this Protestant City from the malicious hearts of barbarous Papists . . .'

A best-selling pamphlet published at that time urged Protestants to go to the top of the tower and imagine the consequences of popish rule: 'The whole town in flames, and amongst the distracted crowd, troops of Papists ravishing their [the Protestants'] wives and daughters, dashing out the brains of their little children against the walls, plundering their houses and cutting their throats in the name of heretic dogs.'

The Monument is the tallest stone column in the world, its height, 202 foot, being the same as the distance between it and the baker's shop on nearby Pudding Lane where the Fire started. The 202-foot measurement was not randomly chosen. The Monument is positioned so that an observer looking east in the morning and west in the afternoon on the day of the summer solstice can see the sun sitting directly on top of the flaming urn of gilt bronze that crowns its top. Ingeniously the Monument also stands a distance of 2,000 cubits (a biblical measurement often used by architects wanting to imbue their buildings with 'divine protection') from Christ Church Spitalfields, designed by Christopher Wren's assistant Nicholas Hawksmoor, and 2,000 cubits from the western end of Wren's own St Paul's Cathedral.

MUGGLETONIANS' BIRTHPLACE, Bishopsgate

A seventeenth-century sect of radical puritans now practically extinct, the Muggletonians were established by Lodowick Muggleton, a Bishopsgate-born tailor, in 1651. That year he claimed that God had appointed him and his cousin, John Reeve, the Two Last Witnesses, as foretold in the verse in the Book of Revelation: 'I will give power unto my two witnesses and they shall prophesy one thousand two hundred and threescore days clothed in sackcloth.'

The main tenets of the Muggletonians' creed were:

1. God and the man Jesus Christ are synonymous expressions.
2. The devil and human reason are synonymous.
3. The soul dies and rises again with the body.

4. Heaven is a place above the stars.
5. At present hell is nowhere, but this earth, darkened after the last judgement, will be hell.
6. Angels are the only beings of pure reason.

Reeve was obsessed with the notion of mankind's impending doom, and claimed he knew whom God had chosen to be saved. He and Muggleton were sent to Bridewell Prison for cursing a vicar, Mr Goffin, who subsequently died. The teachings of the two founders were handed down from generation to generation, but as the Muggletonians did not believe in proselytising, the sect slowly died out. For instance, in 1697 some 250 supporters attended Muggleton's funeral, but by 1803 they were down to just over a hundred members, and a hundred years later only seventeen attended the monthly meeting. According to an article in the *Times Literary Supplement*, in 1974 a handful of believers were left in Kent. By the end of the decade there were only two remaining Muggletonians who by now may have verified tenet Number 4.

→ The Quakers, p. 226

OLD JEWRY

Now a nondescript City street of company offices, this was the centre of medieval Jewish life in London, when the street was known as Jewry. A Jewish community began to take shape here after William the Conqueror invited Jews from Normandy to London in the 1070s to help him improve Britain's primitive trading practices. The king needed an advanced monetary system – payments made in coin not through barter – and such knowledge was the preserve of Jews, barred from most professions and public office throughout the continent but experts in money, commerce and finance because the Church forbade Christians from practising usury.

According to most modern histories there were no Jews in London, or even England, before the Norman Conquest.

However, Jews had been coming to Britain since King Solomon sent tin traders from the Holy Land to negotiate with the miners of Cornwall some time around the year 960 BC. There were almost certainly Jews in London in Roman times: a brick recovered from the excavation of some Roman ruins on Mark Lane near the Tower in 1650 contained a relief of the story of Samson driving foxes into a field of corn – something which could not have been known to pagan, pre-Christian Romans.

Hostility to the Jews increased over the years, especially on anniversaries and celebrations that were particularly English in character. For instance, Jews were barred from attending the coronation of Richard I in 1189, but they sent a delegation to Westminster Hall nonetheless bearing gifts for the king, and a few sneaked into the hall to have a look at the proceedings. The palace guards threw them out, whereupon some onlookers started throwing stones. A rumour began circulating that the king had ordered the destruction of the Jews. In Jewry a mob set fire to Jewish houses and thirty people were killed. One Jew, Benedict of York, saved his life by converting to Christianity on the spot; he was rushed to St Margaret's church and baptised (although he recanted his new views the next day). When the king learned what had happened he ordered the hanging of three of the ringleaders and announced that the Jews must not be so treated.

From that time the Jews were sent to the Tower for their own safety on such days. But soon excuses were being made to send the Jews to the Tower as a punishment for what were mostly fabricated accusations, usually involving coin clipping (chipping away at coins to use the metal), and allegations of murdering children to use their blood in religious sacrificial rituals.

King John treated the Jewish moneylenders well. He even granted them a charter and allowed them to choose a chief rabbi. But this détente didn't last long. In 1210 the king levied a penalty of 66,000 marks on the Jews, and imprisoned, blinded and tortured those who would not pay.

Henry III compelled the Jews to wear two white tablets of linen or parchment on their breasts. Wherever Jews lived, burgesses were chosen to protect them from pilgrims' insults about infidels. But in 1220 the Crown seized the Old Jewry synagogue and handed it to the brothers of St Anthony of Vienna for use as a church. In 1232 more pressure was put on the Jews to reject their religion when Henry built a House for Converted Jews on what is now Chancery Lane.

Jews were then expelled from Newcastle and Southampton. In London the status of the community began to deteriorate sharply after a dead Christian child was found in 1244, its arms and legs embroidered with Hebrew letters – a botched crucifixion, evidently. After a number of further tribulations the Jews asked King Henry if they could leave England officially. The king was outraged. Soon after, eighty-six of London's richest Jews were hanged for supposedly crucifying a Christian child in Lincoln and there was a riot against London's Jews. Five hundred were killed and the synagogue was burnt down. Only those who took refuge in the Tower survived.

Edward I, who came to the throne in 1272, forced the Jews to wear yellow badges so that everyone knew who they were (a symbol Hitler adopted nearly 700 years later). He also levied a tax of threepence on them every Easter. In 1288 all England's Jews were imprisoned and held until they paid a £20,000 ransom, a handy sum to help finance the castles he was building in Wales. It came as no surprise when in 1290 Edward announced on 18 July – the anniversary of the sacking of the Temple in AD 70 – that he was expelling the Jews from England. All Jews (some 15,000) 'with their wives, children and chattels' had to leave the country, and they were given until 1 November, the feast of All Saints, to comply. Any Jew who remained behind after that date would face execution. Ships carrying Jews left St Katharine's Dock near the Tower. When one vessel ran into a sandbank off Queensborough, Kent, the captain invited passengers to stretch their legs. But once they had disembarked he made off, leaving the party to drown as the tide rose.

The Crown seized all the Jews' property and none of their buildings survive locally . . . above ground. Recent excavations of nearby sites during the building of the huge corporate blocks that dominate the area have unearthed well-preserved ritual baths and artefacts.

→ The Jews massacred in York, p. 207

ST DUNSTAN-IN-THE-WEST, Fleet Street at Hen and Chickens Court

Founded *c.* 1185 as St Dunstan's Over Against the Temple, the church was known as St Dunstan-in-the-West from 1278 to differentiate it from St Dunstan-in-the-East in Stepney. It was here that William Tyndale, whose translations of the New Testament from the Greek provided the basis for the later King James Bible, preached in the 1520s. In the seventeenth century St Dunstan's was a centre of Puritanism where Praise-God Barebones, the divinely named Roundhead leader, preached.

The church's unusual-looking clock, the first in London to be marked with minutes, was erected in 1671 as a thanksgiving from parishioners relieved that a sudden burst of wind sent the Fire of London away from the building. The clock features two burly figures, Gog and Magog, biblical characters who appear cryptically in the Book of Revelation: 'And ye shall go out to deceive the nations which are in the four quarters of the earth, Gog and Magog, to gather them together to battle: the number of whom is as the sand of the sea.' However, an ancient London legend tells of a character called Gogmagog – an Ancient Briton beaten in battle around the year 1000 BC by Brutus the Trojan, founder of London.

Today the church unites all major churches of Christendom: 'Old Catholics, the Assyrian Church of the East, the Romanian Orthodox Church, the Anglican Church, the Oriental churches, the Lutheran and Reformed Churches and the Holy Roman and Catholic Church'.

ST LAWRENCE JEWRY

John Wilkins, mid-seventeenth-century vicar of this exquisitely designed Christopher Wren church, devised a new system of measurement in the 1660s based on biblical 'sacred geometry'. He wanted the main unit length to be equal to the 2,000 cubits cited as holy in the Book of Numbers. To make calculations easier the length would be divided not into 2,000 parts but into 1,000 equal divisions, what in the nineteenth century was renamed the metre, now a standard measurement, used extensively throughout the world, but, ironically, not universally in London.

→ London, Sacred City, p. 11

ST PAUL'S CATHEDRAL, St Paul's Churchyard

Britain's major cathedral, the setting for state occasions as well as one of the capital's leading tourist attractions, was founded in 604 by Ethelbert, King of Kent, and Mellitus, Bishop of the East Saxons. The church was destroyed by the Vikings in the ninth century and burnt down in 1087, but at the end of the eleventh century William I granted St Paul's privileges: 'Some lands I give to God and the church of St Paul's, in London, and special franchises, because I wish that this church may be free in all things, as I wish my soul to be on the day of judgment.'

In the thirteenth century Maurice, Bishop of London, decided to build a new grand cathedral on a larger scale than anything witnessed outside central Europe. It was this building, completed in 1240, that is now known as Old St Paul's, to differentiate it from the post-Fire of London cathedral.

Not all clerics have been hospitably received here. In 1093 Anselm, Archbishop of Canterbury, came to St Paul's demanding his tithe of the fruit harvest, only to find the doors closed in his face. In 1259 a mob killed two canons in the papal party. In 1385 Robert Braybroke, Bishop of London, banned various frivolous activities from taking place at St Paul's on Sundays, including barbers shaving customers, worshippers shooting arrows at the pigeons and children playing ball. Nine years later the Lollard reformers nailed a paper listing twelve complaints about the Catholic clergy on the door of the old church – a hundred years before Martin Luther famously posted his ninety-six theses on popish indulgences on the door of the church in Wittenberg.

During the Reformation of the 1530s the high altar was pulled down and replaced by a plain table. Many of the tombs were also destroyed, the reredos was smashed to pieces and St Paul's became more of a social centre than a church. The nave, Paul's Walk, was even used by prostitutes touting for business, and as a market for selling groceries and animals. In 1553 the Common Council of London passed an act forbidding people from carrying beer barrels, baskets of bread, fish, flesh or fruit into St Paul's and from leading mules or horses through the cathedral. Evidently the law didn't go far enough, for in 1558 Elizabeth had to issue a proclamation forbidding the drawing of swords in the church and the shooting of guns inside it or in the churchyard, under pain of two months' imprisonment.

St Paul's collection of holy relics was sold off during the Cromwellian Commonwealth of 1649–60, but there appeared to be an inexhaustible stock of these. The authorities were still selling portions of the Virgin Mary's milk, the hair of Mary Magdalen, the hand of St John, pieces of Thomas à Becket's skull and the blood of St Paul himself – all preserved in jewelled cases – 150 years later.

The Fire of London destroyed Old St Paul's in 1666, but the building was spectacularly redesigned by Christopher Wren, who created what many believe to be the finest example of Renaissance architecture in Britain. Somehow St Paul's escaped destruction during the Second World War Blitz.

Paul's Cross

An open-air pulpit erected by the south wall of the pre-Fire of London St Paul's was known as Paul's Cross. Here papal bulls were broadcast, excommunications pronounced, royal proclamations made and heresies denounced at what was a kind of medieval Speakers' Corner. It was also where the earliest English Bibles were burnt before the authorities decided to allow the people to hear the Scriptures in their native tongue.

In 1422 Richard Walker, a Worcester chaplain, appeared at Paul's Cross on charges of sorcery. Two books on magic which he had been caught reading were then burnt before his eyes. In 1447 Reginald Pecock, Bishop of Chichester, was made to kneel here before the Archbishop of Canterbury and around 20,000 onlookers to make a full confession of his 'errors'. That was how his captors described his writings, which were then cast into the fire as a warning of the fate that might soon befall him.

Preacher Beal stirred up the crowd so passionately on May Day 1517 that riots broke out across London as the mob attacked foreign merchants on what came to be called Evil May Day. Troops managed to restore order and took 400 rioters as prisoners. The leaders of the riots were hanged, drawn and quartered.

On 12 May 1521 an unusual book, *Assertio Septem Sacramentorum* (The Defence of the Seven Sacraments), setting out Catholic arguments against the new Protestant creed being propounded by Martin Luther in Germany, was unveiled at Paul's Cross. The author was supposedly none other than Henry VIII, the jousting, hunting, non-bookish king. Though few believed that Henry was capable of such writing, evidence shows that the king was indeed the author of the work, which he dedicated to the Pope and which earned him the title 'Defender of the Faith'.

Copies of William Tyndale's pioneering English translation of the Bible were burnt here in 1526, shortly after they had been smuggled into the country. They were selling in London for three shillings, but those found with such a Bible were made to ride backward on a donkey and wear a pasteboard mitre emblazoned with some of the offending passages. Tied to their backs were symbolic faggots of wood which they had to hurl into a bonfire as a warning of what would happen to them soon at Smithfield if they continued with their heretical reading.

The Rood of Grace (→ p. 132), a wooden cross bearing an image that could supposedly move and speak if approached by one who had lived a pure life, was smashed to pieces under the king's orders at Paul's Cross in 1538. Two years later it was here that William Jerome, the vicar of St Dunstan and All Saints, was burnt alive for preaching an Anabaptist sermon (belittling infant baptism).

Crowds would gather at Paul's Cross to hear contentious sermons, which often resulted in trouble. For instance in 1549 preachers incited the onlookers to sack the cathedral itself, and a mob tore inside, destroyed the altar and smashed several tombs. At the first sermon preached here following the death of the Protestant king, Edward VI, on 6 July 1553 Bishop Bourne provoked the crowd by denouncing the Protestant Bishop of London, Nicholas Ridley. A group of spectators began shouting: 'He preaches damnation! Pull him down! Pull him down!' Someone threw a dagger at Bourne. It stuck in one of the wooden side posts and the bishop was rushed into St Paul's school for his own safety. In their desperation to exact revenge, the authorities arrested several people and imprisoned them in the Tower, while a priest and a barber had their ears nailed to the pillory at Paul's Cross.

Ridley himself soon made his stand here. On 16 July he denounced both royal princesses, Mary and Elizabeth, daughters of Henry VIII, as illegitimate and singled out Mary for special abuse as she was a papist. Ridley believed that Lady Jane Grey, great-granddaughter of Henry VII, should take the throne as the best way of preserving a Protestant succession – which she did but for only nine days.

In April 1584 the Bishop of London preached here against astrologers who were predicting the end of the world owing to an imminent conjunction of Jupiter and Saturn. On 7 February 1601 the Earl of Essex, at the conclusion of the sermon at Paul's Cross, led a group of 300 rebels through the City shouting: 'Murder, murder, God save the Queen!' in protest at how England was supposedly about to be handed to the Spanish when Queen Elizabeth died. He was arrested and executed on Tower Hill a month later.

The Puritans pulled down Paul's Cross in 1643.

ST PAUL'S CHURCHYARD

When Pope Pius V became pontiff in February 1570 he issued a papal bull, *Regnans in Excelsis*, urging Catholics to overthrow Elizabeth, 'pretended Queen of England'. The Catholics believed Elizabeth was technically illegitimate as they did not recognise her mother, Anne Boleyn, the Protestant who had replaced the Catholic Catherine of Aragon in Henry's favours, as being legitimately married to the king.

Pius V excommunicated Elizabeth, freeing her subjects from their allegiance to her. It was an absurd move as no Catholic European power was in a position to enforce his wishes. It also meant that from now on the queen would treat all Catholics as the enemy. A Catholic called John Felton pinned the papal bull to the gate of the Bishop of London's palace and was duly hanged in St Paul's Churchyard. Cut down while still alive, he supposedly shouted out the holy name of Jesus as the hangman held his heart in his hand.

George Williams was one of a dozen men who established the Young Men's Christian Association above a draper's shop in St Paul's

Churchyard in 1844. Their aim was to unite and direct 'the efforts of Christian young men for the spiritual welfare of their fellows in the various departments of commercial life'. Soon other branches were formed, first in London, and then throughout the world.

SMITHFIELD EXECUTION SITE, West Smithfield

Originally the Smooth Field, this was Britain's major execution site for Protestant martyrs in medieval times, where hundreds lost their lives.

The method of execution used at Smithfield was nearly always burning at the stake before a large crowd. Though gruesome, it was carried out in a far more humane manner than on the continent, where heretics often had their tongues cut off before the pyre was lit. In England burning occurred only after a series of rigorous trials had taken place and the condemned had been given the chance of recanting their views.

A dramatic preamble to the grim fate was the ceremony known as 'carrying the faggot'. The alleged heretic, carrying a faggot of wood, would be taken to the place of execution. There a fire had been lit, and the accused would throw the faggot on to the fire and watch it burn as a warning that if they remained steadfast in their views they would be next for the flames. Before the pyre was lit, the victim's friends and family would try to bribe the executioner to place a bag of gunpowder by the body. That way, when the flames rose, the gunpowder would explode and kill the poor wretch quickly, sparing them the slow torture of burning. This could not happen of course if it had been raining.

The first martyr to meet his death here was William Sawtrey, a priest and follower of the Bible translator John Wycliffe, who went to the stake in 1401. Sawtrey's card was marked when he announced 'instead of adoring the cross on which Christ suffered, I adore Christ who suffered on it'. In 1399 the Bishop of Norwich questioned Sawtrey over his beliefs, and had him arrested and imprisoned on charges of heresy. Sawtrey recanted his views and was released but felt that he had betrayed Christ. Two years later Thomas Arundel, Archbishop of Canterbury, had Sawtrey arrested again. After questioning Sawtrey, the Church authorities deemed 'unacceptable' his views on transubstantiation and the adoration of the cross and declared him indeed a heretic, which meant only one thing – he had to be put to death by burning.

The list of Smithfield martyrs includes:

• **John Badby**, 1410
Badby, a Worcester tailor, got into trouble in 1410 after telling the local diocesan court that when Christ sat at the Last Supper with his disciples he did not have his body in his hand to distribute and that 'if every host consecrated at the altar were the Lord's body, then there be 20,000 Gods in England'. A court at St Paul's sentenced him to be burnt to death. Just before Badby met his fate the watching Prince of Wales (the future Henry V) offered him his life and a pension if he would recant, but Badby would not do so. As the flames began to rise he cried out: 'It is consecrated bread and not the body of God.'

• **John Frith**, 1533
A colleague of the Bible translator William Tyndale, Frith fled to the continent when the persecution of Protestants began in the 1520s. He later returned to England, travelling from congregation to congregation where Catholicism had been ousted following the Reformation. Frith was arrested in 1532 and sent to the Tower of London, where he was chained to a post. Things improved, though, and for a while Frith was allowed to have friends visit his cell. But the authorities soon decided to bring Frith before the bishops to repent his 'heresies', such as denying that the bread and wine at consecration actually turn into Jesus' flesh and blood. When he refused to do so, he was taken to a dungeon under Newgate Prison and, according to Andersen, his biographer, 'laden

with irons, as many as he could bear, neither stand upright, nor stoop down'.

At least Frith had only one night of these horrors, for the next day he and a fellow sufferer, Hewett, were taken to Smithfield and bound to the stake to be burnt. 'The wind made his death somewhat longer, as it bore away the flame from him to his fellow,' Andersen explained, 'but Frith's mind was established with such patience, that, as though he had felt no pain, he seemed rather to rejoice for his fellow than to be careful for himself.'

• **John Lambert**, 1537

Lambert was summoned before a religious court on suspicion of having converted to Protestantism. He remained silent, like Jesus before his accusers, and in doing so was instrumental in bringing about a change in the law whereby it was decreed no man can accuse himself – *nemo tenetur edere contra se*. It didn't save his life, and he was burnt at Smithfield in 1537. When Lambert's legs had been charred to stumps, he was taken from the fire, but he cried out, 'None but Christ, none but Christ,' and was dropped into the flames again.

• **John Forest**, 1538

Forest, a preacher who opposed Henry VIII's divorce from Catherine of Aragon, was the only Catholic to be burnt at the stake at Smithfield for heresy. With Forest on a bed of chains suspended over the pyre, the executioner added a huge wooden holy relic as the martyr slowly roasted. When the flames reached his feet he lifted them up before lowering them again into the fire.

Another who lost his life that year was a man, recorded only as 'Collins', who was executed for mocking the Mass in church by lifting a dog above his head.

• **Edward Powell and others**, 1540

30 July 1540 was a busy day for the Smithfield executioners: that

day three Catholics, Edward Powell, Thomas Abel and Richard Featherstone, went to their doom alongside three Protestants, Robert Barnes, Thomas Gerard and William Jerome.

Powell was that rarity, a Welsh Catholic. He was a rector in Somerset and a preacher favoured by Henry VIII. He was one of four clerics selected to defend the legality of the king's marriage to Catherine of Aragon, the validity of which was questioned as she had been married to Henry's late brother, Arthur. Powell later criticised Henry's marriage to Anne Boleyn (Catherine's replacement) and this resulted in his arraignment for high treason.

Abel had been a chaplain to Catherine of Aragon and continued to support the queen when Henry began divorce proceedings. The king had Abel thrown into the Beauchamp Tower, where he spent six years before being taken to Smithfield and executed for denying royal supremacy over the Church.

Featherstone was also a chaplain to Catherine of Aragon and a tutor to Mary Tudor, her daughter. In 1534 he was asked to take the Oath of Supremacy but refused to do so and was imprisoned in the Tower. After Powell, Abel and Featherstone's execution their limbs were fixed to the gates of the city and their heads displayed on poles on London Bridge.

Barnes, Gerard and Jerome, the Protestants, were prosecuted for supporting the doctrines of the Swiss reformer Huldrych Zwingli. Of the three, Barnes was the most interesting character. Henry VIII sent him to Germany in 1535 to encourage disciples of Martin Luther to give their approval to the king's divorce from Catherine of Aragon. By the year of Barnes's execution Henry had decided to oppose Luther's reforms vehemently. Barnes had made a speech at Paul's Cross attacking a rival cleric, which caused turmoil within the different factions of the king's council. Barnes was forced to apologise but it wasn't enough to save him.

• **John Rogers**, 1555

A Bible translator, Rogers became the first Protestant martyr to be executed during the reign of the Catholic queen, Mary Tudor, when he was burnt at Smithfield on 4 February 1555. Rogers had produced only the second complete English Bible (published 1537), the first to be translated into English from the original Hebrew and Greek. He printed it under the pseudonym Thomas Matthew, but much of it was the work of William Tyndale, whose pioneering English translation had caused the Church such distress.

Prior to his execution, Rogers was asked by Woodroofe, the Newgate Prison sheriff, if he would revoke his 'evil opinion of the Sacrament of the altar'. Rogers replied: 'That which I have preached I will seal with my blood.' When Woodroofe responded, 'Thou art an heretic,' Rogers retorted, 'That shall be known at the Day of Judgment'.

On the way to Smithfield Rogers saw his wife and eleven children in the crowd, but was not allowed to talk to them. He died quickly for the flames soon raged. Nevertheless he was courageous enough to pretend to be washing his hands in the fire as if it had been cold water. He then lifted them in the air and prayed. As he died a flock of doves flew above, leading one supporter to claim that one of the birds was the Holy Ghost himself.

• **Roger Holland**, 1556

Holland was one of forty men and women convicted for staging prayers and Bible study in a walled garden in Islington. With the Catholic Mary Tudor on the throne, such practices were no longer considered acceptable, for the ruling Catholic ideology wanted only priests to read the Bible and even then only in Latin (not its original language). Holland and others believed they were safe from hostile prying eyes, but they were spotted and arrested by the Constable of Islington, who demanded they hand over their books. The Bible readers were taken to Newgate Prison where they were informed they would be released as long as they agreed to hear Mass. Most of them refused to do so.

When Holland was taken to the stake he embraced the bundles of reeds placed there to fuel the fire and announced: 'Lord, I most humbly thank Thy Majesty that Thou hast called me from the state of death, unto the Light of Thy Heavenly Word, and now unto the fellowship of Thy saints that I may sing and say, "Holy holy holy, Lord God of hosts!" Lord, into Thy hands I commit my spirit. Lord bless these Thy people, and save them from idolatry.'

• **Edward Arden**, 1583

A Catholic from the same Warwickshire family as Shakespeare's mother, Arden was probably the innocent victim of a Catholic plot to overthrow Queen Elizabeth. He died protesting his innocence, claiming that his only crime was to be a Catholic. His son-in-law John Somerville, who was implicated alongside him, was tortured on the rack, after which he implicated others. Somerville was found strangled in his cell before he could be executed.

• **Edward Wightman**, 1612

Wightman was the last man burnt alive in England for his religious views – he was a Baptist. At the time, James I, not a particularly bloodthirsty zealot in the Mary manner, was on the throne and the burnings had almost ceased. As the historian Thomas Fuller once noted: 'James preferred heretics should silently and privately waste themselves away in the prison, rather than to grace them, and amuse others, with the solemnity of a public execution.'

→ Hangings at Tyburn, p. 51

SPANISH AND PORTUGUESE SYNAGOGUE, Bevis Marks and Heneage Lane

What is now Britain's oldest synagogue was built in 1701 on the site of the Abbot of Bury St Edmunds's town house with its entrance on the side of the building as the City authorities were worried about the reaction of non-Jews walking past a synagogue door. Bevis Marks was opened for Iberian Jews whom Oliver Cromwell had officially allowed to return to England in 1656. (The community's first synagogue, on nearby Creechurch Lane, no longer exists.)

Bevis Marks's register of births includes that of Benjamin D'Israeli (later Disraeli) in 1804. Despite his Jewish conception, the future Tory prime minister was baptised at St Andrew's, Holborn, after his father rowed with the synagogue authorities. The baptism allowed Disraeli to become a Member of Parliament and later prime minister. Services are still held in Portuguese, as well as Hebrew.

THE TEMPLE

The Inner and Middle Temple, two of London's four Inns of Court where lawyers live and work, takes its name from the Knights Templar, a body of French warrior monks, founded in 1129, who protected pilgrims travelling to the Holy Land. Gradually the Knights Templar became ever more powerful until Pope Clement V disbanded them in 1312 and handed their assets to their rivals, the Knights Hospitaller (the Order of St John of Jerusalem). *They* now became wealthy landowners, buying this estate in London which they leased to lawyers. The Knights Hospitaller themselves had their possessions seized by the English Crown in 1539.

Unofficially the Templars still exist, controlling affairs through their semi-secret offspring organisation, the Freemasons. In recent years various individuals and esoteric groups claiming to represent the Templars have emerged, mostly because of the publicity given to them by the success of the Dan Brown novel

The Da Vinci Code. It remains to be seen whether they will try to claim ownership of Temple Church, especially now that a body calling itself the Association of the Sovereign Order of the Temple of Christ has launched a court case in Spain, demanding that the Pope 'recognise' the seizure of their assets worth some €100 bn.

→ The Knights Templars in Warwickshire, p. 188

TEMPLE BAR

The historical boundary between the ancient cities of London and Westminster, marked by a statue where the Strand meets Fleet Street, was the site of the Pope-burning ceremonies of the late seventeenth century. Every year on 17 November, the anniversary of the accession of Elizabeth I, an effigy of the Pope, seated in his chair of state, would be carried through the local streets in mockery of the papal coronation ceremony, by people dressed as Catholic clergymen. When the train reached Temple Bar bonfires were lit and the 'Pope' was cremated.

TEMPLE CHURCH, Inner Temple Lane

Since the early twenty-first-century publication of Dan Brown's religious thriller *The Da Vinci Code*, much public interest has centred on Temple Church, London's oldest Gothic building, which features in the novel. The church was built from 1160–85 in the style of the Church of the Sepulchre in Jerusalem. A door in the north-west corner of the choir leads to the penitential cell where knights who had broken Temple rules were imprisoned and in some cases starved to death. One such wrongdoer was the deserter Adam de Valaincourt, who was sentenced to eat meat with the dogs for a whole year, to fast four days each week, and to appear naked every Monday at the high altar, where the priest would publicly reprimand him.

→ Rosslyn Chapel, p. 274

TEMPLE OF MITHRAS, **11 Queen Victoria Street**
A Roman temple 60 foot long and 26 foot wide built by the Walbrook stream and dedicated to the light god, Mithras, was discovered in 1954 when the ground was dug up for the construction of an office block. The worship of Mithras, which began in Persia in the first century BC and was open only to men, was carried out in caves, Mithraea, one of which was excavated in London near the site now occupied by Mansion House. The artefacts are housed in the Museum of London.

The East End

The East End has long been the most impoverished part of London, where residents have often turned to religion to ease their predicament. In medieval times the land bordering the East End and the City of London was marked with a line of monasteries, priories and nunneries – Holy Trinity Priory Aldgate, St Katharine's, Minories and Eastminster – all of which vanished with the dissolution of the religious houses in the mid-sixteenth century.

The Bubonic Plague that hit this part of London especially hard in 1665 was seen by locals as a religious punishment foretold by a comet which had passed over the capital the previous December to signify that God was unhappy with London's behaviour. During the Plague clerics explained that it was the punishment outlined in the Old Testament Book of Chronicles in which the Lord smote 'the people, children, wives and all goods [causing] great sickness by disease'. Plague victims often didn't wait to die but threw themselves into pits like the one in St Botolph's churchyard, Aldgate, as noted by Daniel Defoe in his *Journal of the Plague Year*.

At the height of the epidemic a Stepney man, Solomon Eagle,

one of a group of Quakers known for holding fasting matches with Anglican priests and stripping in churchyards to prove their true piety, strode through the area naked, a pan of burning charcoal on his head, proclaiming awful Bible-inspired warnings. Another man paced the streets of Whitechapel crying out like Jonah: 'Yet forty days and Nineveh shall be overthrown!', likening London to the immoral city threatened with destruction in the Book of Jonah. A man wearing nothing other than a pair of underpants wrapped around his head was seen throughout the East End wailing: 'O! the Great and the Dreadful God!' Outside a house in Mile End a crowd gathered as a woman pointed to the sky, claiming she could see a white angel brandishing a fiery sword, warning those who could not see the vision that God's anger had been aroused and that 'dreadful judgments were approaching'.

For centuries the East End was the place where refugees fleeing religious persecution arrived in London, disembarking from boats that moored near the Tower. In the seventeenth century Huguenots (French Protestants) escaping a Catholic backlash settled in the East End's Spitalfields and soon seamlessly assimilated into the local community. In the early nineteenth century Irish (mostly Catholics) turned up in large numbers and, after facing initial hostility, took root in parts of the East End near the Thames, where they eventually assumed control of who worked at the docks. Later that century came a large number of Jews fleeing the pogroms of eastern Europe. They met hostility not just from gentiles but from the Jewish establishment which had partly anglicised itself to win acceptance and was now embarrassed by the influx of chassidic Jews dressed in ritual garb and speaking Yiddish.

Gradually during the twentieth century the Jews moved away from the East End, where now barely a synagogue remains. Since the 1970s the area has become increasingly colonised by immigrants from the Indian subcontinent, mostly Muslims from Bangladesh, who have changed the religious face of the area.

Jacob the Ripper?

When a number of East End prostitutes were murdered in 1888 by an unknown assailant, who later claimed to be 'Jack the Ripper', blame fell on the Jews who had begun to move into the area in large numbers that decade. No gentile could have perpetrated so awful a crime, many locals mused, ignoring the fact that only two Jews had been hanged for murder since the return of the Jews to England in the 1650s. Even the police blamed the Jews. Sir Robert Anderson, the assistant commissioner of police at the time of the murders, once claimed that they had been 'certain that the murderer was a low-class foreign Jew. It is a remarkable fact that people of that class in the East End will not give up one of their number to Gentile Justice.' Or as the Jewish commentator Chaim Bermant put it in the 1960s: 'If Jack the Ripper was a Jew, then one can be fairly certain that his fellows would have kept quiet about it, for the simple reason that the whole community could have been held culpable for his deeds.'

During the spate of murders and attacks Jewish community leaders noticed that the violence occurred on dates significant in the Hebrew calendar. For instance, the first attack on a prostitute that year, when Emma Smith was left for dead at the corner of Wentworth Street and Osborn Street, took place not only on Easter Monday, 3 April 1888, but on the last day of Passover, a Jewish festival rich in associations with slaughter. Jewish leaders hoped that this wasn't a replay of the medieval blood libels in which Jews were accused of ritualistically killing Christians to re-enact Christ's Passion and of using the victims' blood to make the unleavened bread eaten during Passover.

The next attack came on 7 August. The body of Martha Tabram, another prostitute, was discovered on the landing of flats at George Yard Buildings on Aldgate's Gunthorpe Street. She had been stabbed thirty-nine times. Suspicion fell on the Jews, convenient scapegoats, as religious leaders noted that the murder had occurred at the start of the Jewish month of Elul, a time of contrition and repentance in the Jewish calendar. Two more prostitutes were killed on dates significant to Jews over the next few months, including Annie Chapman, who was murdered on 8 September 1888, only a few hours after the ending of the Jewish New Year, the Jewish 'Day of Judgment'.

Some Jewish leaders feared that the slayings might be the work of a deranged Jew enacting some arcane chronological biblical ritual to rid the East End of sin. The community braced itself for another murder on 15 September. For this day was not only the Jewish Sabbath but the Day of Atonement, the most important date in the Jewish calendar, when worshippers beg forgiveness for all their sins. In biblical times the high priest conducted a special Temple ceremony on the Day of Atonement to clean the shrine, slaying a bull and two goats as a special offering. Perhaps there would be a human slaying this time?

Meanwhile, locals poured over the latest edition of the *East London Observer*. The paper contained a bizarre letter on the murders sprinkled with biblical references to 'Pharisees', 'the marriage feast of the Lord' and 'the Kingdom of Heaven', suggesting setting up a national fund to find 'honourable employment for some of the daughters of Eve [prostitutes], which would greatly lessen immorality'. It was signed 'Josephus'. He was a first-century Jewish historian and scholar who, during the war against the Romans, hid in a cave near the fortress of Jotapata with forty others. With dwindling supplies, they realised few could escape, so they drew lots to determine the order of their demise. Whoever drew the first lot was to be killed by the drawer of the second, who in turn would be killed by the drawer of the third, and so on. Only the last one would survive. Josephus was lucky enough to draw one of the last lots. However, he and the penultimate participant chose not to complete their pact but to surrender to the Romans. Many suspected that Josephus had 'fixed' the lots, sending scores to their deaths, a view reinforced when he swiftly moved from the Jewish priesthood to the role of adviser to the Roman emperors Vespasian, Titus and Domitian.

No murder occurred on 15 September 1888. But perhaps the Ripper had been interrupted before he could commit a fresh atrocity? At the start of the Jewish holy day Aldgate police arrested a slightly built shabbily dressed Jewish man, Edward McKenna, of 15 Brick Lane, who had been seen acting suspiciously in the neighbourhood. He had come out of the Tower Subway and asked the attendant: 'Have you caught any of the Whitechapel murderers yet?' He then produced a foot-long knife with a curved blade and jeered, 'This will do for them' before running away. A search of McKenna's pockets at Commercial Street police station yielded what the newspaper described as an 'extraordinary accumulation of articles'. It included a heap of rags, two women's purses and a small leather strap, but no evidence that he might have been responsible for the still unsolved murders.

At the end of the month came the strangest Jewish connection yet. On 30 September the Ripper killed two women, Liz Stride and Catharine Eddowes. Part of Eddowes's white apron was torn during the attack and dropped, presumably by the Ripper, outside Wentworth Model Buildings on Goulston Street. A policeman found it in the early hours of the morning and looking up saw a strange piece of graffiti which read:

'The Juwes are not the men That will be Blamed for nothing'

Fearful of a pogrom, the officer wiped the message – without photographing it – before it could be spotted by the early-morning market traders. Word spread that the graffiti had fingered the Jews, but the word was spelt 'Juwes' as in the Masonic legend of the Three Juwes.

The Three Juwes – Jubela, Jubelo and Jubelum – were apprentices involved with the building of Solomon's Temple. They murdered Hiram Abiff, the Temple architect, in the year 959 BC after he refused to reveal to them the deepest secrets of the Torah. When Jubela, Jubelo and Jubelum were found they were in turn put to death, their throats cut from ear to ear, 'their breasts torn open', and their entrails thrown over the shoulder. All the five 'canonical' Ripper victims were mutilated in this manner.

EMANUEL SWEDENBORG'S BURIAL SITE, Swedenborg Gardens, St George's

Swedenborg Gardens, a now desolate spot in an unlovely part of the East End, was once home to a Swedish church that contained Emanuel Swedenborg's tomb. Swedenborg was a Swedish mystic and one of the eighteenth-century's greatest theologians, who believed that the spirit of the dead rose from the body and assumed a different physical shape in another world.

When the church was demolished in 1908 his corpse was taken to Sweden so that it could be placed in a marble sarcophagus in Uppsala Cathedral. By that time the skull was missing. It had been removed by a Swedish sailor who hoped to sell it as a relic. The skull was later recovered and returned to London, but was then lost again while being exhibited with other skulls in a phrenological collection. In a bizarre mix-up the wrong skull was later returned to Swedenborg's body while the genuine one went on sale in an antique shop and was auctioned at Sotheby's in London in 1978 for £2,500.

HOLY TRINITY MINORIES, Minories, Aldgate

Edmund Crouchback, Earl of Lancaster and brother of Edward I, established the Abbey of the Grace of the Blessed Virgin Mary and St Francis to the north of St Katharine's in 1293 for women belonging to the Franciscan Order. The institution soon had a string of names: the Covenant of the Order of St Clare, the Little Sisters, *Sorores Minores*, the House of Minoresses without Aldgate and Holy Trinity Minories, the latter name surviving in that of the modern-day street that connects Aldgate and Tower Hill.

From the privacy of their rooms the sisters had clear views of the executions on the Tower Hill gallows. They also enjoyed special privileges, for the abbey's status as a Papal Peculiar rendered it beyond the powers of the Bishop of London. But Minories turned out to be even beyond the powers of the Bishop of Rome, for most of the inhabitants were wiped out during a plague in 1515.

By this time the nunnery, despite the sisters' original vow of poverty, had become the richest religious house in England. Fifteen years later the Archbishop of Canterbury brought an end to the sisters' pledge of chastity, declaring that 'no person may make a vowe or promyse to lyve chaste and single; And that none is bounde to keep any suche vowes, but rather to breke them'. Henry VIII dissolved the nunnery soon after and the buildings were used as an armoury and workhouse until demolition in 1810.

→ Glastonbury Abbey, p. 255

JAMME MASJID MOSQUE, 59 Brick Lane, Spitalfields

The only building outside the Holy Land to have housed the world's three major monotheistic faiths – Christianity, Judaism and Islam – was built in 1742 as a Huguenot chapel, the Neuve Eglise. It was one of a number of local places where John Wesley, founder of Methodism, hosted the earliest Methodist services, in 1755. Later it became a Methodist chapel and was also the headquarters of the Christian Evangelical Society for promoting Christianity among Jews, a body which opened a school in Bethnal Green and whose governors offered to pay the fees of any Jew that wished to be Christianised.

In 1892 the Brick Lane building reopened as the Spitalfields Great Synagogue. It was now run by the Jewish sect Machzikei Hadas V'Shomrei Shabbas ('strengtheners of the law and guardians of the Sabbath'). So extreme were they in their worship of the Sabbath, followers even refused to carry handkerchiefs on the day of rest, tying them around their waists instead, and for vital tasks that needed doing on that day they would employ a flunkey known by the quasi-insulting Yiddish term 'Shobbos Goy', who could not be directly ordered but had to guess the nature of his or her tasks by suggestions and inferences.

Ironically, the Machzikei found harassment not so much from gentiles but from non-religious Jews. In 1904 on the Day of Atonement, a day of fasting when a Jew must do no manual work, worshippers taking a break from the service were pelted with bacon sandwiches hurled by members of a Jewish anarchist group driving a food van up and down the street outside. The orthodox Jews in turn pelted the anarchists with stones and broken bottles. The synagogue closed in 1965 and in 1976 was converted into a mosque.

PRITHI CURRY HOUSE, 126 Brick Lane, Spitalfields

The Lord Maitreya, a Bodhisattva or enlightened being intent on saving souls, was expected to appear at this curry house – of all places – on 31 July 1985. Adverts had been printed in the papers for the previous few months explaining that as Christians await the return of Christ, Muslims the Imam Mahdi, Hindus a reincarnation of Krishna, and the Jews the Messiah, those knowledgeable in mysticism would recognise that all those names refer to the same being – the Lord Maitreya – who manifested himself 2,000 years ago in Palestine by overshadowing his disciple Jesus.

Behind the event was the artist Benjamin Crème. When asked how the public would recognise the Maitreya, he responded: 'When Lord Maitreya appears, it will be as different beings to different people. He will appear as a man to a man, as a woman to a woman. He will appear as a white to a white, as a black to a black, as an Indian to an Indian.'

Crème invited a number of Fleet Street journalists to meet the Maitreya at what was then the Clifton curry house that July day. The journalists waiting for the Maitreya drank lager after lager to pass the time, but no Maitreya appeared. They left, disappointed and drunk. 'Once again, I am afraid God did not show,' read the *Guardian*.

• No. 126 already had an interesting religious history. Here just over 200 years previously the silk weaver Samuel Best, a pauper who lived on bread, cheese and gin tinctured with rhubarb, had announced himself as a prophet, chosen to lead the children of Israel back to Jerusalem.

ST GEORGE-IN-THE-EAST, Cannon Street Road, St George's

This Nicholas Hawksmoor church by Cable Street was the setting for the 'No Popery' riots of 1859 and 1860. Trouble broke out after parishioners discovered that the vicar, Bryan King, had co-founded a secret brotherhood for priests, the Society of the Holy Cross. So angry were they at King for indulging in Romish practices, they pelted the altar with bread and butter, and orange peel, brought in barking dogs to disrupt services, seized the choir stalls, tore down the altar cross and spat on and kicked the clergy. They even urinated on the pews.

The mob would have thrown the Revd King into the docks had his friends not made a cordon across a bridge, enabling him to get to the Mission House safely. The church was forced to close and allowed to reopen only when King promised not to wear ceremonial vestments during Mass. Even when services began again there were often as many as fifty police officers stationed in the wings ready in case of trouble.

→ Riots at St Giles Cathedral, p. 262

SALVATION ARMY BIRTHPLACE, outside the Blind Beggar pub, 337 Whitechapel Road, Whitechapel

One evening in June 1865 William Booth, a tall, fierce-looking revivalist preacher sporting a long black beard down to his chest, heard two missionaries preaching at an open-air meeting outside the Blind Beggar pub. When they invited any Christian bystander to join them, Booth exclaimed: 'There is heaven in East London for everyone who will stop to think and look to Christ as a personal saviour.' He told them of the love of God in offering salvation through Jesus Christ in such clear terms that they invited him to take charge of a special mission tent they were holding nearby.

This was the beginning of what became the Salvation Army. Within a year Booth's mission had more than sixty converts and he was returning home 'night after night haggard with fatigue', as his wife Catherine later explained, 'his clothes torn and bloody, bandages swathing his head where a stone had struck'.

Booth had moved to London in 1849 and drawn up a personal code of conduct which read:

I do promise – my God helping – that I will rise every morning sufficiently early (say 20 minutes before seven o'clock) to wash, dress, and have a few minutes, not less than five, in private prayer. That I will as much as possible avoid all that babbling and idle talking in which I have lately so sinfully indulged. That I will endeavour in my conduct and deportment before the world and my fellow servants especially to conduct myself as a humble, meek, and zealous follower of the bleeding Lamb.

Booth preached regularly across the East End, condemning the usual vices: drinking, gambling, watching cricket and football – anything that people enjoyed but which could lead to unchristian behaviour – surrounded by what a supporter called 'blaspheming infidels and boisterous drunkards'. In 1878 he reorganised the mission along quasi-military lines and began using the name Salvation Army. His preachers were given military-style ranks such as major and captain, with Booth himself as the general. The Salvation Army's banner in red, blue and gold sported a sun symbol and the motto 'Blood and Fire', the blood that of Christ and the fire that of the Holy Spirit.

Salvation Army bands would march into town 'to do battle with the Devil and his Hosts and make a special attack on his territory'. Their services provided the model for what became known disparagingly the following century as 'happy clappy' – joyous singing, Hallelujahs, beseeching for repentance, hand-clapping. Evil-doers and lost souls flocked to repent, even when the organisation's enemies, the so-called 'Skeleton Army', marching under a skull and crossbones banner, attempted to drive the Salvation Army off the streets. Within ten years Booth had 10,000 officers, and had opened branches in Iceland, Argentina and Germany. By the time he died the Salvation Army had spread to fifty-eight countries worldwide.

TOWER HILL EXECUTION SITE

The hill to the north of the Tower of London was one of the capital's main sites for religiously motivated executions, along with Smithfield and Tyburn. Its victims include perhaps the most famous of all British martyrs, Thomas More, who has since been canonised by the Catholic Church.

Ancient British tribes treated Tower Hill at the edge of the East End as holy and buried the head of Bran, a Celtic god king, under the ground there. Bran's head supposedly had magical powers and was interred facing France to ward off invaders. Nevertheless it failed to repel the Romans, who came to London shortly after the death of Christ. It also failed to repel the Saxons, the Danes and the Normans, who took over London at the end of the eleventh century and built what is still the capital's greatest landmark – the Tower – by the ancient tribes' sacred hill. Those executed here include:

• **John Fisher**, 1535

John Fisher, Bishop of Rochester, made a famous speech at Paul's Cross in 1526 denouncing Martin Luther. He was beheaded on Tower Hill on 22 June 1535 after opposing Henry VIII's divorce from Catherine of Aragon and the king's wish to make himself head of the English Church. Originally Fisher was supposed to be hanged, drawn and quartered at Tyburn, but Henry magnanimously commuted the sentence to beheading. The corpse was stripped naked and hung on the scaffold till evening when it was thrown into a pit at the nearby church of All Hallows, Barking. Fisher's head was later stuck on a pole on London Bridge where it remained for a fortnight before being thrown into the Thames.

• **Thomas More**, 1535

Lawyer, MP and fêted author, More was one of Henry VIII's leading aides, who resigned the chancellorship when the king declared himself supreme head of the Church in England after the Pope refused to support his divorce from Catherine of Aragon. More continued to argue against Henry's divorce and the split with Rome, and was arrested for treason in 1534. Before going to the scaffold on Tower Hill on 6 July 1535 More urged the governor of the Tower: 'I pray you, see me safe up, and for my coming down let me shift for myself.' He then joked with the executioner: 'Pluck up thy spirits, man. My neck is very short!' On the block More moved his beard away with the quip: 'It were a pity it should be cut off, it has done no treason.' He was later canonised by the Pope, but has been singled out for criticism by anti-Catholic commentators. They condemn his persecution of the Bible translator William Tyndale, whom he allegedly had arrested and burnt alive for translating the Book of Matthew.

• **Margaret Pole**, 1541

When Margaret Pole was taken for execution in 1541 after

refusing to support Henry VIII's break with the Roman Church, she would not agree that she was a traitor and had to have her head forcibly secured to the block. Pole struggled free and ran off closely pursued by the axe-wielding executioner, who killed her by hacking away at her.

• **William Laud**, Archbishop of Canterbury, 1645
One of the major religious figures of the seventeenth century, Laud was a chaplain to James I and became Charles I's main religious adviser. He was influenced by the Dutch theologian Jacob Arminius, who championed free will over predestination and loved ceremony at his services, what he called the 'beauty of holiness'.

The Puritans became increasingly powerful during Charles's reign and they hated such ceremonies, which they saw as being dangerously close to Roman Catholicism. In November 1640 the Long Parliament instituted proceedings against what it called King Charles's 'evil councillors', including Laud, who was impeached for high treason. He was accused of subverting the true religion with popish superstition, such as reintroducing stained glass into churches, and of causing the recent disastrous wars against the Scots.

Laud was sent to the Tower in 1641 and tried before the House of Lords in 1644. He defended himself admirably and the peers adjourned without voting. However, the Commons passed a Bill condemning him and he was beheaded on 10 January 1645. Laud was buried at the nearby church of All Hallows Barking, and after the Restoration was reburied in the vault under the altar at the chapel of St John's College, Oxford.

• **Christopher Love**, 1651
Love was a Puritan who was condemned for plotting to put Charles II on the throne during Oliver Cromwell's Commonwealth. In his final speech on 22 August 1651 he

announced: 'I am exchanging a pulpit for a scaffold and a scaffold for a throne. I am exchanging a guard of soldiers for a guard of angels to carry me to Abraham's bosom.' An onlooker watching Love go to the scaffold repented and claimed to be born again as the martyr died.

• **Simon, Lord Lovat**, 1747

The last Tower Hill execution took place in 1747 when Simon, Lord Lovat, was beheaded for supporting the Jacobite attempt to seize the throne of England.

→ Smithfield execution site, p. 33

TOWER OF LONDON, Tower Hill

Britain's major tourist attraction has been palace, mint, menagerie and most notably a prison, especially to London's medieval Jewish population who endured much misery here in the twelfth and thirteenth centuries (→ Old Jewry, p. 24).

Sir John Oldcastle, the most famous of the Lollard Bible reformers, escaped from the Tower in October 1413 after being imprisoned here for heresy. With a group of followers he had made a botched attempt to seize the capital, planning to kidnap the royal family from Eltham Palace. The plot failed when one of the group betrayed them. Oldcastle was eventually executed at St Giles, central London.

John Gerard, a Jesuit priest during a period of severe restrictions on Catholics, escaped from the Salt Tower, one of the wings of the complex, in 1589. He had been arrested soon after landing in England after a spell on the continent. In the Tower he was tortured by being suspended from chains on the dungeon wall, but managed to escape using a rope strung across the moat, which he somehow managed to negotiate despite his ravaged hands. Gerard fled to Morecrofts, a house in Uxbridge that was home to Robert Catesby, the Gunpowder Plotter of 1605. Thanks to his daring escape Gerard managed to avoid execution and died in Rome aged seventy-three.

William Penn, one of the first Quakers, was imprisoned in the Tower in 1668–9 for publishing controversial religious pamphlets. Here he wrote another, No Cross No Crown, 'to show the nature and discipline of the Holy Cross of Christ; and that the denial of self . . . is the alone way to the Rest and Kingdom of God'.

WELLCLOSE SQUARE, St George's

Now a ravaged location overlooked by fearsome tower blocks and slum estates, Wellclose Square has an extraordinary religious history. It was built as Marine Square, the first planned residential estate in east London, and was aimed at intellectuals and free-thinkers. Indeed it was the apex of the new London devised by the team around Christopher Wren that reshaped London after the 1666 Fire. Using biblical measurements connected with the ancient notion of 'sacred geometry' (→ p. 38), Wren and his assistants created the square 2,000 cubits (a biblical measurement, around ⅔ of a mile) from St Dunstan-in-the-East, his favourite church, which itself stands the same distance from St Paul's. Smart houses lined the square around a railed-off grassed area at the centre of which stood a church designed by Nicholas Hawksmoor and the Danish architect Caius Gabriel Cibber, the designer of the relief on the Monument based on the Book of Lamentations.

In the eighteenth century two illustrious religious figures – the Kabbalist *extraordinaire* Chaim Jacob Samuel Falk and the scientist-cum-theologian Emanuel Swedenborg – lived on Wellclose Square. Falk was known as the Ba'al Shem of London, a master of the secret names of God which in biblical times the high priest used to invoke special powers.

Over the years a succession of legends arose regarding Falk's stay here. He could work miracles, such as saving the Great Synagogue from fire (→ p. 20). He could re-enact the ancient Kabbalistic experiment in which the essence of God, containing the ten stages of primal divine light, appears from holy vessels. As Falk's reputation grew, so did the invitations to impart Kabbalistic advice. In London he was visited by the lothario Giacomo Casanova, who wanted to gain insights into Kabbalistic sexual techniques. He met the great occultist Cagliostro with whom he discussed the idea of founding a new Freemasonry that would restore the religion of Adam, Noah, Seth and Abraham. But he also had many detractors.

A feature in the *Gentleman's Magazine* of September 1762 lampooned Falk as a 'Christened Jew and the biggest rogue and villain in all the world, who had been imprisoned everywhere and banished out of all countries in Germany'. The anonymous writer explained that when he asked the Kabbalist to reveal one of his 'mysteries' Falk told him to avoid all churches and places of worship, steal a Hebrew Bible and obtain 'one pound of blood out of the veins of an honest Protestant'.

Emanuel Swedenborg, the Swedish visionary, scientist, philosopher and Christian theologian whose work was a major influence on William Blake, moved to Wellclose Square in 1766 at the age of seventy-eight. Twenty-one years earlier Swedenborg had given up science after experiencing an epiphany, and from then on he devoted himself to God. He wrote voluminous works interpreting the Scriptures and warned that 'no flesh could be saved', according to Christ's words in Matthew 24, unless a New Church was founded. It was, in London, after his death.

Swedenborg and Falk met to discuss the history of knowledge – the earliest knowledge saved by Noah before the Flood, which, according to ancient myth, was recorded on two indestructible pillars: one of marble, which could not be destroyed by fire, the other of brick, which could not be dissolved by water.

In 1845 St Saviour, the Wellclose Square church, was let to the Anglo-Catholic movement, led locally by the charismatic Revd Charles Lowder. He converted the church into a mission hall, which imposed a strict ascetic regime, and co-founded a secret brotherhood for priests, the Society of the Holy Cross. Its members worshipped the True Cross – the cross on which Jesus Christ was crucified – fragments of which had come into Lowder's possession by a circuitous route.

One night in 1862 a woman knocked at the mission in some distress. Her daughter had died. Two missionaries, Joseph Redman and Father Ignatius of Llanthony, left for the woman's house with a fragment of the True Cross. Father Ignatius laid the relic on the dead girl's breast and proclaimed: 'In the name of Jesus Christ I say unto thee, "Arise!"' Remarkably the girl's right hand moved slowly, tracing a cross in the air. The shocked Redman quietly breathed: 'Father, what have you done?', to which Father Ignatius replied: 'I have done nothing, but our Lord has done a great thing indeed.' Doctors soon explained away the 'miracle'. Evidently the girl had been unconscious, not dead, and the clerics' arrival had merely catalysed her revival. Those involved with the mission and Lowder's society believed otherwise.

Father Ignatius made a name for himself locally when he burst into Wilton's Music Hall one night and oblivious to the intoxicating atmosphere of mild ale and shag tobacco, gingerly made his way to the centre of the dance floor and announced to the startled crowd: 'We must all appear before the Judgment Seat of Christ,' before stealing away.

→ Little Gidding, p. 106

Hampton

HAMPTON COURT PALACE, Hampton Court Road

The palace was built in the twelfth century for the Knights Hospitallers, religious warriors who took over from the Knights Templars as protectors of pilgrims travelling to the Holy Land. It became a royal palace under Thomas Wolsey, Henry VIII's Lord Chancellor 400 years later, and was where in 1604 a conference led to the production of the greatest English Bible – the King James.

The Hampton conference was organised not to produce a new Bible but to seek a settlement between the Puritan and Anglican wings of the Church. The Puritans expected James to be sympathetic to their cause. But John Reynolds, one of their leaders, made a tactical error during the conference by using the word 'presbytery'. James was sensitive about the way the Presbyterians had restricted his power as a monarch in Scotland and felt he had to assert his role as head of the Church by supporting bishops. Viewing the Puritans' motion as a move to limit his power, he voiced the infamous threat: 'No bishop, no king!' and won the day.

As the conference proceeded, Reynolds suggested delegates discuss producing a new translation of the Bible. It was a timely move, for even though the Geneva version was popular, the clergy didn't like its marginal notes which proclaimed the Pope as the Antichrist. Reynolds explained that 'Those which were allowed in the reigns of Henry the eighth, and Edward the sixth, were corrupt and not answerable to the truth of the original.'

James was keen that 'some special pains were taken for a uniform translation, which should be done by the best learned men in both Universities'. The conference agreed that a translation be made of the whole Bible 'as consonant as can be to the original Hebrew and Greek; and this to be set out and printed, without any marginal notes, and only to be used in all churches of England in time of divine service'.

The king appointed fifty-four 'learned men', including Reynolds, Lancelot Andrewes and William Barlow (though, oddly, not Hugh Broughton, the foremost English Hebrew scholar of the time), to work on the new translation, dividing them in six groups at Westminster, Cambridge and Oxford. They based their new edition on the 1568 Bishops' Bible, but also consulted previous milestone works by William Tyndale and Miles Coverdale. The task took four years, including nine months of refining carried out in London. Thomas Bilson and Myles Smith, who wrote the preface, conducted the final revision, which was then printed in London by Robert Barker, printer to the king.

The King James Bible or Authorised Version (it was authorised by the king) stands as a masterpiece, but more for its literary content than its religious validity. Phrases that are now a rich part of English vocabulary – 'coat of many colours', 'fight the good fight' – were first found within, alongside passages of unmatchable quality and clarity: 'Though I speak with the tongues of men and of angels, and have not charity, I am become as sounding brass, or a tinkling cymbal . . .' and 'His body also was like the beryl, and his face as the appearance of lightning, and his eyes as lamps of fire, and his arms and his feet like in colour to polished brass, and the voice of his words like the voice of a multitude', for instance.

In the eighteenth century the King James replaced the Latin Vulgate as the standard version for English-speaking scholars. But disingenuously it also came to be seen as *the* divine text, refutation of which was a cardinal sin. Subsequent versions, while trying to jazz up the translation to make it more 'relevant', have come little nearer to capturing the original intention of the Scriptures and have fallen well short of the King James version in literary qualities.

→ The Gunpowder Plot, p. 81

Islington

ALEXANDER CRUDEN'S ADDRESS, Camden Passage

The alleyway near Angel tube station, which contains one of the greatest concentration of antique shops in Britain, was home in the early eighteenth century to the biblical expert Alexander Cruden. In 1737 he completed the first English concordance to the Bible, a monumental production, longer than the complete works of Shakespeare. It lists alphabetically every significant word in the Scriptures and indicates where in the Old and New Testaments it can be found.

Cruden was something of an eccentric. He would stride through the streets of Islington removing all traces of the number 45 to show his contempt for the radical orator and pamphleteer John Wilkes, whose issue No. 45 of the *North Briton* magazine had criticised George III. The king must have been pleased, for in 1758, the year the second edition of the Concordance appeared, he gave Cruden £100.

Lambeth

LAMBETH PALACE, Lambeth Palace Road

The London residence and offices of the Archbishop of Canterbury date back to the thirteenth century. It was here in April 1378 that John Wycliffe, the first man to translate the Bible into English, was ordered to appear before William Courtenay, Archbishop of Canterbury, accused of heresy after rejecting the idea of transubstantiation – that the Communion wafer actually becomes the body of Christ during the service. As the trial began a message came to the judges from the Queen Mother, Joan of Kent, forbidding the council to pass sentence upon Wycliffe, which left them dumbfounded. This gave him some time to resubmit his case. He also handed the judges a statement of his principles:

1. The Pope of Rome has no political authority.
2. All popes are sinners just as other men and need to be reproved.

3. The Pope has no right to the national resources of England.
4. Priests have no power to forgive sins.
5. Neither the Pope nor his priests have the power of excommunication.
6. The Church is a plunderer of the world's goods.
7. No tithes should be paid to Rome.
8. The Mass is blasphemous.

The archbishop reprimanded Wycliffe for his teachings, but the trial ended inconclusively.

Wycliffe's followers, the Lollards, were imprisoned here in 1434–5 in what was known as the Lollard's Tower, destroyed by Second World War bombs but since rebuilt.

→ William Tyndale translates the Bible into English, p. 250

THOMAS TANY BIBLE BURNING SITE, St George's Fields, Lambeth Road

Thomas Tany, a London silversmith, was found in St George's Fields in December 1654 burning the Bible, armed with a sword and pistols. He had rowed over the Thames towards the Houses of Parliament earlier that day, trying to deliver a petition which backed his claim that he was directly descended from Aaron, Moses' brother, High Priest of the Israelite, when God gave the Ten Commandments on Mount Sinai. The petition also alleged that Tany was now Theauraujohn, High Priest of the Jews, who would soon rebuild the Temple in Jerusalem with himself as High Priest.

By a remarkable coincidence, the same day that Tany was jailed John Reeve, a local tailor, supposedly received a divine visitor who told him he had been chosen as the Lord's 'last messenger'. With his cousin, Lodowick Muggleton, Reeve formed the Muggletonian sect (→ p. 16), which later condemned Tany as a 'counterfeit high priest and pretend prophet, the spawn of Cain'.

Tany was sent to jail, but while he was inside a series of fires began to blaze in the City. Tany claimed that these were a sign of the imminent destruction of the world. A more likely explanation came with the arrest of an arsonist who may have been in his pay. The self-styled 'High Priest' later perished at sea while journeying to the Holy Land 'to recover Jerusalem for the true Jews'.

→ Prophet John Wroe, p. 200

Moorfields

THOMAS EAMES RESURRECTION SITE, Bunhill Fields Cemetery, City Road

When Dr Thomas Emes, a self-styled prophet, died in December 1707 his supporters claimed that he would be resurrected five months later. Huge crowds turned up at Bunhill Fields Cemetery the next May. When there was no sign of Emes his followers explained that the miracle had been cancelled because of fears that the sizeable crowd would have endangered the safety of the risen prophet.

JOHN ROBINS'S ADDRESS, Ling Alley

Robins, a mid-seventeenth-century Moorfields mystic, failed in his plan to take nearly 150,000 followers to the Holy Land, and feed them solely on dry bread, raw vegetables and water. Robins explained that he had previously spent time on earth both as Adam and Melchizedek (an Old Testament high priest), but when he claimed in 1651 that his wife, Joan, would give birth to Jesus Christ, the authorities committed her to the Clerkenwell House of Correction and his scheme withered away.

Chapter 1

Peckham

WILLIAM BLAKE'S VISION, Goose Green

At the age of nine in 1766 William Blake, who went on to become England's greatest religiously inspired painter, claimed that he saw a tree filled with angels on Peckham Rye, then in the countryside at the south-eastern fringe of London. He went home and told his father, who thrashed him until his mother intervened. Blake also once described seeing the face of God pressed against the window of his parents' Soho shop. Blake later discovered, to his great pleasure, that his birth year – 1757 – had already been marked down by his mentor, the Swedish visionary Emanuel Swedenborg, as a special one when the last judgment would come to pass in the spiritual world.

Although many of Blake's paintings and poems were inspired by biblical imagery, confusion has long surrounded the identity of the Nonconformist sect he was born into. That his parents were Nonconformists was certain, for they were buried in Bunhill Fields, Moorgate, like Blake himself. Peter Ackroyd, Blake's most extensive biographer, has debated whether William's father, James, was a Baptist on Grafton Street, a Moravian on Fetter Lane, a Muggletonian, Sandemanian, Hutchinsonian, Thraskite or Salmonist, such were the bewildering number of non-establishment Protestant groups present in London in the mid-eighteenth century.

Blake's own views were idiosyncratic. He designed a mythology based upon the Bible and the Greek classics, and rejected what he called 'arid atheism and tepid deism'. He was wary of conventional religion, and in *The Marriage of Heaven and Hell* (1790) wrote: 'Prisons are built with stones of Law, Brothels with bricks of Religion . . . as the caterpillar chooses the fairest leaves to lay her eggs on, so the priest lays his curse on the fairest joys,' a line borrowed from the Book of Proverbs.

In his epic poem *Jerusalem* (1804–20) Blake posed the ancient queries of the Christian Kabbalists that James I had revived when he moved to London from Scotland in 1603 to take the throne: was Britain the primitive seat of the patriarchal religion? Was Britain home of a purer Christianity than Rome? Was London *the* Holy City, the New Jerusalem, the centre of a world of one God, one religion, one nation?

If it is true, my title-page is also True, that Jerusalem was & is the Emanation of the Giant Albion. It is True, and cannot be controverted. Ye are united O ye Inhabitants of Earth in One Religion. The Religion of Jesus: the most Ancient, the Eternal: & the Everlasting Gospel – The Wicked will turn it to Wickedness, the Righteous to Righteousness. Amen! Huzza! Selah! All things Begin & End in Albion's Ancient Druid Rocky Shore.

Plumstead

The south-east London suburb beyond Woolwich was home in the mid-nineteenth century to one of the capital's most esoteric and strictest religious cults, the Peculiar People of Plumstead. They took their name from the verse in the Book of Deuteronomy which runs: 'And the Lord hath avouched thee this day to be his peculiar people.' Although the Peculiar People merited an entry in the 1911 Encyclopaedia Britannica, they soon died out as their religion forbade them from seeking medical help, a stance that presaged their doom during a typhoid epidemic.

Primrose Hill

William Blake, walking here early in the nineteenth century, had a vision of the 'spiritual sun, not like a golden disc the size of a guinea but like an innumerable company of the heavenly host crying "Holy, holy, holy"'.

According to the fifteenth-century soothsayer Mother Shipton, if Primrose Hill were ever surrounded, the streets of London would become rivers of blood.

→ Intrigue involving James II at St James's Palace, p. 94

The Popish Plot

One of the most infamous religious conspiracies in London history, the Popish Plot unfolded after the body of Sir Edmund Berry Godfrey, MP, JP and well-known Protestant, was found on Primrose Hill in October 1678, impaled on his own sword.

As speculation mounted about who could have murdered Godfrey, the conspiracy theories began to emerge. Perhaps the murder was connected with an anonymous pamphlet, believed to have been written by the poet Andrew Marvell, which suggested that the Catholics were plotting to take control of London, and make their religion that of England?

Back in August the king, Charles II, had been told by his chemist, Christopher Kirkby, while walking in St James's Park, that the Catholics were planning to massacre Protestants, burn down the staunchly Protestant City of London (as the papists had been accused of doing after the 1666 Fire), overthrow the government, and replace Charles with his brother, the Catholic Duke of York (later James II).

Kirkby told the king he knew the names of assassins who planned to shoot him. If that failed, the queen's physician would poison him. Now Godfrey was dead, so perhaps the putsch had begun. The House of Commons was searched in case another Gunpowder Plot was imminent. The grapevine buzzed with talk of how the letters of Godfrey's name could be rearranged into the anagram 'Died by Rome's revenged fury'. A cutler made a special 'Godfrey' dagger. On one side were the words 'Remember the murder of Edmund Berry Godfrey', on the other, 'Remember Religion'. He sold 3,000 in one day.

A cleric called Titus Oates told the authorities that there definitely was a Popish Plot to take over the country. He made more than forty allegations against various Catholics, and even accused the queen's physician and the secretary to the Duchess of York of planning to assassinate Charles II. Soldiers were seconded to help Oates root out these saboteurs, and on 3 December 1678 the Duke of York's former secretary, Edward Colman, was sentenced to death.

Parliament passed a bill barring Catholics from membership of both Houses (a law not repealed until 1829), while Oates received a state apartment in Whitehall and an annual allowance of £1,200. Far from being sated with his illicitly gained power, Oates succumbed to megalomania. He claimed assassins would soon shoot the king with silver bullets causing wounds that would not heal. But public opinion began to turn against him after he had fifteen mostly innocent men executed. Oates was eventually arrested for sedition (accusing the Duke of York of treason) and fined £100,000.

When the Catholic Duke of York took the throne in 1685 as James II he sought revenge. Oates was sentenced for perjury and given a life term. He was removed from his cell wearing a hat emblazoned with the slogan 'Titus Oates, convicted upon full evidence of two horrid perjuries' and put into the pillory in Westminster so that passers-by could pelt him with unwanted food. William of Orange pardoned him in 1688.

It later transpired that Godfrey had been murdered not on Primrose Hill but at Somerset House, by a silversmith called Prance, hired by Titus Oates and his associate Israel Tongue, and that the body was then taken to Primrose Hill.

Chapter 1

Putney

ST MARY'S, Putney High Street

The church where Oliver Cromwell's New Model Army debated notions of political freedom in 1647 was the setting for one of the most dramatic incidents in London's recent religious history. On Sunday 13 July 2008 the Right Revd Gene Robinson, the world's first openly gay Anglican bishop, was preaching, remarking how sad it was that the Anglican Communion was 'tearing itself apart' over the issue of gay priests, when a heckler rose and interrupted with the taunt 'because of heretics like you'.

The congregation turned to stare at the source of the cry. It was a long-haired man clutching a motorcycle helmet, who continued: 'Go back, go back. Repent, repent, repent.' Some began to boo and slow handclap until the vicar, Dr Giles Fraser, stepped in to calm down proceedings, urging everyone to open their hymn sheets. The singing drowned out the barracking, and when Bishop Robinson resumed his sermon he urged the congregation to 'pray for that man', who by that time had been escorted outside back to his bike.

The incident occurred during a highly charged Lambeth Conference at Canterbury that many feared might result in serious schism over the issue of gay clergy and women bishops. When asked about the heckling, Dr Fraser told reporters: 'Some of us are struggling for the dream of an inclusive Church. I'm proud that Bishop Robinson is speaking here.'

→ Canterbury Cathedral, p. 142

River Thames

There are no records of the first Jews to arrive in east London, but Jews have been coming to Britain since King Solomon sent tin traders over some time around the year 960 BC to negotiate with the miners of Cornwall. The tin traders included a number of Phoenicians – inhabitants of what is now the Gaza Strip – whose word for this island was 'Berat-Anach' – 'country of tin' – which is phonetically similar to 'Britain'.

Some time around the year AD 20, according to a once popular legend, Joseph of Arimathea, a merchant from the Holy Land, journeyed across the Mediterranean, past the Straits of Gibraltar, and landed in Cornwall to trade tin. His party allegedly included his great-nephew, Jesus Christ. Better known is the legend of how after Jesus' crucifixion Joseph of Arimathea returned to Britain with the Holy Grail, the vessel used by Jesus and the Apostles at the Last Supper, and at Glastonbury preached the first Christian teachings heard in England.

Yet if Joseph did visit Britain on an evangelical mission – with or without the Holy Grail – it is more likely that after crossing the Channel from France at the closest point (Calais to Dover) he would have explored the nearest estuary (the Thames), rather than heading a long distance west and journeying seventy miles through woodland to get to a remote spot such as Glastonbury. If so, he may well have disembarked only once the marshland on the riverbank gave way to the settlements dotted around the huge lake known to locals as Llyndin, which was later drained to form Wapping.

CHAIM FALK'S LABORATORY, **London Bridge**

The eighteenth-century Kabbalist *extraordinaire* Chaim Jacob Samuel Falk, known popularly as the Ba'al Shem of London, had an alchemical laboratory on London Bridge. Here, according to rumours that swept London's Jewish community in the 1740s and 1750s, Falk was creating a golem of Jewish legend. A golem is an artificial being made of clay that a Kabbalist creates by whipping himself into a state of ecstasy using rituals and chants. When the Kabbalist engraves a Hebrew word on the golem's forehead and places under its tongue a piece of paper bearing one of the secret names of God the being supposedly comes to life. Sometimes the creator engraves the Hebrew word אמה ('emmes' – truth), later disabling the Golem by rubbing out the 'א', leaving the word מה ('mes' – death).

According to Hebrew lore, the first golem was Adam – the first man – created out of each of the four letters of the main name of God – י, ה, ו, ה – stacked one on top of the other: Yod (י) being the head, Heh (ה) the arms and shoulders, Vav (ו) the spine and sexual organs, and the final Heh the hips and legs.

Despite all expectation, no golem was ever officially seen appearing from the Ba'al Shem's London Bridge workshop.

SHABBATAI ZEVI'S BARGE

A barque with silken sails and rigging and manned by a Hebrew crew was believed to be waiting on the Thames at Ratcliffe, the river's main medieval emigration point, to take believers to the Promised Land in 1666. There followers would meet the Messiah – Shabbatai Zevi – a Turkish Jew known for indulging in religious ecstasies and mystical speculations, who had declared he would appear as the Anointed One that September.

At the beginning of the year scholars had nervously noted the juxtaposition of 1,000 (Christ's millennium) and 666, the Number of the Beast of the Revelation, in the numerical construction of the year. In case Zevi *was* the Messiah, many London Jews prepared for his arrival. Hebrew prayer books fronted by pictures of Zevi sitting on a royal throne circulated within the community. Members of the Exchange even began to wager large sums on whether Zevi would take control of the Ottoman Empire, and Samuel Pepys noted in his diary for 19 February 1666 that speculators were offering 10–1 if a 'certain person now at Smyrna [Turkey] be within these two years owned by all the Princes of the East, and particularly the grand Signor as the King of the world, in the same manner we do the King of England here, and that this man is the true Messiah'.

In April 1666 Zevi landed in Constantinople, Turkey, where he was captured by the sultan's troops. The sultan gave Zevi the chance to prove himself. Troops would fire arrows at him, and using his divine powers he would surely be able to ward them off. Rather than risk humiliation, or even martyrdom, Zevi immediately renounced his views and converted to Islam. This shocking news led many, understandably, to denounce Zevi as a false messiah.

→ False messiah Joanna Southcott, p. 73

The West End

GEORGE ORWELL'S MINISTRY OF LOVE, All Saints, Margaret Street, Fitzrovia

The political author partly modelled the nightmarish Ministry of Love in *1984*, his bleak totalitarian novel, on this Anglo-Catholic church. In *1984* the Ministry is a prison where non-believers are punished, where they confess to their thoughtcrimes. But *1984* is also a bleak black satire of mid-twentieth-century bureaucratic bumptiousness, and one of its targets is the Church, where the phrase 'Ministry of Love' has long been used to describe the circle of followers around Jesus.

Orwell often targeted the Anglo-Catholic Church in his writings, and All Saints, with its exquisite polychromatic Gothic design, is a superb example of the group's places of worship. 'Its influence is and always must be against freedom of thought and speech, against human equality,' the author once explained. Orwell's 1935 novel *A Clergyman's Daughter* features a character described as an 'Anglo-Catholic of the most truculent Church Times breed – more clerical than the clerics, knowledgeable about Church history, expert on vestments, and ready at any moment with a furious tirade against Modernists, Protestants, scientists, Bolshevists, and atheists'.

1984, though not at first glance a 'religious' novel, contains a covert religious subtext. Infallible Big Brother, the unseen hero of the book, equates with God. O'Brien, the personification of all that is righteous in the utopian society depicted in the book, is Jesus Christ. Goldstein, the traitor who betrayed the revolution, Satan. Winston Smith is Adam, and Julia, Eve, for the manner in which Julia lures Winston into rebellion against Big Brother is reminiscent of Eve's behaviour in the Garden of Eden in Genesis.

Orwell spent much time in this area during the Second World War while working nearby at the BBC, and would pass the church when heading from the studio to the pubs of Fitzrovia. Evidence that he entered All Saints, presumably for inspiration, comes from his use of one of the church's favoured biblical passages, displayed on its walls, from Matthew 28, 'I am with you always, even unto the end of the world', which Orwell adapts in the novel for the first meeting between Winston and O'Brien.

HERMETIC ORDER OF THE GOLDEN DAWN, 17 Fitzroy Street, Fitzrovia

A mystical order with similarities to the Masons, the Hermetic Order of the Golden Dawn was a major influence on modern occultism. It was founded in 1888 by Dr William Wynn Westcott, a coroner and Master Freemason, who deliberately shrouded its origins in mystery. Nevertheless the year the order came into being was significant, for 1888 was the strangest in London since 1666 (→ Fire of London, p. 18; → Shabbatai Zevi, p. 19), the year when a murderer (or murderers) unknown – Jack the Ripper – killed at least five prostitutes in the East End according to Masonic rite (→ p. 21).

Westcott claimed he had discovered in a bookstall on Farringdon Road an encrypted sixteenth-century document written in an arcane alphabet. It contained details of the alchemical and mystical rituals of a secret Germanic occult order, Die Goldene Dammerung. On Fitzroy Street Westcott set up the enticingly named Isis-Urania Temple, which attracted the cream of London bohemia, intrigued by the promise of obtaining a glimpse of eternity. Those who joined the order included the poet W. B. Yeats. At the Fitzroy Street temple the poet assumed the title *Demon est Deus Inversus* (D. E. D. I., 'The Devil is God Inverted') and underwent a 'spiritual' marriage with one Maud Gonne, also known as *Per Ignum ad Lucem* ('Through the Fire to the Light').

By the end of the year the Temple had thirty-two members being schooled in astrology, alchemy, Enochian magic and *The Egyptian Book of the Dead*. Rituals would begin with a recitation of the eleven Magick Commandments:

> Thee I invoke, O Bornless One.
> Thee, that didst create the Earth and the Heavens.
> Thee, that didst create the Night and the Day.
> Thee, that didst create the Darkness and the Light.
> Thou art ASAR UN-NEFER ('Myself made Perfect'): Whom no man hath seen at any time.
> Thou art IA-BESZ ('the Truth in Matter').
> Thou art IA-APOPHRASZ ('the Truth in Motion').
> Thou hast distinguished between the Just and the Unjust.
> Thou didst make the Female and the Male.
> Thou didst produce the Seeds and the Fruit.
> Thou didst form Men to love one another, and to hate one another.

Within a few years the order was well established. But it soon suffered a schism. MacGregor L. Mathers, a pioneer of the Tarot, wrested control from Westcott. He wanted a mystical order in which initiates would study the esoteric knowledge centred around the Kabbalist notion of how all things in the universe connect via the Tree of Life. In 1900 Mathers was exposed as a fraud and expelled from the order. By then there were branches in America and a Thoth-Hermes Temple had been founded in Chicago. The order died out in the 1970s.

→ The Rosicrucians, p. 9.

JOANNA SOUTHCOTT'S ADDRESS, 38 Manchester Street

The most infamous of all English prophetesses was a Devonian upholsterer who in the 1790s began hearing a voice that told her: 'The Lord is awakened out of sleep. He will terribly shake the earth.' Joanna Southcott thought this must be the work of Satan until the same voice began to make accurate prophecies about imminent events. When she asked for proof of divinity, there were three knocks on the bedstead and then she found her hand writing messages as if guided by another.

Southcott moved to the West End in 1801. There she began to describe herself as 'the woman clothed with the sun' of Revelation 12 and the 'bride of the lamb' of Revelation 19. She issued pamphlets and went on speaking tours, amassing some 20,000 followers who believed her a true visionary. Thousands signed a petition in support of her desire to overthrow Satan and establish Christ's kingdom on earth. In turn they each received a piece of paper inscribed: 'The Sealed of the Lord, the Elect precious. Man's Redemption to inherit the Tree of Life, to be made Heirs of God and Joint-Heirs with Jesus Christ', with their name written above the inscription and Southcott's signature below it.

At the age of sixty-four in 1814 Southcott announced she was pregnant. It was to be a virgin birth and the child would be 'Shiloh', as prophesied by Jacob in Genesis 49:10; he would 'rule all the nations with a rod of iron' as outlined in Revelation 12:5. Doctors confirmed Southcott was pregnant. Supporters sent gifts and a cradle decorated with a gold crown, the name 'Shiloh' embroidered in Hebrew letters at the head. They urged her to acquire a husband prior to the birth, lest the child be declared illegitimate, and so she married John Smith, a steward to the Earl of Darnley.

Some of Southcott's followers travelled to the capital, camping on the outskirts to await the great event. The newspapers of the day were not enthusiastic, however. Many journalists alleged that the birth would be of the 'baby-smuggled-in-warming-pan' variety, similar to that allegedly staged by Mary of Modena, wife of James II, at St James's Palace (→ p. 94). Typical of these was the *Morning Chronicle*, which on 18 October 1814 announced: 'Tomorrow is the great, the important, day, *big* with fate of multitudes of miserable sinners, anxiously waiting to be white-washed through the merits of the forthcoming little Shiloh. The happy news of the coming of Shiloh is to be announced to the Faithful by the sound of ten thousand Jew's-harps and penny trumpets!'

The detractors were right, for the signs of pregnancy disappeared and there was no birth. Supporters claimed the birth failed to take place because of a 'want of faith' among the people, just as a modern-day medium might blame failure to contact the dead on the number of sceptics present. Southcott, meanwhile, grew increasingly weak, and on 27 December 1814 she died, while a mob jeered and raved outside her house. She had dropsy, not pregnancy.

Lord Byron weaved the story into his epic poem *Don Juan*, noting 'So few are the elect/And the new births of both their stale virginities/Have proved but dropsies taken for divinities.' William Blake was equivocal and commented: 'Whate'er is done to her she cannot know/And if you'll ask her she will swear it so./Whether 'tis good or evil none's to blame/No one can take the pride, no one the shame.'

To Southcott's supporters her death was only a temporary

setback. Some believed that Shiloh had indeed been born – on Christmas Day – and had immediately soared to heaven. They placed hot-water bottles around the late prophetess's body, to keep it warm in expectation of either a resurrection or the appearance of Shiloh, and when neither happened after four days took her remains to St John's Wood Cemetery, where she was buried. They vowed not to shave their beards until she was reborn, but their wait is still not over.

Southcott left a box which was opened over a hundred years later at Church House, Westminster (→ p. 80).

LORD GEORGE GORDON'S ADDRESS, 64 Welbeck Street, Marylebone

Five years after the anti-Catholic Gordon Riots of June 1780 (→ p. 4), their instigator, Lord George Gordon, leader of the Protestant Association, was visited at his Marylebone home by two Jesuits carrying a vial of liquid. They had a note supposedly written by the local chemist urging the peer to drink the mixture. Suspicious of the strangers with the unusual request, Gordon had the contents of the vial examined, which proved to be a noxious poison. It turned out that the two Jesuits were emissaries of the Vatican sent to kill Lord Gordon for inflaming opinion against Catholics.

RICHARD BROTHERS' ADDRESS, 57 Paddington Street, Marylebone

Brothers was a late eighteenth-century false messiah who claimed to be descended from King David and described himself as the 'Prince of the Hebrews'. He was born in Newfoundland, Canada, in 1757, on 25 December no less, came to London to work in the Woolwich shipyards, and in 1790, after studying various ancient tracts, announced that 'the Spirit of God began to enlighten my understanding' – not that this was enough to keep him out of debt and Newgate Prison where he shared a cell of fifteen.

Following his release in 1792, Brothers decided to return to Canada. But on his way to Bristol to catch a ship, he found that 'God by his power stopped the action of every joint and limb, commanding me at the same instant to return and wait.' Brothers walked back to London, and took lodgings on Paddington Street in the West End. Here he wrote a book, *A Revealed Knowledge of the Prophecies and Times*. It contained little more than extracts from the Bible, annotated with his own commentary, which adopted some of the more extreme Protestant teachings of the day: Rome as the great whore of Revelations 17, the Pope as the scarlet-coloured beast, the cardinals as the ten horns and so on, although he did issue a precise date for the Second Coming: 19 November 1795.

The book became a bestseller – *The Time*s nicknamed Brothers 'The Great Prophet of Paddington Street' – and he was visited by large numbers of people. But the authorities took fright at his claim that the royal family would have to step down at the coming of the 'King of Heaven and Earth'. He was arrested in March 1795 and accused by the Privy Council of 'maliciously publishing fantastical prophecies with intent to cause disturbances'. The Privy Council declared Brothers insane and imprisoned him inside the austere brick walls of Canonbury Tower (→ p. 8).

After 19 November passed with no Second Coming of the Messiah, Brothers's influence waned. When he was again a free man, he came up with a new plan, to return the Jews to the Holy Land. He tried to enlist help from the kings of England, Denmark, Sweden and Prussia, who he hoped would provide building materials to create the city of sacred geometry outlined in Ezekiel chapters 40–48. Alas they didn't.

SOCIETY OF THE HOLY CROSS, House of St Barnabas, 1 Greek Street, Soho

The charismatic Revd Charles Lowder founded a brotherhood for priests, the Society of the Holy Cross, at what was then the Chapel of the House of Charity, in 1855. Lowder and his associates strongly believed in the legends surrounding the True Cross – the cross on which Jesus Christ was crucified. It had allegedly been discovered in 1326 in a Jerusalem cave, along with two similar crosses, by Empress Helena, mother of Constantine I. The empress had found out which was the authentic one by placing a sick woman on each of the three in turn. When the woman rested on the third she was healed.

The True Cross passed through the hands of many people over the centuries, not all of whom treated it reverentially. Saladin, twelfth-century master of the Muslim world, rode through the streets of Damascus with the captured cross tied to his horse's tail, dragging in the dust. It was later broken up into fragments, one of which came into Lowder's possession. In London it was then used to perform 'miracles', particularly in the East End (→ p. 57).

TYBURN, **Edgware Road at Oxford Street**

England's most famous execution site was an 11-foot gallows, the Tyburn Tree, which stood by the Tyburn stream from 1388 to 1783. It could be used to hang eight people simultaneously. The nearby Tyburn Convent on Bayswater Road contains the remains of over a hundred Roman Catholic martyrs executed at Tyburn. They include:

• **Elizabeth Barton**, 1534

The 28-year-old Holy Maid of Kent saw visions of 'wondrous things done in other places whilst she was neither herself present nor yet heard no report thereof', according to the leading cleric of the time Thomas Cranmer. She refused to back Henry VIII in his bid to divorce Catherine of Aragon, and prophesied that if Henry married Anne Boleyn against the Pope's wishes he would be dead within a few months. The authorities initially ignored Barton, but she was executed at Tyburn for treason on 20 April 1534.

• **John Houghton**, 1535
Some members of the clergy were not enthusiastic about recognising Henry VIII as head of the English Church, as prescribed by the 1534 Act of Supremacy. One of these was John Houghton, prior of London's Charterhouse monastery, whose disobedience left the authorities with no option but to imprison him in the Tower. Continued attempts to make Houghton and similar thinkers see the king's point of view were unsuccessful and they were sentenced to hang at Tyburn. From a prison cell in the Tower they were spotted by Thomas More, once Henry VIII's favourite, who exclaimed to his daughter: 'Look, Meg, these blessed Fathers be now as cheerfully going to their deaths as bridegrooms to their marriage!' Houghton and his fellow heretics were hanged in their habits and disembowelled while still conscious. As the executioner went to tear out Houghton's heart, he shouted: 'O Jesu, what wouldst thou do with my heart?'

• **Edmund Campion**, 1581
Campion was a Jesuit priest who after being arrested for heresy was tortured on the rack and questioned in front of Elizabeth I. When asked if he accepted Elizabeth as queen, Campion replied: 'I will willingly pay to her Majesty what is hers, yet I must pay to God what is his.' On being found guilty and sentenced to death, Campion thundered: 'In condemning us you condemn all your own ancestors, all the ancient priests, bishops and kings, all that was once the glory of England, the island of saints, and the most devoted child of the See of Peter.' Standing on the scaffold, Campion exclaimed: '*Spectaculum facti sumus Deo, angelis et hominibus* . . .', words first uttered by St Paul (though not in Latin), which translate roughly into English as 'we are made a spectacle unto God, unto his angels as unto men . . .'

In 1970 Campion was canonised as one of the forty English martyrs. The ropes which were used to hang him are kept at Stonyhurst College, Lancashire.

• **Robert Southwell**, 1595
Any subject of Queen Elizabeth who had become a Roman Catholic priest after her accession in 1558 could remain in England for only forty days or would forfeit his life. Southwell was a Jesuit and poet who in 1584 returned to England from Rome, despite the ruling, and travelled from one Catholic family to another administering Catholic rites. After six years he was arrested, not just on religious grounds but for supposedly plotting against the queen. He suffered the misfortune of being taken to the bloodthirsty royal torturer Richard Topcliffe, an expert of the rack. Topcliffe used his best techniques to extract information about other priests from Southwell, to little avail. For three years Southwell languished in the Tower and was tortured on ten occasions. Tried at the King's Bench, he denied he was a traitor and explained that he had come back to England simply to administer the sacraments according to the rites of the Catholic Church. Southwell was hanged, drawn and quartered on 20 February 1595.

• **Philip Powel**, 1646
Powel was a Benedictine monk who, when sentenced to death exclaimed: 'Oh what am I that God thus honours me and will have me to die for his sake?' and called for a glass of sherry. From the Tyburn Tree he announced: 'This is the happiest day and the greatest joy that ever befell me, for I am brought hither for no other cause or reason than that I am a Roman Catholic priest and a monk of the Order of St Benedict.' Pope Pius XI beatified him in 1929.

• **Robert Hubert**, 1666
Hubert, a French silversmith, was executed after admitting starting the 1666 Fire of London – on the Pope's orders – to punish London for turning to Protestantism. This was later shown to be a false confession, but by then the damage had been done.

Hubert was hanged at Tyburn alongside an effigy of the Pope, its head filled with live cats, which was set alight. As the flames rose the cats screamed in torment but, as the animals could not be seen, it looked as if it was the 'Pope' that was being burnt alive, which brought whoops of delight from the large crowd.

• **Oliver Plunkett**, 1681
The last Catholic martyr to be executed in England, Plunkett was Archbishop of Armagh and was convicted of treason. He was beatified in 1920 and canonised in 1975 – the first new Irish saint for almost 700 years.

Westminster

CHURCH HOUSE, Dean's Yard
A conference centre used instead of the Houses of Parliament during the Second World War, Church House was where Joanna Southcott's infamous box was finally opened in July 1927. Southcott was an early nineteenth-century prophetess who claimed she would give the virgin birth to the messianic child Shiloh as prophesied in the Book of Revelation. When she died on 27 December 1814 without achieving this extraordinary feat her supporters kept her flame alive. Southcott had left a box of mementoes, which she had insisted should be opened only in the presence of twenty-four bishops, but it proved difficult to find that many bishops willing to take part in the ceremony.

However, in April 1927 Harry Price of the National Laboratory of Psychical Research was sent a sealed wooden casket with an accompanying letter claiming that the box in question belonged to the religious visionary Joanna Southcott and 'undoubtedly contains some of her private property'. The contents of the box would reveal to an astonished nation 'means of saving the country

. . . I do not know how many boxes Joanna left, and there are bound to be spurious ones, but the history of the one I am sending you can be traced from the time the dying hand of Joanna entrusted it.'

Was this really the famed box? Price invited a number of mediums to speculate on its contents. A Mrs Stahl Wright sensed 'a little box – a jewel – and the names "Edith" and "Yates".' Mr Vout Peters went into a trance and detailed that the box contained 'three documents, one bound as a book, scripts, curious drawings, something that is opaque, something long, the name Jehovah, the year 1812 and something to do with fabric'. Harry Price X-rayed the box without opening it and discovered inside a pistol, a dice-box, a bone puzzle with rings and a pair of gold earrings. Newspapers reported that, if the box were opened wires attached to a pistol would release the trigger and kill a bishop or two. Perhaps that was why twenty-four bishops could not be found despite Southcott's supporters parading through the streets of London bearing sandwichboards proclaiming 'The Bishops must open Joanna's Box to save England from ruin.'

Eventually one bishop was found, Dr Hine of Grantham, and Joanna Southcott's box was opened. As well as the pistol (which didn't fire) it contained fifty-six items, the most interesting of which were a lottery ticket, a 2d William and Mary coin and a cheap novel. Predictably, supporters retorted that this was not the correct box.

→ The Panacea Society of Bedford takes up the case, p. 158

HOUSES OF PARLIAMENT, St Margaret Street

The most infamous botched terrorist attack in British history was Guy Fawkes and his fellow conspirators' attempt to blow up the Palace of Westminster in November 1605. Fawkes and his allies planned to carry out the explosion during the state opening of

Parliament in revenge for James I's attacks on Catholicism.

Yet when James took the throne in 1603 Catholics were enthusiastic. One Oxfordshire woman was heard to remark: 'Now we have a king who is of our religion and will restore us to our rights.' James was, after all, the son of the Catholic Mary, Queen of Scots, and had been baptised. He had, however, been brought up a Protestant. After intimating that he would relax anti-Catholic legislation, he took the opposite position, ordering all Catholic clergy to leave England and passing a law that fined those who did not attend Protestant church services.

A gang was assembled to assassinate the king. It comprised thirteen disaffected Catholics including Robert Catesby (the leader), Thomas Percy and Guy Fawkes, and they met in the Duck and Drake inn on the Strand. They had a grand scheme planned. Were James to die in the explosion, Catesby, Fawkes and the others planned to kidnap the royal princess, Elizabeth, from Coombe Abbey, marry her to a Catholic nobleman and make her queen. Fawkes, the explosives expert, was left in the parliamentary cellars to light the fuse, but he was caught at the last moment when a group of guards checked the rooms.

The guards knew what they were doing for they had information. One of the gang, Francis Tresham, worried that the explosion would kill his brother-in-law, Lord Monteagle, warned the latter not to attend Parliament on 5 November. Monteagle informed Robert Cecil, the king's chief minister, and he organised a search of Parliament. Fawkes was arrested, gave his name as John Johnson, and was taken to the Tower of London for questioning. Under torture he revealed his real name and gave away those of his co-conspirators. Troops surrounded Holbeche House, Staffordshire, where the gang had agreed to meet and when the conspirators refused to surrender a gunfight broke out in which Catesby, Percy and the two Wright brothers, Christopher and John, were killed. Three members of the gang, Everard Digby, Robert Wintour and Thomas Bates, were executed on 30 January

1606. Digby was disembowelled while still alive. Fawkes and Robert Wintour were hanged, drawn and quartered the following day.

A number of questions remain about the plot. The government had a monopoly on storing gunpowder, so how did the conspirators find thirty-six barrels of the explosive? Most of the nation's gunpowder was stored at the Tower of London, so how did Fawkes and his gang get their stash to Westminster without anyone noticing, especially given the unsuitability of river transport for fear of damp? And why were known Catholics allowed to rent a house so near Parliament?

Some historians believe the gang was set up and encouraged – just so far – by Tresham as part of a plot hatched by Robert Cecil, head of the secret service, to get the king to clamp down hard on Catholics. Indeed, following the unmasking of the plot, stricter measures against papists were enacted. For instance, in May 1606 Parliament passed the Oath of Allegiance requiring subjects to deny the Pope's authority over the king.

There was trouble outside the Houses of Parliament in 1641 when peers debated the Bishops' Exclusion Bill. The mob, encouraged by the leading parliamentarian John Pym, obstructed bishops trying to take their seats in the Lords. In the mêlée one officer accidentally coined one of the era's major new words – 'roundhead' – after drawing his sword and threatening to 'cut the throat of those round-headed dogs that bawled against the bishops'. The following February both Houses voted to ban bishops from the House of Lords. (They've since been allowed to return.)

A year later Charles I burst into the House of Commons looking for five MPs he believed were conspiring against his Catholic wife, Henrietta Maria. Realising they were absent, the king cursed: 'The birds have flown,' and demanded that the Speaker reveal their whereabouts. Speaker Lenthall responded with one of the most extraordinary and powerful statements in political history: 'I have neither eyes to see, nor tongue to speak in this place, but as this House is pleased to direct me.' No monarch has since been allowed into the House of Commons.

When Parliament met in June 1780 to debate laws that would give further civil rights to Catholics, some 60,000 protesters wearing blue cockades and carrying blue flags, spurred on by Lord George Gordon, head of the Protestant Association, gathered outside to demonstrate. As the peers arrived they jostled, hissed and booed. Some even went as far as pulling Lord Bathurst, the Lord President of the Council, from his carriage and jeering at him for being 'the Pope and a silly old woman'.

Inside the House demonstrators shouting 'No popery!' tried to storm the doors as peers picked up their swords, threatening to use them if attacked. The motion was postponed, but violence soon shook London (→ The Gordon Riots, p. 4). Parliament met again the following Tuesday when the mob again prevented normal business. The prime minister, Lord North, had his hat torn into pieces which were then handed out as trophies. He was lucky to escape with his life.

Catholic emancipation didn't follow until the 1820s.

* * *

Parliament and religion

In medieval times religion was the cause of more parliamentary debate than any other subject, other than notions of personal liberty. Since the liberalisation of laws governing Catholics early in the nineteenth century and Jews a few decades later there has been considerably less discussion of religion. Among the most significant debates over the centuries are:

• **The Statute of Provisors**, 1306
Edward I curtailed the right of the Pope to impose taxes on the English. Three acts of Parliament passed in 1353, 1365 and 1393 aimed to prevent appeal to the Pope against the powers of the king.

• **The Pope's authority**, 1365
When Pope Urban V demanded that England submit to the authority of the Bishop of Rome as the only legitimate sovereign of England the government discussed how best to resist him, even if it meant using military force. They invited John Wycliffe, the Bible translator, to comment and he concluded: 'There cannot be two temporal sovereigns in one country: either Edward is king or Urban is king. We make our choice. We accept Edward of England and reject Urban of Rome.'

• **John Wycliffe's views**, 1377
In October 1377 the Bible translator was again sought for advice on the Pope's demands for total authority over England, this time by the new eleven-year-old king, Richard II. Wycliffe explained to the king and Parliament that the papacy had no moral, legal or spiritual right to claim sovereignty over the country and was spurred on by financial rather than religious motives. He declared that nowhere in the Scriptures did Peter or Paul suggest themselves to be the supreme authority in the Church or over all men: 'We must oppose the first beginning of mischief. Christ himself is the Lord paramount, and the Pope is a fallible man who must lose his lordship in the event of his falling into mortal sin.'

• **On the Burning of Heretics**, 1401
Parliament passed a law *De Haeretico Comburend* ('On the Burning of Heretics') so that the reformist Lollards could be arrested and tried.

→ The Lollards, p. 121

• **Act in Restraint of Appeals**, 1533

Parliament once again decreed that the Church of England could decide its own cases without referring to Rome. This allowed Henry VIII to divorce Catherine of Aragon and validate his marriage to Anne Boleyn. But it resulted in the Pope's excommunication of the king. Parliament retaliated by abandoning Peter's Pence, a tax the Pope levied on all householders for the construction of St Peter's Church in Rome.

• **Act of Supremacy**, 1534

In one of the most far-reaching pieces of religious legislation ever passed in Westminster, Parliament declared Henry VIII supreme head of the English Church and ordered all references to the Pope removed from prayer books. The rampant and often violent dissolution of the monasteries followed. Mary Tudor, Henry's daughter, repealed the Act in 1554, but her decision was itself overturned five years later by her replacement, Elizabeth.

• **Act for the Dissolution of the Smaller Monasteries**, 1536

The Commons debated the king's proposal to close down the smaller religious houses and passed the bill reluctantly, questioning the claim that the smaller monasteries were abodes of vice. Eventually, MPs decided that all religious houses with an income lower than £200 a year should be given to the Crown. The heads of the houses were to receive pensions, and the clergy transferred to the larger monasteries or be licensed as secular priests.

The House needed to calculate the value of the places being dissolved, so they measured the lead upon the roof and counted the bells. They seized the best plate and vestments. Once officers had passed on to the next house they left behind workmen to strip the roofs, pull down the gutters and rain pipes, and break the bells with sledgehammers.

Parliament then set up a Court of Augmentation to deal with

all lands and movables coming into the king's possession through the suppression or surrender of the religious houses. No sooner had Henry gained possession of the smaller houses, than he refounded more than fifty 'in perpetuity' under a new charter.

• **Act for the Dissolution of the Greater Monasteries**, 1539
In dissolving the larger religious houses the king's officers presented the abbots with prepared deeds of surrender. If the abbot and the monks agreed with the deeds they were given life pensions. If not, the officers would 'take possession of the house and lands, the jewels, plate, cattle, stuff and all other things belonging to them', and turn them out with no pension. The first targeted monasteries were in the North, where opposition under the Pilgrimage of Grace (→ p. 207) had taken place. The last house to go, on 10 April 1540, was Waltham Abbey, Essex, which had been founded by Harold II in the eleventh century. Some Benedictine cathedral priories were converted to cathedrals with a dean and a chapter. These included Gloucester, Ely, Chester, Durham, Norwich, St Albans, Peterborough and Winchester.

• **The Six Articles**, 1539
Henry VIII, despite breaking with Rome in 1531, was determined to keep England a Catholic country. In 1539 he laid down the Six Articles of anti-Protestant doctrine. These included support for the notion of transubstantiation – that the communion bread and wine change into the body and blood of Christ – denial of which could lead to being burnt for heresy.

• **The Act of Uniformity**, 1549
This law established the Book of Common Prayer as the sole legal form of worship in England at the expense of the Latin Missal.

• **Oath of Supremacy**, 1559
Anyone taking public office in England now had to swear

allegiance to the monarch (Elizabeth), rather than the Pope, as Supreme Head of the Church of England. This was later extended to include MPs and university students. The new Act of Uniformity, also passed that year, ordered everyone to conform to Anglicanism, and failure to attend Sunday church would lead to a fine of one shilling. Attending Mass would attract ever larger fines and eventually imprisonment.

• **The Thirty-Nine Articles**, 1563
Parliament declared that 'the Bishop of Rome hath no jurisdiction in this Realm of England' and that Mass offered for the souls of the living and dead was 'blasphemous fables, and dangerous deceits'.

• **William Prynne's punishment**, 1633
After writing a series of attacks on the government's High Church policies, Prynne was tried in the Palace of Westminster's Star Chamber. He was imprisoned, fined £5,000 and sentenced to the punishment of having part of his ears removed. Two years later, Prynne, having continued his religious writings in prison, was sentenced to having the rest of his ears removed and his cheeks branded with the letters S L (Seditious Libeller). He later became a Member of Parliament.

• **John Liliburne**, 1638
Parliament's Star Chamber began a long campaign of victimisation against the 22-year-old Liliburne in 1638 for importing religious publications from Holland that hadn't been licensed by the Stationers' Company. Liliburne demanded to be charged in English, not Latin, but had his request turned down. He was flogged on his bare back with a three-thonged whip, tied to an ox cart, and dragged from Fleet Prison back to Westminster where he was put in the pillory. Even this didn't stop him distributing unlicensed religious material to the crowds, and the

ABOVE The Old Testament prophet Moses looks somewhat underwhelmed at the phenomenon of the Burning Bush, a story the painter William Blake adapted from the Book of Exodus early in the 19th century.

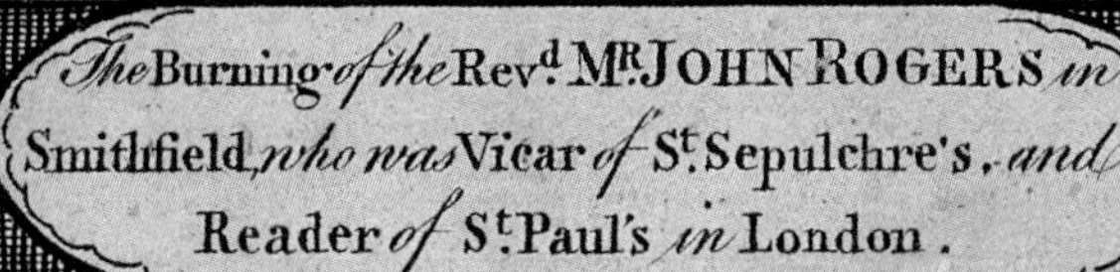

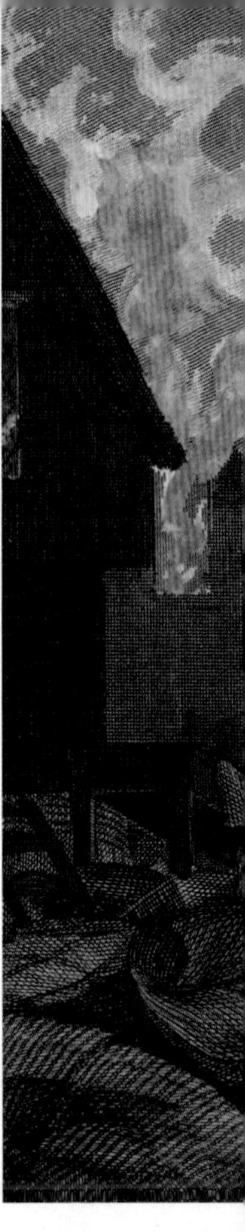

ABOVE John Rogers was the first Protestant martyr executed during the reign of the Catholic queen, Mary Tudor. He was burnt at Smithfield in 1555 for translating the Bible into English, an act that upset the clergy who were keen to protect their hold on the scriptures.

ABOVE RIGHT Perhaps the great conflagration of 1666 was an accident, or perhaps God was punishing London for being a city of sin? Either way, much of the ancient city was destroyed.

RIGHT A group of Catholic terrorists including Guy Fawkes plotted to blow up the king, James I, in the Houses of Parliament in 1605. They were not successful.

Iohn wright
Thomas Percy
Guido Fawkes
Robert Catesby
Thomas Winter

LEFT The Monument stands the same distance as its height from the site of the outbreak of the Fire of London, and its height and location also fit astronomical and mystical settings imposed by its creators, Robert Hooke and Christopher Wren.

RIGHT The Gordon Riots of 1780 against the granting of more rights to Catholics took their name from Protestant peer Lord George Gordon, who whipped up the crowds into protesting.

BELOW At Hampton Court in 1604, King James set into motion work on what became the greatest of English Bibles, named after himself.

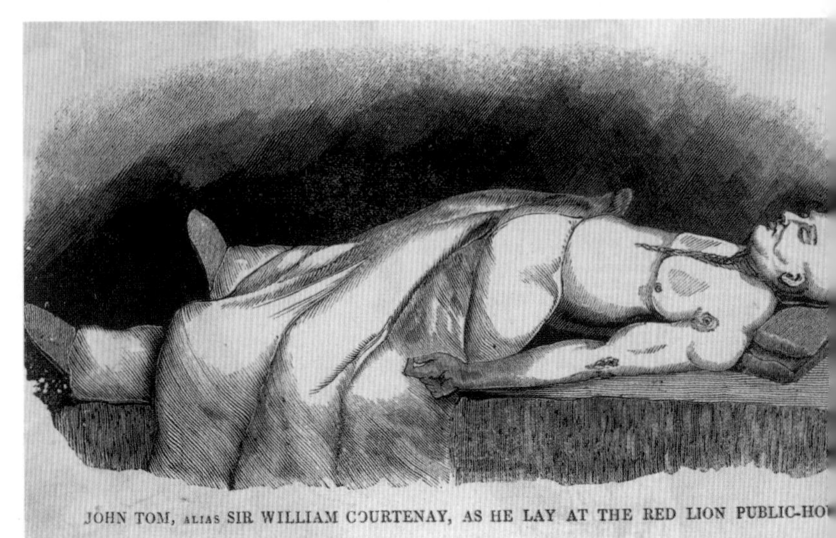

JOHN TOM, ALIAS SIR WILLIAM COURTENAY, AS HE LAY AT THE RED LION PUBLIC-HO

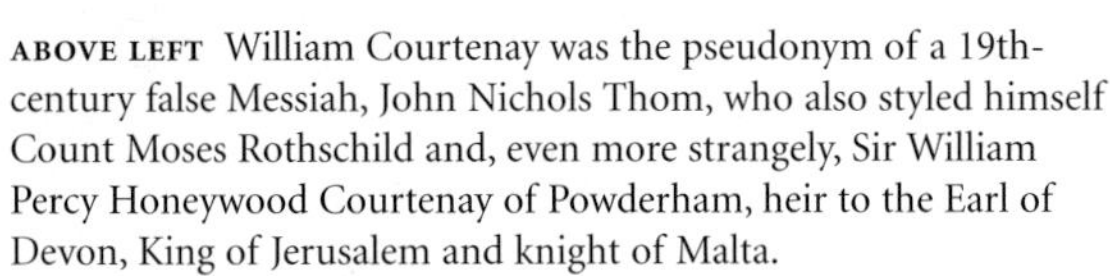

ABOVE LEFT William Courtenay was the pseudonym of a 19th-century false Messiah, John Nichols Thom, who also styled himself Count Moses Rothschild and, even more strangely, Sir William Percy Honeywood Courtenay of Powderham, heir to the Earl of Devon, King of Jerusalem and knight of Malta.

LEFT The most important Protestant cathedral in the land, Canterbury Cathedral, seat of the Archbishop of Canterbury, was also where knights working for Henry II killed archbishop Thomas à Becket in 1170.

ABOVE The Sussex town of Lewes has long been fiercely anti-Papist. Anti-Gunpowder Plot celebrations are held every 5th November, during which effigies of the Pope are burned.

LEFT The Children of God were a hippy-era religious cult whose most famous acolyte was the Fleetwood Mac guitarist Jeremy Spencer. Preaching free love, they curtailed their sexual activity during the AIDS years.

BELOW Matthew Hopkins was the Witchfinder General of the 1640s who terrorised the women of Essex with accusations of sorcery that led to 19 local hangings.

charges and trials continued for years. Liliburne's story was an influence on the thinking behind the 5th Amendment of the United States Constitution.

• **Barebones Parliament**, 1653

During the height of Oliver Cromwell's power in 1653 the authorities spent much time discussing how to form a new Parliament. Major-General Thomas Harrison, one of the extraordinary Fifth Monarchists (→ p. 14), wanted a ruling body based on the Old Testament Sanhedrin of seventy selected elders or saints. He didn't quite get his way. Instead Cromwell established a watered-down version of Harrison's demands in the form of a Parliament chosen through nominations made by church congregations from a shortlist approved by himself. This method was adopted rather than having an election, limited though the franchise was in those days, for fear that royalist sympathisers might be returned. It became known as the Barebones Parliament after one of its most colourful members, the City of London representative Mr Barebones, best known for his unusual first name, Praise-God.

• **The Act of Uniformity**, 1662

With this Act Charles II re-established the Church of England, but some 2,000 ministers, mainly Puritans and Presbyterians, were expelled in what became known as the Great Ejection. Outside the Church of England such believers soon came to be called Dissenters and eventually split into countless denominations – Muggletonian, Sandemanian, Hutchinsonian, Thraskite, Salmonist and others. Following the Glorious Revolution of 1689 Dissenters were allowed further rights of worship.

• **Test Act**, 1673

Parliament, distraught at the conversion of James, Duke of York (the future James II) to Catholicism, passed the Test Act. This required all those holding public office to take the sacrament according to the rites of the Church of England, and to renounce the Catholic belief in transubstantiation – that the bread and wine of the Eucharist *literally* become the body and blood of Christ. Now James himself had to resign his post as Lord High Admiral of the Fleet.

Five years later a second Test Act barred Catholics from the House of Commons. But this was not the end of anti-Catholic measures in the House. Following the discovery of the Popish Plot in 1678 (→ p. 65), fears of a Catholic rebellion soared, and in May 1679 the Commons passed the Exclusion Bill to prevent James from taking the throne.

The bill passed two readings, but before the third could take place the king, Charles II, dissolved Parliament. To appease the anti-James lobby, Charles banished his brother from court – for his own safety – and for the next three years the heir to the throne spent much of his time outside London. When on one occasion James returned to the capital the crowd taunted him with cries of 'A Pope! A Pope!' The Act was repealed in 1829 by the Catholic Relief Act.

• **Declaration of Indulgence**, 1688

Although James II was a Catholic when he took the throne in 1685, by which time Protestantism was firmly established in England, he was greeted enthusiastically at first. People were pleased with the orderly succession after the shenanigans involving his father Charles I, who had been executed, and brother, Charles II, who took the throne only through the support of the military.

James's honeymoon didn't last long. In April 1688 he issued a Declaration of Indulgence giving rights of public worship to Catholics and Protestant Nonconformists. 'We cannot but heartily wish,' the king stated, 'that all the people of our dominions were members of the Catholic Church; yet . . . conscience ought not to be constrained nor people forced in matters of mere religion.'

Seven Anglican bishops were imprisoned for signing a petition against the Declaration, yet James didn't remain on the throne for long. In June 1688 five English peers and two commoners conspired to replace him with his daughter Mary and her Dutch husband, William of Orange. Public support for James to give up the throne because of his religious beliefs grew and he was encouraged to flee the country in 1688 after only three years as king.

The Protestant William of Orange travelled to England and was offered the throne by the country's leading politicians in February 1689, James deemed to have abdicated after fleeing the country in December 1688. William's accession took place with remarkably little bloodshed. Indeed so bloodless was the coup, it has gone down popularly in English history as the Glorious Revolution. In Ireland, where James's and William's forces clashed in July 1690 in the Battle of the Boyne (→ p. 299), the repercussions from the *coup d'état* are still being felt.

• **Bill of Rights**, 1688-89.

One of the most far-reaching pieces of legislation in English history ended the Stuart notion of the 'Divine Right' of kings to rule, and with it enshrined freedom from royal interference in the law. The bill allowed Protestants to bear arms to defend themselves and crucially stated that no monarch could be, or could marry, a Catholic – 'It hath been found by experience that it is inconsistent with the safety and welfare of this protestant kingdom to be governed by a papist prince.' There has been no Catholic British monarch since, although George II did marry his Catholic mistress in secret in Park Street, Mayfair, in 1785. When Prince Michael of Kent married Baroness Marie-Christine von Reibnitz in 1978 he lost his place as No. 15 in line to the throne.

• **Act of Toleration**, 1689
Freedom of worship was granted to Nonconformists as long as they formally rejected the Catholic notion of transubstantiation. The act didn't, however, extend that right to Quakers.

• **Blasphemy Act**, 1698
It was now illegal for anyone to deny that the members of the Holy Trinity were God; to claim there was more than one god, to deny the truth of the Christian religion, and to deny the divine authority of the Scriptures. An amendment which would have rendered Jews liable for persecution on some of these grounds was rejected by 140 votes to 78. The Act was rarely applied and was repealed by the Criminal Law Act 1967.

• **The Popery Act**, 1698
Known officially as An Act for the Further Preventing the Growth of Popery, it entitled any individual who apprehended a 'Popish Bishop, Priest or Jesuit', who was then prosecuted for saying Mass, to receive £100 from the county sheriff. The Act was repealed in 1846.

• **Act of Settlement**, 1701
This key piece of legislation, still being debated today, reinforced elements of the earlier Bill of Rights and ensured that the royal succession passed through the Protestant wing of the Stuart dynasty, first to Sophia, Electress of Hanover (James I's granddaughter), and then to her Protestant descendants who had not married a Catholic.

• **Catholic Relief Act**, 1778
Roman Catholics could now own property, inherit land and join the army as long as they renounced Stuart claims to the throne and the civil jurisdiction of the Pope. The Act was received with much hostility in London, resulting in the Gordon Riots of 1780 (→ p. 4).

• **Catholic Relief Act**, 1791
Catholics were now allowed to worship in public, although priests had to be registered and services had to be held behind locked doors. Churches with steeples were forbidden.

• **Catholic Relief Act**, 1829
Following a campaign led by Daniel O'Connell, the Irish lawyer and MP, under this act (passed to avoid an Irish uprising) Catholics could now sit in the Westminster Parliament. O'Connell, who had formed the Catholic Association in 1823, had won a by-election in County Clare five years later but was forbidden under the law to take his seat in the House of Commons. However, Catholics were not allowed to take degrees at Oxford, Cambridge and Durham until 1871.

• **Jewish Relief Act**, 1858
After many years of campaigning, Jews were finally allowed full civil rights, including being able to sit as MPs without having to take the Christian oath. Consequently, on Monday 26 July 1858, Lionel de Rothschild took the oath with his head covered in the Jewish manner, substituting 'so help me, Jehovah' (absurdly, because it is not the Jewish name for God) for the usual Christian words.

• **Accession Declaration Act**, 1910
The Act reiterated the requirement of a new sovereign taking the throne to 'solemnly and sincerely declare [to be] a faithful Protestant, and secure the Protestant succession to the Throne of my Realm'.

PALACE YARD

Following the death of the early nineteenth-century millennial prophetess Joanna Southcott after failing to give birth to the messianic child Shiloh (p. 73), one of her disciples, George Turner, a Leeds businessman, tried to take over the leadership of her group of devotees and delivered a Proclamation of the Final Days in Palace Yard outside the Houses of Parliament.

Calling himself the 'Herald of Shiloh', Turner explained that the holy child had been taken from Southcott's womb into paradise until the Day of Judgment. He warned that 'the Treasury, Horse Guards, Carlton House, the Playhouses, Churches and Chapels, the Tower, Somerset House, and other public places . . . shall all sink by earthquake', instigated by the 'Angel of the Lord'. Turner also urged that the dead be carried in carts three miles from the city and 'put into deep pits covered with pigs' flesh', and claimed that the earthquake predicted in Revelation 6 would occur on 28 January 1817, when the stars would fall and the sun would turn black.

The evening before the predicted earthquake a number of Londoners threw their money out of the window as it would soon be worthless. However, no earthquake occurred and Turner was sent to an asylum. After being released in 1820 he announced that Shiloh would appear in London on 14 October. He/it didn't.

→ The opening of Joanna Southcott's box, Church House, p. 80

ST JAMES'S PALACE

London's senior palace – foreign ambassadors are still officially sent to the Court of St James – was where Charles I spent the last night before his execution. When he woke up the following morning, 30 January 1649, he called to his servant: 'I will get up. I have a great work to do this day. This is my second marriage day; I would be as trim today as may be for before tonight I hope to be espoused to my beloved Jesus.' The king then received the Sacrament of Holy Communion and made his way across the park to Banqueting House, Whitehall, where he was beheaded.

James II outraged public (Protestant) opinion by sinking to his knees before a papal nuncio, Cardinal d'Adda, at the palace in

1687. A year later St James's was at the centre of one of the biggest scandals in royal history, again involving the king. On 10 June 1688 a boy, James Francis Edward Stuart, was born here to James's queen, Mary d'Este (irreverently nicknamed Mother East by the masses).

By a remarkable coincidence exactly nine months previously the king had prayed for a male heir who could continue the Catholic-worshipping line. Indeed no sooner had James's prayer session at Holywell, north Wales, ended than Mary announced her pregnancy. The news of the pregnancy alarmed the Protestant majority in England. Courtiers opposed to James's religion spread a rumour that the queen would give birth to two sons, one of whom would be king of England, the other Pope of Rome.

But was James Francis Edward Stuart royal at all? Some historians believe that the pregnancy was a fabrication; that Mary's size was due to obesity not fecundity, that she had miscarried in April, and that James's 'son' was a foundling, smuggled into the royal chamber to provide the king with a male heir. Even though a crowd of around thirty people gathered by the queen's bedside at St James's Palace, no one actually saw the birth as she asked for the curtains to be drawn around her at the last minute.

James Stuart was later christened at the palace with the Pope designated as his godfather *in absentia*. He never did become king for James was shooed out of office the following year and attempts by him and his son, Charles (Bonnie Prince Charles), to regain the throne in adulthood failed ignominiously.

→ Palace of Holyroodhouse, p. 268

WAR OFFICE, Whitehall

When the British army was trapped at Dunkirk in 1940 with little possibility of rescue, officers, unable to fully explain their plight but determined to carry on resisting the Nazis, hastily sent

Whitehall a three-word telegram: 'But if not.' War chiefs at Whitehall recognised the words as being from the Book of Daniel (see box, below). They quickly began preparing the famous Dunkirk evacuation in which hundreds of small boats headed for France to evacuate the trapped army, taking more than 300,000 British and French soldiers off the beach.

'But if not'

The soldiers stranded at Dunkirk equated their plight with that of the three Jews from the Book of Daniel – Shadrach, Meshach and Abednego – cast into the fire by Nebuchadnezzar after refusing to worship the statue the Babylonian king had erected. Although the three hoped God would deliver them from the burning furnace, they reassured themselves with the thought 'but if not, be it known unto thee, O king, that we will not serve thy gods, nor worship the golden image'. Similarly the Dunkirk troops hoped that the allies would save them. But if not, they would not surrender to the enemy.

→ Isaac Newton and the Book of Daniel, p. 103

WESTMINSTER ABBEY, Broad Sanctuary

A legend invented in the thirteenth century claimed that St Peter himself consecrated what is now Westminster Abbey in the year 616. Appearing on the riverbank, he persuaded a fisherman to ferry him across and, when he landed, he struck the ground twice, producing two springs of fresh water, before returning to heaven.

The church founded here, St Peter's, later became a monastery, ruled by an abbot rather than by a bishop sitting on a cathedra chair. Consequently it was not a cathedral but a minster – West

Minster – to distinguish it from the now demolished East Minster near the Tower. St Dunstan, tenth-century Bishop of London, refounded West Minster as a Benedictine monastery, in 950. The kings of England have been crowned here since William I in 1066. The abbey was consecrated in October 1269 when the bones of St Edward the Confessor were moved to a shrine.

After ascending to the throne in 1553, Mary Tudor restored the abbey and renounced the title of Supreme Head of the Church of England so that she could bring the country back to the faith of Rome. Given the widespread dissolution of the monasteries, Mary was never going to be able to reconstitute the great religious houses and return England to how it had been in pre-Reformation days. Her sister Elizabeth, who became queen five years later, soon revealed her distaste for Catholic practices. At the opening of Parliament in January 1559, Elizabeth entered the abbey but when the abbot and monks met her with candles, incense and holy water she quickly ushered them off with a curt 'Away with those torches, for we see very well.' Elizabeth expelled the monks that Mary had invited back and established Westminster as a Royal Peculiar – a church responsible directly to the sovereign rather than to a bishop, what is still officially the Collegiate Church of St Peter.

→York Minster, p. 208

WHITEHALL PALACE, Whitehall

It was at London's main medieval palace, which burnt down in January 1697, never to be rebuilt, that Henry VIII passed the Act of Supremacy in 1534, following Rome's refusal to grant him a divorce from Catherine of Aragon. The Act laid down that the king, not the Pope, was the head of the Church of England.

Twenty years later in January 1554 Henry's daughter, Mary Tudor, moved into Whitehall. Some 15,000 armed men, unhappy at having a Catholic monarch, marched on London and attacked the palace. At one stage one of the rioters threw a dead dog, its ears cropped, through the window of one of the royal buildings; attached to it was a note saying that all Catholic priests should be hanged.

Mary remained unpopular with the masses by peddling a fundamentalist version of Catholicism. One of her fiercest critics was the Protestant writer Christopher Goodman, who denounced the queen as a bastard born of an incestuous relationship (her mother was Catherine of Aragon who had married her late husband's brother, Henry VIII) and a 'tormentor of the saints of God'.

When Gerard Winstanley, leader of the proto-communist Diggers, was summoned before Lord Fairfax at the palace in 1649 to explain why he and his followers had dug up a tract of land in Surrey (→ p. 151), he revealed that he was 'of the race of the Jews'. Since the arrival in England of William the Conqueror, Winstanley continued, 'the people of God had lived under tyranny and oppression worse than that of our forefathers under the Egyptians'. His assistant, William Everard, added in suitably apocalyptic fashion: 'The time of deliverance is at hand. God will bring his people out of this slavery and restore them to their freedom in enjoying the fruits and benefits of the Earth.'

A century later, in 1656, it was at Whitehall Palace that the authorities held a conference to discuss readmitting the Jews to England. Some of those close to Oliver Cromwell, ruler of England as Lord Protector, were motivated by the cynical notion that they could convert the Jews to Christianity to complete Jesus' work; others thought that the restoration of the Jews would lead to the beginning of a Messianic age in England.

Many Puritans were fascinated by all things Judaic. They believed that God's message to Israel in the 68th Psalm was addressed to them – that they had been chosen by God to preside over the establishment of His rule on earth. Their ideology had been shaped by an enthusiasm for reading the Bible in English, a language in which it had only recently been made available, and they were excited by the notion that not only must God have created the world in Hebrew, but that Adam, the first man, must have spoken it.

Cromwell's concerns were of a more financial nature. He had cast envious eyes at cities like Hamburg, Amsterdam and Leghorn in Italy, where Jews had been instrumental in creating a new prosperity, and so he invited the Dutch rabbi Menasseh Ben Israel to England to discuss the 'official' return of the Jews to the country. The December 1656 conference was dramatically interrupted when a Flemish Jew approached England's ruler and proceeded carefully and deliberately to touch him all over. A minion rushed up to stop the man and seek an apology or explanation for this outrageous behaviour. The Jew explained that he meant no harm, but that he had journeyed from Antwerp to London purely to ascertain whether 'his Highness, the Lord Protector, was of flesh and blood, as his superhuman deeds indicated that he was more than a man and must have emanated directly from heaven'.

After much deliberation the meeting decided that the law expelling Jews from England in 1290 applied only to those who lived here then. Jews could return. A synagogue was built in a house on Creechurch Lane in the City in December 1656, but the demise of Cromwell's Commonwealth and the restoration of the throne in 1660 left the thirty-five Jewish families in London with no legal protection. However, fears that the advances made under Cromwell would be lost proved groundless when Charles II showed himself to be amicably disposed towards the community because of the help the Jews of Amsterdam had afforded him in exile.

James II was crowned according to the rites of the Catholic Church in secret at the palace on 22 April 1685. It had to be in secret, for Catholicism was then frowned upon by most Britons, not just through fear that the religion might return through royal assent but that behind the altar, metaphorically speaking, lurked not only the Pope but the ominous figure of Louis XIV, king of France, champion of the notion of the monarch as absolute ruler and self-appointed leader of the anti-Protestant counter-Reformation in Europe. Louis had invaded the Spanish Netherlands (now Belgium) in 1667 and probably had his sights on Britain. James lasted only three years as king and no invasion took place.

→ Palace of Holyroodhouse, p. 268

CHAPTER 2

EAST ANGLIA

Three ancient urban centres dominate religious history in East Anglia: Cambridge, Norwich and Lincoln. At Cambridge University in the sixteenth century some of England's first Protestant thinkers met soon after Martin Luther famously nailed his ninety-five points of view critical of Rome to the door of his local church in Germany. These proto-Protestant scholars – Thomas Bilney, Robert Barnes and Hugh Latimer – all ended up burnt at the stake for their trouble.

Norwich, England's second largest city in medieval times, was where the first accusations of ritual murder and 'blood libel' against Jews in Europe were made in 1144. Blood libel alleged that Jews murdered Christian children before Easter to mock Christ's Passion and used their blood to make the unleavened bread Jews eat during Passover. And this despite the fact that Norwich had been one of the main areas of Jewish settlement in England after William I invited Jewish financiers from Normandy to help build England's economy. Norwich's Jews thrived until the twelfth century when tension against them increased, and things reached an awful climax on 6 February 1190, when hundreds of local Jews were slaughtered – apart from those few who took refuge in the castle.

Similar hostility occurred in Lincoln in 1255 when the body of Little Hugh, an English boy, was found at the bottom of a well. Once again Jews were accused of conducting a blood libel. Scores were sent to the Tower in London and eighteen executed. The region is no longer quite so hostile to those whose religious views differ from those of the majority.

Key events

_c._ 60 **Boadicea launches an attack on the pre-Christian Roman temple of the divine Claudius in Colchester.**

1144 **The first accusations of ritual murder and blood libel against Jews in Europe are made in Norwich.**

1255 **The discovery of the body of an English boy at the bottom of a Lincoln well in a Jewish area sparks off a series of attacks on local Jews, many of whom are later executed.**

1520s **Cambridge scholars Thomas Bilney, Robert Barnes and Hugh Latimer proclaim the new reformist teachings of Martin Luther. They are later burnt at the stake as heretics.**

1572 **A prison is created especially for Catholics at Wisbech.**

1626 **Ascetic Nicholas Ferrer creates the celebrated Anglican community of Little Gidding, later captured in verse by T. S. Eliot.**

1656 **Thomas Tillam occupies the Colchester parish church for Oliver Cromwell's forces and transfers Sabbath worship from Sunday to Saturday.**

1838 **The enticingly named Peculiar People sect develop in Essex. They are inspired by the biblical line: 'You are a chosen generation, a royal priesthood, a holy nation, a peculiar people.'**

Chapter 2

Cambridgeshire

Cambridge

Cambridge University's most celebrated scholar is Isaac Newton, early eighteenth-century pioneer of the science of gravity, light and calculus. Rather than devoting his time to science, Newton spent much of his stay in the ancient university city engaged in religious issues. The great scientist was obsessed with the Old Testament Book of Daniel; along with a number of other scholars he considered it to be the key to unlocking the secrets of the universe. A clue comes in Chapter 12 which states: 'But thou, O Daniel, shut up the words, and seal the book, even to the time of the end: many shall run to and fro, and knowledge shall be increased.' Some contemporary scholars believe he came closer than any other researcher to finding some satisfaction from his study of the biblical book but failed mainly through not having a computer.

Newton was hostile to the Catholic Church. He identified it with the 'scarlet coloured beast, full of names of blasphemy, having seven heads and ten horns' from the Book of Revelation. When James II tried to have a Catholic priest admitted to Cambridge University in 1685 without taking the oath of allegiance to the Church of England, Newton raged: 'A mixture of Papists and Protestants in the same university can neither subsist happily nor long together.' He denied the trinity and divinity of Jesus, and believed the Church founders had distorted the biblical message – not that it would have been prudent of him to admit so at the time, these details emerging only in 1936.

Newton also had considerable interest in sacred architecture – architecture based on instructions outlined in the Bible. He believed that Solomon's Temple would one day be rebuilt in Jerusalem and that its structure would be understood as a blueprint for creation. Newton was still searching the Book of Daniel for the answers when he died.

→ Canonbury Tower, p. 8

EMMANUEL COLLEGE, St Andrews Street

Walter Mildmay, Chancellor of the Exchequer, founded the college in 1584 on the site of a Dominican priory for the training of church ministers. The first Master of the College was Laurence Chadderton who early in the seventeenth century served on the committee that produced the King James Bible. In the 1640s William Laud, Charles I's controversial Archbishop of Canterbury, whose practices many claimed were too Romish, denounced Emmanuel as 'that nest of Puritans' thanks to its group of scholars (William Gurnall, Thomas Brooks and Thomas Watson) producing major works on Protestant theology.

PETERHOUSE COLLEGE, Trumpington Street

The constant switching of religious fashion in the late Tudor period saw many leading figures veer between different strains of Catholicism and Protestantism with bewildering frequency. The most capricious of these was Peterhouse's Dr Andrew Perne who changed his religion at least three times to suit the taste of the monarch and when asked to explain 'honestly and simply' what he really believed in replied:

I beg you never to tell anyone what I am going to say . . . if you wish you can live in the religion which the queen and the whole kingdom profess [and] you will have a good life, you will have none of the vexations which the Catholics have to suffer. But don't die in it. Die in the faith and communion with the Catholic Church if you want to save your soul.

Alas Perne wasn't able to follow his own advice. He died suddenly on the way back to his room after lunch with the

(Protestant) Archbishop of Canterbury . . . in the Protestant headquarters, Lambeth Palace, to boot.

→ All Souls College Oxford, p. 173

ST EDWARD KING AND MARTYR, Peas Hill

Now a centre for 'meditative Christianity', this church was known as the 'cradle of the English Reformation' in the sixteenth century as it was here that some of the earliest Protestant scholars – Thomas Bilney, Robert Barnes and Hugh Latimer – proclaimed the new reformist teachings. They called themselves Lutherans, in honour of their mentor, Martin Luther, but gradually came to be known as Protestants, a term first used in Germany to describe those Lutheran princes who had sent a letter to the Pope protesting about various Catholic decisions. These Protestants also met to discuss religious theory at the now demolished White Horse tavern near Queen's College, where they indulged in the then unusual practice of reading the Bible in English.

Barnes, who had been prior of a local Augustinian friary until Bilney converted him, was summoned to appear before the university vice-chancellor in 1526 for preaching an unorthodox sermon. Recant or be burnt at the stake was the sentence. Barnes took the safe option and was sent to London's Fleet Prison. On his release, he left for Antwerp and visited Martin Luther himself in Wittenberg. Barnes returned to England in 1531 and acted as intermediary between the English government and Germany. Four years later he was sent to Germany to check whether the Lutheran clerics approved of Henry's divorce from Catherine of Aragon. Barnes's star fell after he attacked Bishop Gardner in a sermon at Paul's Cross in 1540. He was forced to apologise, but was burnt at the stake at Smithfield nonetheless on 30 July 1540.

Bilney was at the stake in 1531, and Latimer burnt in October 1555 outside Balliol College, Oxford (→ p. 178).

A chaplain to the church in the 1870s was F. D. Maurice,

pioneer of Christian socialism, who is believed to have died of overwork and who according to the author Charles Kingsley had the 'most beautiful human soul'.

→ Paul's Cross, p. 30

Little Gidding

Nicholas Ferrer, a seventeenth-century ascetic, created an Anglican community at Little Gidding in 1626 with thirty people including his extended family. After restoring the local Church of St John the Evangelist, they devoted themselves to a life of prayer, fasting and meditation based around the Book of Common Prayer which included the daily recital of the complete Book of Psalms. At all times there was at least one member of the community praying before the altar so that they might keep to the pledge of praying 'without ceasing'.

Charles I visited Little Gidding in 1633, and again in 1646, although on that occasion he was fleeing from parliamentary troops who ransacked and destroyed the place when they arrived. The poet T. S. Eliot visited the village in 1936 seeking inspiration for what became his acclaimed *Four Quartets*, one of which is named 'Little Gidding'. A new ecumenical group, the Community of Christ the Sower, was formed here in 1970 but disbanded in 1998.

Wisbech

WISBECH CASTLE, Museum Square

A prison was created especially for Catholics at Wisbech on the

Isle of Ely in 1572, a time when it was illegal not to attend Church of England services. Although thirty-three priests were incarcerated here they were held under what was little more than house arrest and spent most of their time quarrelling about points of theology. One of their number, Thomas Bluet, was even allowed to go to London to raise funds for his fellow prisoners, although when he arrived he was arrested by Richard Bancroft, the Bishop of London, who showed him a huge cache of letters and books implicating English Jesuits in a plot to seize the throne. The Jesuits wanted the King of Spain to invade the country, kill Queen Elizabeth 'by poison or sword', and take his supposedly rightful place as monarch (he had been married to Elizabeth's predecessor, Mary Tudor). Bluet denied any knowledge of the plot and was granted an audience with the queen to protest his innocence. He tried to convince her that there was no Jesuit conspiracy but Elizabeth was not to be swayed, explaining; 'If I grant this liberty to Catholics, by this very fact I lay at their feet myself, my honour, my crown and my life.'

→ The Catholics lose the Battle of the Diamond, p. 292

Essex

Chelmsford

PALACE OF BEAULIEU/NEW HALL, White Hart Lane

Mary Tudor, first in line to the throne in the late 1540s, illegally attended Mass when living in this ancient house (now New Hall Catholic girls' school). Mass had been banned by the fundamentalist Protestants in charge of the country on behalf of the boy king, Edward VI.

Although Edward was concerned to hear about his half sister's activities, he was advised by Thomas Cranmer (author of the Book of Common Prayer) and Nicholas Ridley, Bishop of London, to turn a blind eye for diplomatic reasons – Mary had been encouraged to break the law by her cousin Charles V, Holy Roman Emperor.

Once Charles began to wage war against France and Protestant Germany, the English Church authorities toughened their stance. They arrested several of Mary's priests and sent the Lord Chancellor, Richard Rich, to Beaulieu to warn her that Mass was illegal. Mary refused to allow Rich into the house, taunting him from an upstairs window and laughing at the idea that such a law could exist. The authorities soon dropped their opposition and she was free to continue worshipping.

Coggeshall

Before Thomas Haukes was burnt in this market town in June 1555 for not baptising his son, he arranged with friends that he would make a sign from the flames to show how much pain he was suffering. He told them that if he could bear the pain he would raise his hands lifted up to the skies. During his ordeal Haukes duly kept his hands towards heaven – even after his fingers had been burnt off – and managed to clap them together before he died.

Colchester

First-century Britons led by Boadicea launched an attack on the pre-Christian Roman temple of the divine Claudius in Colchester. Boadicea and her followers were appalled at the Roman belief that the soul of Claudius, conqueror of Britain, would now join the gods, deriding the temple as a 'citadel of everlasting subjugation', as Tacitus noted in his history of the Roman conquest.

ST NICHOLAS, **High Street**
Thomas Tillam, a fiery preacher keen on rousing the congregation with dramatic interpretations of the Book of Revelation, occupied the parish church for Oliver Cromwell's forces in 1656. To the amazement of the locals he also transferred Sabbath worship from Sunday to Saturday. Tillam explained that the Sunday Sabbath had 'the Mark of the Beast' and outlined how adopting Saturday as the Sabbath could help convert to Christianity the Jews who had just been let back into England for the first time in around 350 years. The authorities soon cut short Tillam's career and sent him to prison, where he wrote a tract called *The Seventh Day: Sabbath Sought Out and Celebrated.*

Earls Colne

Ralph Josselin, an Earls Colne vicar in the mid-seventeenth century, was a vociferous supporter of the Puritans' banning of Christmas. The most important pressure group in the land once the king, Charles I, had lost his head, the Puritans derided what is now seen as the key Christian celebration as a superstition, because it was 'the darling of rude and licentious persons' and, even worse, as the 'Antichrist's Mass'. William Prynne, a regular critic of Charles's High Church stance, who once had part of his ears removed for opposing the king's religious views, summed up the Puritan hostility to Christmas:

When our Saviour was born into the world at first we hear of no feasting, drinking, healthing, carding, dicing, stage plays, mummeries, masques or heathenish Christmas pastimes; those puritanical angels, saints and shepherds knew no such pompous Christmas courtships which the devil and his accursed instruments have since appropriated to his most blessed Nativity.

→ The Fifth Monarchy Men, p. 14

Manningtree

It was in Manningtree in 1644 that Matthew Hopkins, a shipping clerk, overheard a group of women discussing their meetings with the devil, and it was these conversations that inspired him to become England's self-styled 'Witchfinder General'. Due to Hopkins's accusations nineteen local witches were hanged, and he was soon travelling through eastern England uncovering diabolical practices, often resorting to torture, such as sleep deprivation, to achieve the result he wanted.

There was a popular belief that because witches had renounced baptism, they would in turn be rejected by water. So Hopkins devised his infamous 'sink or swim' test. If a woman accused of being a witch sank, she was innocent; if she didn't, she was deemed to be a witch and therefore had to be put to death.

Milton Shore

The early Protestant reformer John Frith was apprehended at Milton Shore on the Essex coast in 1529 for illegally distributing Bibles in English. Frith had been working in Holland with William Tyndale, the first man to publish the Bible translated into English, and came home at great risk with the new volumes. About to return to the continent, he was stopped by a constable who suspected he might be a smuggler. The policeman searched Frith's bag and came upon loot of far greater interest than the expected contraband. It was the Good Book itself, printed not in the acceptable Latin that only the priests and learned could understand but in English. The authorities sent Frith to the Bishop of London for a rebuke and he was eventually burnt at the stake at Smithfield.

Rochford

The oddly named Peculiar People sect developed in Rochford from 1838 around James Banyard, a faith healer. He was inspired by two biblical entries, a line from Deuteronomy 18 that runs: 'And the Lord hath avouched thee this day to be his peculiar people, as he hath promised thee, and that thou shouldest keep all his commandments,' and an extract from 1 Peter 2: 9: 'But you are a chosen generation, a royal priesthood, a holy nation, a peculiar people . . .' The sect rejected most medical treatment, relying instead on prayer and anointment with oil. Their chapel six miles north of Burnham on Crouch and built in 1877, survives as a residential property.

→ The Peculiar People of Plumstead, p. 64

Tillingham

Mary Adams of Tillingham declared in the 1650s that she was the Virgin Mary, blessed with carrying a child conceived with the help of the Holy Ghost that would become the true messiah. Adams was one of the Ranters, free-thinkers who did not believe in the

Bible too literally, in life after death, or heaven. Instead they adopted practices which were more hedonistic than those of most Christian groups of the time – dancing, singing and joyful fornicating.

Adams did indeed give birth but it was to a disabled child which had 'neither hands nor feet but claws like a toad in the place where the hands should have been and every part odious to behold'. The child died soon after and Mary herself then suffered, 'rotting away and consumed as she lay, being from head to foot as full of blotches, blains, boils and stinking scabs as ever one could stand by another', according to contemporary reports.

Woodham Walter

ST MICHAEL THE ARCHANGEL

The world's oldest purpose-built Anglican church, constructed in 1563–4, still survives in Woodham Water in south Essex. It was the first of only six constructed during the reign of Elizabeth I.

LINCOLNSHIRE

Gainsborough

The Gainsborough Separatists were a group of seventy pioneering Baptists who in the early seventeenth century promoted the idea that Christians had free will to choose their own path rather than being at the mercy of predestination, as the Calvinists maintained. They elected their pastors by the casting of lots, regarded set prayers as being inimical to true religion, and believed that infant baptism was pointless.

Led by John Smyth, a clergyman disillusioned with the Anglican Church, the Gainsborough Separatists fled England in 1607 for Amsterdam. There they fell in with the Dutch Mennonites, a sect which claimed to practise a pure form of Christianity similar to that of the pre-Romish Church. After Smyth died in 1611 Thomas Helwys took over the congregation and moved the Gainsborough Separatists to Spitalfields, east London, where they founded England's first Baptist church. Eventually the group joined forces with the better-known pilgrims on board the *Mayflower* in 1620, emigrating to America.

→ The Pilgrim Fathers, p. 241

Lincoln

The discovery of the body of Little Hugh of Lincoln, an English boy, at the bottom of a well in 1255 sparked off violent recriminations against Lincoln's Jews. Locals claimed the Jews had killed Hugh as part of a blood libel, a ritual killing of Christian children by Jews for their blood in the days leading up to Easter as a re-enactment of Christ's Passion, the blood being used to make the unleavened bread that Jews eat during Passover.

Copin, a Lincoln Jew, soon admitted, probably under duress, to killing the boy. He explained that it was a Jewish custom to crucify a Christian child every year. He was hanged, and ninety-one other Lincoln Jews were sent to the Tower in London, eighteen of whom were executed. Meanwhile Hugh's corpse in Lincoln Cathedral (see below) became a site of pilgrimage.

The Reformation of the 1530s, which followed Henry VIII's failure to persuade the Pope to recognise his divorce from Catherine of Aragon so that he could marry Anne Boleyn, did not go down too well in Lincoln initially. Catherine was well liked in

Lincoln, Anne Boleyn not so. Indeed one Lincolnshire woman was accused of rejoicing when Anne's child was stillborn in February 1535 and of calling her 'a goggle-eyed whore'. Nevertheless the local monasteries were disbanded, the buildings demolished or their roofs pulled off, and the estates handed to absentee landlords. On a visit to Lincoln the royal representative, Richard Layton, urged that 'there can be no better way to beat the King's authority into the heads of the rude people of the north than to show them that the King intends reformation and correction of religion.' Churches were stripped of all jewels and ceremonial vessels, which were replaced with tin and brass, and this according to some calculations was more widespread in Lincoln and surrounding towns than in any other region.

LINCOLN CATHEDRAL, Minster Yard

One of Britain's most handsome cathedrals was for centuries a major pilgrimage site. Tens of thousands came to pay their respects to Hugh, a local boy found dead down a well in 1255, victim of a ritualistic killing by an unknown assailant locals claimed was a Jew. According to legend the bottom of the well where Hugh's corpse was found had been filled with a brilliant light and sweet odour, the body floating on the water. This proved that the boy was holy, and Lincoln Cathedral soon benefited from the story as thousands came to pay their respects – and pay their admission money to see the body of Little Hugh, the martyr.

After some time the child's head was removed from his body and placed in a gold and silver box decorated with jewels. Twice a year the box was opened so that pilgrims who gave enough money could see it, that is until it was stolen and thrown into a field. The head was later found and restored to the cathedral. The more outré manifestations of the site were destroyed during the sixteenth-century Reformation, but the pilgrimages continued into the early twentieth century. In 1955 the Church replaced the shrine at Lincoln Cathedral with a plaque that reads:

Trumped up stories of 'ritual murders' of Christian boys by Jewish communities were common throughout Europe during the Middle Ages and even much later. These fictions cost many innocent Jews their lives. Lincoln had its own legend and the alleged victim was buried in the Cathedral in the year 1255.

Such stories do not redound to the credit of Christendom, and so we pray:

Lord, forgive what we have been,
amend what we are,
and direct what we shall be.

There was also religious conflict in Lincoln not involving Jews. Philip Repyngdon, one of the first Lollards, Protestant-style preachers of the early fifteenth century, recanted his views after much persuasion by the authorities. He swiftly won promotion through the Church ranks, becoming confessor to Henry IV and a cardinal in Lincoln. He was denied his burial wish, to be interred naked in a sack in a churchyard under the open sky, and had to make do instead with Lincoln Cathedral itself and full honours.

In October 1536 a mob of around 40,000 Lincolnshire residents, unhappy with Henry VIII's Reformation of the Church, seized the cathedral, demanding the right to continue practising as Catholics and the protection of the treasures of Lincolnshire churches. Henry VIII sent in the army to crush the uprising but was unsure who should lead it as some of his generals were still loyal to the old religion. He chose the Duke of Suffolk, who arrived in Stamford that October with 5,000 soldiers. In Lincoln Cathedral the rebels were waiting to hear the king's response to their petition. It was not positive.

How presumptuous then are ye, the rude commons of one shire . . . to find fault with your Prince . . . Wherefore, Sirs, remember your follies and traitorous demeanours, and shame not your undoubted King and natural Prince . . . ; and remember your duty of allegiance, and that ye are bound to obey us, your King, both by God's commandment and law of nature . . . Withdraw yourselves to your own houses, every man; and no more assemble, contrary to our laws and your allegiances.

Many wanted to continue their revolt. They discussed charging Suffolk, whose troops were disorganised and poorly armed, but they were worried about losing their lands if they were beaten and the prospect of civil war if they were successful, so they urged the people to desist. The rebellion collapsed on 10 October 1536.

Ten years later Anne Askew, a Lincoln woman, was burnt at the stake for heresy and Protestant practices. Askew first got into trouble with her husband, a devout Catholic, for reading the Bible in English in Lincoln Cathedral. He banished her from their house, and he and their son testified against her. In July 1546 she was sent to the Tower of London. There she was tortured on the rack so that she would reveal the names of other Protestants. 'They did put me on the rack,' she recalled, 'because I confessed no ladies or gentlemen to be of my opinion, and thereon they kept me a long time; and because I lay still and did not cry. My Lord Chancellor and Master Rich took pains to rack me with their own hands till I was nigh dead.'

Askew remains the only woman tortured in the Tower and, though she did not break despite the months of suffering, she was too crippled to walk to the stake in Smithfield where she was burnt to death.

• The cathedral stood in for Westminster Abbey during the 2005 filming of *The Da Vinci Code.*

JEWS HOUSE, The Strait

One of the oldest occupied houses in Europe is a two-storey stone building from around 1150 which was then owned by a Jewish woman, Bellaset of Wallingford, executed in 1287 for clipping coins (cutting away some of the metal to sell it off).

→ Massacre of the Jews in York, p. 207

Louth

ST JAMES, Upgate

A sermon preached on Sunday 1 October 1536 at St James, Louth, was the catalyst for a local revolt against the Reformation. The rebels were not just Catholics but traditionalists who wanted to preserve their long-standing customs. The mob went on the rampage throughout the county, demanding the freedom to continue worshipping as Catholics and, protection for the treasures of Lincolnshire churches.

Sempringham

Gilbert of Sempringham, a twelfth-century member of the Bishop of Lincoln's household, was the only medieval Englishman to found a religious order, the Gilbertines, which unusually for the time included women.

Gilbert became lord of the manor of Sempringham in 1130 after his father died and used his wealth to build a large number of convents and monasteries. He was imprisoned in 1165 for helping Thomas à Becket after the latter rowed with the king, Henry II, but was eventually cleared. Shortly before Gilbert died in 1189 aged ninety, some of the lay brothers in Sempringham rebelled against him, complaining that the Gilbertine system involved too much work and too little food. The rebels even took their grievance to Rome, after which he improved their conditions. Gilbert was canonised in 1202. By the time of the Dissolution there were twenty-six Gilbertine houses. The last prior, Robert Holgate, was promoted to Archbishop of York.

Skegness

Harold Davidson, the incorrigible Rector of Stiffkey (pronounced Stewkey), was mauled to death by a lion while reading the Bible inside the beast's cage on Skegness beach in 1938. Davidson was already a household name at that stage as the Sunday papers had lapped up the story that he was using a house in London's Bloomsbury as a retreat for 'fallen women'. On Sunday mornings the Revd would catch a train to his church in Norfolk, deliver a sermon, say hello to his wife and return as quickly as he could to London.

A reporter stumbled upon the story, and Davidson's activities developed into a major vicar-and-tart sex scandal. When the Church realised he had been more intimate with more women than they deemed appropriate the Revd Davidson was defrocked. He joined the circus, applied unsuccessfully for the post of Blackpool football manager and started a naturist colony, before heading for Skegness where he met his bloody end.

Ken Russell made a film, *Lion's Mouth*, inspired by the Davidson scandal, in 2000.

→ Matthew Hopkins, Witchfinder General, p. 110

Norfolk

Broomholm

The now ruined priory on Abbey Street was one of the holiest places in Europe in the twelfth century as it was home to a piece of the True Cross – the actual cross on which Christ was crucified, so locals claimed. The Broomholm monks used the relic to cure disease and raise people from the dead, but it disappeared when

Henry VIII sent commissioners to Norfolk to suppress the monasteries and other religious houses in 1537.

King's Lynn

The Church sought special parliamentary permission in March 1401 to execute William Sawtrey, a Lollard priest – an early type of Protestant reformer – and the first heretic to be executed since 1216. Sawtrey raged at being sentenced to death. 'I am sent by God to tell thee that thou and thy whole clergy, and the King also, will shortly die an evil death.' But it was he who went first, burnt at the stake at Smithfield, London.

Norwich

The first accusations of ritual murder and blood libel against Jews in Europe were made in Norwich in 1144. Blood libel asserted that Jews murdered Christian children before Easter to mock Christ's Passion and used the blood to make the unleavened bread eaten during Passover. During Passover that year a boy who became known as William of Norwich was found stabbed to death. He became a martyr and large numbers of pilgrims journeyed to the city.

Norwich had been one of the main areas of Jewish settlement in England after William I invited Jewish financiers from Normandy into the country to help the burgeoning English economy. The Jews, officially the property of the king, lived near the castle, and by the twelfth century were thriving in what was then England's second largest city. They supplied most of Norwich's doctors and ran much of the city's trade. Ironically, as moneylenders, a role supposedly forbidden to Christians, they helped finance the building of Norwich Cathedral.

All this changed during the twelfth century when tension against local Jews increased. A poem by Meir ben Elijah (Meir of Norwich), 'Put a Curse on my Enemy', a copy of which survives in the Vatican archive, relates the woe of Norwich's Jews from those days. 'The land exhausts us by demanding payments, and the people's disgust is heard . . . When I hoped for good, evil arrived, yet I will wait for the light.'

Things reached a terrible climax on 6 February 1190 when, due to the hostility of Bishop, William de Turbeville hundreds of Norwich Jews were slaughtered. A few who took refuge in the castle escaped, but by 1194 only eight were left. Norwich's Jews were expelled in 1290 as part of Edward I's nationwide purge and didn't return to the city until 1789.

So destructive was the Black Death of the 1340s in Norfolk that 527 priests out of 799 died. As a result William Bateman, Bishop of Norwich, obtained from Pope Clement VII a bull allowing him to promote sixty clerks who were just twenty-one years old and 'only shavelings' to fill around 1,000 vacant posts.

Julian of Norwich was a famous medieval mystic who during a severe illness in her late twenties in May 1373 began to have religious visions. After she recovered she became an anchoress (a hermit), spending her life in a cell attached to the Norwich church of St Julian, whose name she took. There were three windows in her cell which contained only a crucifix, a hard bed and an altar. One window, the Squint, opened into the church so that she could receive communion and follow services. The second enabled her attendant to pass her food and remove waste. The third allowed visitors access. In the cell Julian wrote *Sixteen Revelations of Divine Love* about her visions, the first book written in English by a woman.

→ Massacre of the Jews in York, p. 207

LOLLARDS PIT, by Bridge House pub, Rosary Road

Protestant martyrs were burnt to death at the stake in the fifteenth century in what became known as the 'Lollards' Pit'. It took its name from the quasi-insulting term, Lollard, taken from the Dutch word for mumbler, which was given to fifteenth-century Christian reformers. The first to die was William White, a priest who had moved up to Norfolk from Kent, in 1428. White was a vociferous opponent of the Roman Catholic Church. He claimed priests and bishops had no power to hear confessions and that men should seek forgiveness for their sins from God alone. Lest anyone remained confused about White's views, he claimed the Pope presided over a 'Devilish estate' and that monks were 'soldiers of Lucifer'.

Another who met an unfortunate end in the Lollards' Pit was Thomas Bilney, one of England's first Protestant martyrs. It was Bilney who managed to convert Hugh Latimer (a future Bishop of Worcester, famously burned to death in Oxford) when in Cambridge in the early 1520s. Bilney was dragged from the pulpit as he preached in St George's Chapel, Ipswich, in 1526 and imprisoned in the Tower of London. The leading bishops of the day found him guilty of heresy, but instead of immediately sending Bilney to his execution, they deferred pronouncing sentence while they tried to make him recant his views – which eventually he did.

Back in East Anglia, in Cambridge not Ipswich, Bilney was overcome with guilt over his recantation and began to preach proscribed views again. As the churches were no longer open to him, he preached in the fields, arriving after some time in Norwich where the bishop, Richard Nix, had him arrested. This time there was no reprieve. He was sentenced to be burnt to death on 19 August 1531. The night before his execution, he read aloud the passage from Isaiah 42:2 that says: 'When thou walkest through the fire thou shalt not be burnt.' Watching Bilney burn at the stake the following day was Bishop Nix, who exclaimed: 'I fear I have burned Abel and let Cain go.'

When Queen Mary took the throne in 1553 and returned England to the Roman Church she appointed as Bishop of Norwich Dr John Hopton, one of England's most devout Catholics, who had been her confessor. He appointed as his chancellor one Dr Dunning, another extremist intent on making Protestants suffer as much as possible. Those now convicted for heresy had to spend the week between their conviction and being burnt at the stake tied up with their hands drawn high above their heads and standing on tiptoe. More than 170 Protestants were burnt in Norwich – more than in any other English city other than London and Canterbury.

→ The Lollards at St Paul's Cathedral, p. 28

MUSIC HOUSE, King Street

The Music House is one of Norwich's oldest surviving properties. It belonged to the Jurnets, wealthy thirteenth-century Jews, whose paterfamilias, the merchant Isaac Jurnet, was immortalised in a contemporary cartoon, held in the National Archives. It shows him sporting three heads, surrounded by demons frolicking above the castle, figures brandishing weighing scales and a devil in the foreground tweaking the noses of local Jews.

Oxburgh

OXBURGH HALL, Meadowgate Lane

A well-concealed priest hole at the moated mansion of the Bedingfield family, now a National Trust property, was used to conceal Father John Huddleston from the authorities in the seventeenth century. Fr Huddleston was the priest who helped

Charles II escape from England and Oliver Cromwell's forces after the Battle of Worcester in 1651. He was taken to Charles's deathbed through a secret staircase in Whitehall Palace in 1685 so that the king could convert to Catholicism. There Charles's brother, the Duke of York, who was about to become James II, introduced Huddleston with the words: 'Sire, this good man once saved your life. He now comes to save your soul.' Charles then took the communion of the Roman Catholic Church. The seven-foot square Oxburgh priest's hole is in a closet in one of the entrance turrets and is revealed when pressure is applied to a particular spot on the floor.

Suffolk

Bury St Edmunds

Robert Browne, father of Congregationalism, was imprisoned at Bury St Edmunds, once home of the richest Benedictine monastery in England, in 1581 after denouncing the local bishops. The Bishop of Norwich complained that Browne had seduced 'the vulgar sort of people', and this led to the first of thirty-two prison terms. Each time it was after preaching controversial doctrines, and he was held in a cell so dark he could not see his own hand.

One local man who got into trouble for distributing Browne's works was John Coppin who refused to have his child baptised by an 'unpreaching minister'. Coppin was hanged here in 1583 for claiming that Queen Elizabeth was an idolater and perjurer.

Hadleigh

Rowland Taylor, rector of Hadleigh in the mid-sixteenth century, promoted the new Protestant ideology he had picked up at Cambridge from the sermons of Hugh Latimer. His status in society came under threat after the accession of the Catholic queen, Mary Tudor.

Encountering a Catholic priest celebrating Mass in St Mary's church, he made his opposition clear. The authorities summoned Taylor to London, sent him to prison for two years, and then sentenced him to be burnt at the stake at Suffolk's Aldham Common. Before Taylor went to the pyre he declared:

I say to my wife, and to my children, the Lord gave you unto me, and the Lord hath taken me from you, and you from me: blessed be the name of the Lord! I believe that they are blessed which die in the Lord. God careth for sparrows, and for the hairs of our heads . . . Count me not dead, for I shall certainly live, and never die. I go before, and you shall follow after, to our long home.

When Taylor arrived at the stake he asked: 'What place is this?' and on being told it was Aldham Common, replied: 'God be thanked. I am even at home.' He was burnt at midnight on 9 February 1555, a time chosen so that most townsfolk would not witness the event.

→ The Tyburn executions, p. 51

CHAPTER 3

THE HOME COUNTIES

In the ancient towns and low-lying hills around London many far-reaching religious measures have been implemented. For instance, it was in Windsor Castle in 1548 that clerics met to create a body of prayers written in English, rather than the usual Latin, that became the landmark Book of Common Prayer. Once it was introduced church congregations became participants in the service rather than just spectators and the clergy were no longer so revered. Ironically, it was here that the decapitated corpse of Charles I was brought for burial in 1649. It was ironic because Charles's demise followed his unwise attempt to impose the English Book of Common Prayer on the Scots in 1637.

Much plotting by Protestants seeking to overthrow Catholicism took place at various Home Counties retreats in the sixteenth and seventeenth centuries. For instance, at Rye House, Hoddesdon, Hertfordshire, in 1683 Whig sympathisers hatched a plan to keep Catholics from the British throne. They were unsuccessful, and couldn't stop James II from becoming king, but within five years Protestant members of the aristocracy were plotting in the cellars of the Ladye Place house in Hurley, Berkshire, to replace James with William of Orange – successfully, it turned out.

No Home Counties city and few in Britain have played a greater role in Christianity's progress than Canterbury, the seat of the most powerful Church figure in the country, the Archbishop of Canterbury. It was here that Christianity officially arrived in

England in 597, and it was in Canterbury Cathedral in 1170 that Thomas à Becket was murdered by knights working for Henry II.

The cathedral is still the setting for major theological debates. At the 2008 Lambeth Conference – boycotted by some 250 bishops following the consecration of Gene Robinson, the gay Bishop of New Hampshire – delegates heard that the continuing row in the Anglican Communion over gay clergy had left the Church a 'wounded community'.

Key events

597 **Augustine, a Roman monk sent by Pope Gregory, lands in Kent to bring Christianity to Britain. He becomes the first Archbishop of Canterbury.**

1154 **Nicholas Breakspear, a St Albans monk, becomes the only Englishman to be Pope.**

1170 **Archbishop Thomas à Becket is murdered in Canterbury Cathedral by Henry II's agents.**

1212 **At Dover King John hands over the kingdoms of England and Ireland to the Pope, immediately receiving them back in exchange for an annual payment.**

1548 **Thirteen clerics led by Thomas Cranmer, Archbishop of Canterbury, meet at Windsor Castle to create a body of prayers written in English following the banning of the Latin Mass. From this comes the landmark Book of Common Prayer.**

1649 **Soldiers enter St Mary's church, Walton-on-Thames, lead worshippers outside and inform them that the Sabbath has been abolished as 'unnecessary, Jewish and ceremonial'.**

1870s **The Christian Israelites of Gillingham build a 95-foot high temple and prepare to be among the 144,000 to be saved in the 'final gathering of AD 2000'.**

2008 **Current Archbishop of Canterbury Rowan Williams is vilified after suggesting that sharia law may have to be introduced into parts of the United Kingdom.**

BERKSHIRE

Bray

A once well-known satirical seventeenth-century song, 'The Vicar of Bray', was based on the life of a cleric from this Berkshire village, whose support for the prevalent fashionable religious mood of the country would remain steadfast until it changed along with a new monarch. The song begins: 'In good King Charles's golden days/When loyalty had no harm in't/A zealous High Churchman I was . . .' and takes the protagonist on to the time of Charles's successor, James II, when 'Popery grew in fashion'.

The original vicar of Bray may have been Simon Simonds, a Congregationalist during Oliver Cromwell's Protectorate, a Church of England man under Charles II, a Catholic in James II's reign, and an Anglican once more under William and Mary. However, some historians point to Simon Aleyn, sixteenth-century vicar of Bray, as the model. He had witnessed the burning of a Windsor man who refused to accept Henry's legislation preventing the spread of Protestant teaching and vowed not to risk his own life by standing up for his religious beliefs, which meant he kept keep his job until to the reign of Elizabeth I.

Hurley

LADYE PLACE, Mill Lane

Members of the aristocracy who plotted to replace the Catholic king, James II, with the Protestant William of Orange in the 1680s met in the cellars of this ancient property. When William landed in Devon in November 1688 with 15,000 troops Lord Lovelace, who then owned Ladye Place, set out with seventy followers to join him. He reached Gloucester but there met resistance from the army and was imprisoned in Gloucester Castle. William of Orange threatened to burn the mansion of Badminton House unless Lovelace was set free. A month later William reached Berkshire, staying at the Bear Inn on the old London to Bath road, where he was visited by James's commissioners, looking to negotiate.

The cellars of Ladye Place still exist by Hurley parish church.

→ William of Orange lands at Torbay, p. 212

Windsor

Five Protestant men – Robert Testwood, Henry Filmer, Anthony Pierson, John Marbeck and Robert Bennett – were executed for heresy in 1544 and became known as the Windsor Martyrs.

Testwood, already known for making trouble against the local Catholic church, did his chances of having an easy life no good at all by pushing past a group of pilgrims gathered around the Virgin Mary's statue in Windsor Castle and breaking off her nose. A lawyer called Simons picked up the broken nose and put it in his pocket, commenting 'That shall be a dear nose to Testwood some day.'

Filmer was indicted by his own brother who stood up in the witness-box and revealed how Filmer, when asked if he was going to Mass to partake of communion, replied: 'If that be God, I have eaten twenty Gods in my day.'

WINDSOR CASTLE, Castle Hill

In late medieval times pilgrims would visit the castle's fifteenth-century chapel to pay homage at the shrine of King Henry VI, murdered at prayer in the Tower of London, probably by the future Richard III. They would bring gifts of candles and waxen images, crowd along the southern aisle of the choir to kiss Henry's 'holy' spur, and place his 'sacred' hat on their heads as a cure for headaches.

A group of thirteen clerics known as the Windsor Commission met at Windsor Castle in 1548 to create a body of prayers written in English following the banning of the Latin Mass. Out of this came the Book of Common Prayer, one of the landmark works of English Christianity. Its instigator was Thomas Cranmer, Archbishop of Canterbury (1533–56), although experts aren't clear exactly which parts he wrote and which were based on the works of German clerics.

With the new prayer book, Cranmer wanted to ensure that church congregations became participants in the service rather than just spectators watching the clergy perform their mysterious rites. Use of the new book was made compulsory in June 1549, which led to protests in some areas such as Devon and Cornwall (→ p. 244), and inevitable denunciations by Cranmer of the 'wickedness of the rebellion'.

After the execution of Charles I in January 1649, the

decapitated royal corpse was brought for burial to the castle's St George's Chapel. The mourners asked the Bishop of London, William Juxon, whether the Book of Common Prayer could be used for the service but, as Thomas Cranmer's great work had been banned in 1645, their wish was refused.

→ Whitby Abbey, p. 215

HERTFORDSHIRE

Hoddesdon

RYE HOUSE, **Rye Road**

Little remains of the medieval manor house where in 1683 Whig sympathisers hatched the Rye House plot to keep Catholics from the British throne. Behind the conspiracy was a gang that included Lord Shaftesbury, the Earl of Essex and the Earl of Bedford. Some of them wanted a monarchy with limited powers, led by Charles's illegitimate son, the Protestant Duke of Monmouth, and others a republic, as there had been a generation earlier under Oliver Cromwell.

The conspirators planned to gather a force of around a hundred men to ambush Charles II and his brother and heir, the Duke of York (later James II), as they passed by Rye House on their way back to London from the Newmarket races. They would then assassinate them.

The plot failed when the king's house in Newmarket caught fire, which forced Charles to leave earlier than expected, before the conspirators were ready. The Rye House conspirators were rounded up and executed, except for the Earl of Essex, who committed suicide in the Tower of London. Some experts believe that Charles fabricated the plot to remove his enemies.

Rye House later became the parish workhouse, then a hotel.

St Albans

A twelfth-century St Albans monk, Nicholas Breakspear, became the only Englishman ever to be Pope when he took office in 1154. Breakspear's was a remarkable progression, for at the age of eighteen he was rejected by the monks of St Albans Abbey for having too little schooling. He went abroad to study, staying in St Denys, Paris, and in Avignon where in 1130 he became a monk in the Augustinian Abbey of St Rufus. There Pope Eugenius III spotted Breakspear's talents and made him first a bishop and then a cardinal. He sent him on a peace-keeping mission to Norway where he restored peace and rearranged the local church administration.

When Pope Anastasius IV died in 1154 Breakspear was unanimously elected Pope. He took the name Adrian IV and announced: 'The Lord has long since placed me between the hammer and the anvil, and now He must Himself support the burden that He has placed upon me, for I cannot carry it.'

Breakspear's reign was not a happy one. He became unpopular, especially after placing Rome under martial law, and died after only five years as pontiff, having possibly been poisoned.

KENT

Aldington

A village near Romney Marsh ravaged by the Black Death of the fourteenth century, Aldington was where Erasmus, the famous Dutch theologian, was made vicar in 1511, resigning after a year because he spoke no English.

Eight years later Mary Barton, the so-called 'Maid' or 'Nun of Kent', was born in Aldington. Following an illness at the age of nineteen, she began seeing visions – 'of wondrous things done in other places whilst she was neither herself present nor yet heard no report thereof', as the leading cleric of the time, Thomas Cranmer, put it. The local priest was convinced Mary Barton was genuine and informed the Archbishop of Canterbury who sent a commission of priests to check her claims. They believed her. Barton then claimed the Virgin Mary would cure her afflictions at a particular chapel. Before a large crowd she emerged restored to health. She became a Benedictine nun and received royal support from Henry VIII who was pleased that her visions supported his religious views.

However, when Henry planned his divorce from Catherine of Aragon, Barton refused to back the king. She prophesied that, if Henry married Anne Boleyn against the Pope's wishes, he would be dead within a few months. The authorities ignored Barton for a year, despite the extreme nature of this claim, but supporters of Henry then began to allege that she was having sex with priests and arrested her for treason. Although Barton recanted her views, she was executed at Tyburn on 20 April 1534.

→ The plague hits Eyam, Derbyshire, p. 170

Boxley

BOXLEY ABBEY

A tithe barn and a private house enclose what little remains of Boxley Abbey, famous in medieval times for the Rood of Grace. This was a wooden cross bearing an image that could supposedly move and speak if approached by one who had lived a pure life, especially if they came bearing a large purse. Thousands came to witness these 'divine' demonstrations at a spot which Archbishop William Warham once described as 'so holy a place where so many miracles be showed'. When the monasteries were dissolved in 1538 those examining Boxley found the relic to be a fake, and that the miracles were worked not by God but by a mechanic pushing levers and wires. The rood was sent to Paul's Cross, London, where it was destroyed.

→ Debunking myths at Paul's Cross, p. 30

Canterbury

Canterbury – Durovernum to the Romans and Cantwarabyrig ('fortress of the men of Kent') to the Saxons – was where Christianity officially arrived in England in 597 with Augustine. He was a Roman monk sent by Pope Gregory the Great with the instruction to 'Destroy the idols; purify the temples with holy water, set relics there and let them become temples of the true God.'

The city has long been the major religious seat for the Church of England, home to Britain's most visited cathedral outside London and the location of the oldest church in the country in St Martin's. It also features a rare remaining set of city walls which enclose it on three sides.

The 1534 Convocation of Canterbury petitioned Henry VIII to allow the Bible to be translated into English. Miles Coverdale's Bible appeared a year later. His second edition of 1537 featured the king's licence but it was preceded by the Matthew Bible, produced by John Rogers, a friend of the ill-fated William Tyndale, to whom Tyndale entrusted his unpublished manuscripts. It was the Great Bible of April 1539 that was the first 'authorised' Bible. The authorities ordered that copies be placed in every church, which led to its being nicknamed 'the Chained Bible'.

John Nichols Thom, a nineteenth-century false messiah who

led the last battle to be fought on English soil, stood for the parliamentary seat of Canterbury in 1832. He did not win, but soon stood again, this time under the name Count Moses Rothschild, campaigning in a crimson velvet suit with gold lacings and carrying a sword. Thom later assumed an even more bizarre name: Sir William Percy Honeywood Courtenay of Powderham, heir to the Earl of Devon, King of Jerusalem and Knight of Malta. In 1833 he published a theological journal, *The Lion*, in which he claimed that all churches just wanted to hoard gold. Soon he was plain Sir William Courtenay, supposedly a reincarnation of the fourteenth-century Archbishop of Canterbury who had opposed the Bible translator John Wycliffe.

Declaring himself the 'saviour of the world', Thom became a wandering preacher, brandishing a sword he claimed was Excalibur of Arthurian legend, and gathering together around a hundred disciples, most of them absconding farm-workers. The authorities sent three policemen to arrest Thom, whereupon he shot one constable, mutilated the body and threw it into a ditch. About a hundred soldiers were now sent to arrest the deranged preacher. Battle flared, and Thom and nine of his followers were killed. Thom's surviving disciples tore the shirt from his body and divided it up for relics. Meanwhile the coroner, worried about claims that Thom would rise on the third day, ordered that his heart should be removed and pickled in a jar. It survived until the 1950s.

Archbishops of Canterbury

The Archbishop of Canterbury is the leading figure in the Church of England. His main residence is London's Lambeth Palace but in Canterbury he has lodgings in the Old Palace next to the cathedral. Within the British Constitution the archbishop ranks below only the monarch and the main members of the royal family.

Since Henry VIII broke the church's ties with Rome the sovereign (now helped by the prime minister) chooses the archbishop. The most noteworthy Archbishops of Canterbury have included the following:

• **Augustine** (597–604)
The first Archbishop of Canterbury was Augustine sent to Kent by the Pope to establish Romish Christianity in England (see below).

• **Alfege** (1005–12)
Alfege was killed by a group of Danes in Greenwich in April 1012 at a site now marked by St Alfege church. The Danes seized the Archbishop in Canterbury Cathedral and kept him in near starvation on a ship on the Thames for seven months. They demanded a ransom – 3,000 pieces of silver – and when that was not forthcoming killed him following a drunken feast.

• **Stigand** (1052–70)
Five popes excommunicated Stigand, who officiated at William the Conqueror's coronation, for holding the sees of Canterbury and Winchester at the same time. The support of Benedict X, an anti-Pope (a self-proclaimed Pope rivalling the valid pontiff) didn't help, and in 1070 the papal legate deposed Stigand.

• **Anselm** (1093–1109)
Anselm, an Italian, was the founder of scholasticism, a school of thought within the Church that debated the metaphysical existence of God. He openly opposed the Crusades and after clashing with William II, the late eleventh-century English king, left for Rome to seek help from the Pope, only to find the king refusing to let him back in the country. William's successor, Henry I, invited Anselm back, but there was another clash and Anselm was again briefly banned from England.

• **Thomas à Becket** (1162–1170)
Becket is the most famous of all Archbishops of Canterbury simply because he was murdered in Canterbury Cathedral by knights working for Henry II (see below).

• **Simon Sudbury** (1375–81)
The rebels behind the 1381 Peasants' Revolt saw Sudbury as the figurehead of a corrupt Church. After freeing John Ball, one of their leaders, from Maidstone Prison, they attacked Sudbury's Canterbury base and headed for the Tower of London to find him. The Tower guards let the rebels in and they dragged Sudbury to Tower Hill where they beheaded him. Sudbury was buried in Canterbury Cathedral minus his head, which was displayed on a spike on London Bridge and taken to St Gregory's in Sudbury, Suffolk.

• **William Courtenay** (1381–96)
A fierce opponent of the Bible translator John Wycliffe and the reformist Lollards, it was Courtenay who called a synod in London in May 1382 to condemn Wycliffe's translations of the Bible into English, proceedings famously interrupted by a supposedly divine earthquake (→ p. 25).

• **Thomas Arundel** (1396–7, 1399–1414)
After a row with the king, Richard II, and the House of Lords in 1397 Arundel was charged with high treason and banished from England. He headed for Rome where the Pope, Boniface IX, made him head of the see of St Andrews, a pointless move given that St Andrews didn't recognise Boniface's authority.

With the accession of Henry IV, Arundel was back in favour and he reassumed the position of Archbishop of Canterbury. Now he began to campaign vigorously against the reformist Lollards, particularly their founder, John Wycliffe ,and his revolutionary move of translating the Bible into English. He colourfully described Wycliffe as the 'son of the serpent, herald and child of the Antichrist' in a letter to Pope John XXII in 1411, but the Bible translator retorted:

You say it is heresy to speak of the Holy Scriptures in English. You call me a heretic because I have translated the Bible into the common tongue of the people. Do you know whom you blaspheme? Did not the Holy Ghost give the word of God first in the mother tongue of the nations to whom it was addressed? You say that the Church of God is in danger from this book. How can that be? Is it not from the Bible only that we learn that God hath set up such a society as the Church on earth? Is it not the Bible that gives all its authority to the Church? Is it not from the Bible that we learn who is the builder and sovereign of the Church. What are the laws by which she is to be governed, and the rights and privileges of her members? Without the Bible, what proof has the Church to show for all these? It is you who place the Church in peril by hiding the divine warrant, the epistle of her King, for the authority she wields and the faith she enjoins.

Christ and his apostles taught the people in the language best known to them. It is certain that the truth of the Christian faith becomes more evident the more the faith itself is known. Therefore the doctrine should not only be in Latin but also in the common tongue, and as the faith of the Church is contained in the Scriptures, the more these are known in the true sense the better.

If thou condemnest the word of God in any language as heresy, then you condemn God as a heretic that spoke the word, for He and His word are all one, and if His word is the life of the world how many Antichrists take it away from us that are Christian men, and allow the people to die for hunger in heresy?

In 2006 *BBC History* magazine named Arundel among the ten worst Britons of the last 1,000 years.

• **Thomas Cranmer** (1533–55)

Cranmer is one of the most famous archbishops, and was in charge of Canterbury during the most momentous period in

English Christianity, the Reformation of the 1530s. He supported Henry VIII's controversial divorce from Catherine of Aragon, declaring it was no marriage, and when England broke from Rome in 1533 the Pope, unsurprisingly, excommunicated him. But Cranmer's legacy was immense, for it was he who compiled the Book of Common Prayer, the staple of Protestantism. When Mary Tudor took the throne in 1553 and reintroduced Catholicism, Cranmer was accused of heresy and burnt to death in Oxford on 21 March 1556 (→ p. 174).

• **Reginald Pole** (1556–59)
Britain's last Catholic Archbishop of Canterbury presided over the burning of scores of Protestant 'heretics' which simply had the effect of turning many Englishmen against Catholicism.

• **Matthew Parker** (1559–75)
Parker was responsible for a new English translation of the Bible, the Bishops' Bible of 1568. The new translation derived from his hatred of the Geneva Bible, which contained annotations he found controversial and unwelcome. The Bishops' Bible, also known as the Treacle Bible thanks to its unusual translation: 'Is there not treacle at Gilead', (it should be balm), was substantially revised four years later and provided the foundation for what became the greatest of all English Bibles, the King James Bible of 1611.

But Parker is perhaps best known for being the butt of a farcical rumour circulating London in 1590. Opponents claimed the archbishop had been consecrated not at Lambeth Palace but at the Nag's Head tavern on Cheapside. There, with John Scory, ex-Bishop of Chichester who had been expelled by Queen Mary, attending, Parker supposedly knelt on the floor of the tavern, a Bible on his neck, and announced: 'Receive the power of preaching the word of God sincerely.' The story was probably false, spread by Jesuits unhappy with Parker's Anglican beliefs.

• **George Abbot** (1611–33)
Abbott eccentrically preached a sermon on the Book of Jonah every Thursday morning from 1594–9. He once had 140 Oxford undergraduates arrested for not removing their hats on entering St Mary's church. Abbott descended into profound melancholy after accidentally shooting a park-keeper dead during a hunt. A commission set up by the king, Charles I, ruled that 'an angel might have miscarried after this sort', and narrowly found in his favour at his trial.

• **Richard Bancroft** (1604–10)
Bancroft was the main organiser of the team who wrote the King James Bible (→ p. 57).

• **William Laud** (1633–45)
One of the most controversial archbishops, Laud presided over Charles I's coronation in Scotland, where his love of ceremony was deemed too Catholic for local taste. His determination that Scotland should adopt the English prayer book made him a hate figure and led to much conflict. Under Laud's tenure the High Commission of the Church wasted much time on bureaucratic trivia, dealing with cases such as that of a man who christened his cat and that of a man caught urinating in St Paul's Cathedral.

Laud polarised the country by inflicting savage punishments on critics such as William Prynne, Henry Burton and John Bastwick, who in 1637 had their ears cut off for opposing him. However, in 1640 the Long Parliament impeached Laud for high treason. They accused him of assuming tyrannical powers and 'subverting the true religion with popish superstition'.

After three years in the Tower, Laud was brought to trial before the House of Lords where the prosecution was led by Prynne of all people. The Lords couldn't make the charges stick until the House of Commons voted to condemn the archbishop by special decree. Laud was executed on Tower Hill in January 1645.

• **John Potter** (1737–47)
Though Potter took a High Church position, he failed to restore the Convocation (a Catholic-style synod), as many had hoped, which saw him ridiculed by the poet Alexander Pope in *The Dunciad.*

• **Frederick Temple** (1896–1902)
Temple made his name as late-Victorian headmaster of the famous public school Rugby, where he built its first laboratory, reformed sport, and preached many powerful sermons. A Liberal, he backed the disestablishment of the Church of Ireland, and as archbishop had to respond to Rome's questioning of the validity of Anglican orders. He moved against the introduction of incense into Anglican services and urged that Britain should take the lead in evangelising non-Christian nations.

• **Donald Coggan** (1974–80)
Coggan, an expert in Oriental languages, made a remarkable gesture of conciliation with Rome on a visit in 1977, when he called for harmony between the Anglican Communion and the Roman Catholic Church. He controversially supported the ordination of women, which became reality a decade after his departure. Coggan was well known for the charitable remark: 'The art of hospitality is to make guests feel at home when you wish they were.'

• **Rowan Williams** (2002–)
The most controversial incumbent for centuries, Rowan Williams received the kind of public opprobrium usually reserved for unsuccessful England football team managers, when he suggested in February 2008 that sharia law might have to be introduced in parts of the United Kingdom.

Williams told Radio 4 that Britain had to 'face up to the fact' that some of its citizens did not relate to the British legal system, and argued that adopting certain aspects of sharia law would maintain social cohesion. 'An approach to law which simply said, "There's one law for everybody" – I think that's a bit of a danger.' Inevitably there was a public outcry, and, with a series of confusing and tortuously phrased pronouncements, Williams failed to allay public disquiet about being associated with the kind of inhuman practices adopted in the name of sharia law.

No sooner had the fuss generated by his remarks died down than Williams was at the centre of a new storm – not one attributable to him, admittedly – as the Anglican Church moved towards irrevocable schism over the issues of gay clergy and women bishops. The archbishop was never likely to placate everyone. Peter Akinola, Archbishop of Nigeria, accused him of apostasy, manipulation and leading the Church into turmoil when traditionalists attacked the Church's liberal leadership at an Anglican summit in Jerusalem.

ABBEY OF ST AUGUSTINE, Longport

The abbey, now in ruins, covers a substantial area east of the cathedral and is named after Augustine, a Roman abbot, buried here, who brought Christianity to Britain in 597. Scholars are divided over whether Augustine truly was responsible for introducing Christianity into Britain. Some religious historians believe the good news arrived in England immediately after Jesus' crucifixion, maybe at Glastonbury, in the year AD 30, courtesy of Joseph of Arimathea, Jesus' uncle. The Augustine story dates back to the Venerable Bede who in his eighth century *Ecclesiastical History of the English People* described how Pope Gregory, before becoming pontiff, spotted a group of fair-haired youths in a Roman slave market. He was told they were Angles (English) and replied (roughly translated into English): 'Not Angles, but Angels – for they have an angelic face'.

Determined to save such a divine-looking people, when he

became Pope, Gregory sent over a group of monks including Augustine. They landed in Thanet, then an isle at the edge of Kent, and made their way to the nearest big town, Canterbury, where the local king, Æthelbert, met them in the open air so that the visitors could not practise any black magic. According to Bede, Augustine and his men sang to the court: 'We beseech Thee, O Lord, in all Thy mercy, that thy anger and wrath be turned away from this city, and from the holy house, because we have sinned. Hallelujah.' They converted the king to Christianity, and he granted Augustine a palace, which became Canterbury Cathedral, and land just outside the city walls to build a Benedictine abbey dedicated to Peter and Paul. The abbey became the burial place for Kent's kings and bishops, and was one of Europe's great religious centres until Henry VIII dissolved it in 1538.

→ Glastonbury Abbey, p. 255

CATHEDRAL CHURCH OF CHRIST, CANTERBURY (CANTERBURY CATHEDRAL), The Precincts

The history of Canterbury Cathedral is the history of English Christianity. It is the seat of the head of the English Church (the Archbishop of Canterbury), was the destination of countless pilgrimages in medieval days and because of Kent's close links to Europe long enjoyed special status in the eyes of Rome.

An infamous tragic incident on 29 December 1170 earned Canterbury a special place in the spiritual life of the country – the killing of Archbishop Thomas à Becket by knights working for Henry II. The king had clashed frequently with the strong-willed cleric and, when he shouted in frustration 'Who will rid me of this meddlesome priest?', a group of knights took the remark literally. They sought out Becket, killing him in the cathedral quire as he was on his way to vespers, prising out part of his brain and spreading it on the floor. Soon after Becket's murder local worshippers were claiming that miracles were taking place at the late archbishop's tomb in the cathedral crypt. The blind wife of a Sussex knight made a vow to 'Saint Thomas, martyr precious to Christ' and was supposedly cured. Other worshippers found that Becket's blood, scraped off the floor, healed the deaf, lame and blind, and cured leprosy and epilepsy.

News spread and pilgrims began journeying to the tomb to seek inspiration from the tomb of Becket. Those that entered the building were taken from Trinity Chapel back to the nave along the south choir aisle, their easy pace resulting in the coining of a new phrase – to canter. They would often leave with small flasks of holy water (ampullae) supposedly mixed with the blood and brains of the murdered archbishop. One of the first Canterbury pilgrims in 1174 after Becket was canonised was the king himself, Henry II, seeking forgiveness for any part he might have played in the murder.

By the thirteenth century Canterbury was one of Europe's great pilgrimage sites, rivalling Santiago de Compostela in Spain, and the donations of the pilgrims were used to carry out repairs and extensions on the building.

However, the most famous Canterbury pilgrims are fictional, those of Chaucer in his *Canterbury Tales*.

During Henry VIII's dissolution of the monasteries in the 1530s Becket was declared 'a false saint and a traitor to the Supreme Head of the Church'. The king's agents destroyed the shrine, carting away twenty-six wagon loads of loot said to include the clay out of which God made Adam and pieces of the crown of thorns. In 1538 a courtier read a writ denouncing Becket, dead nearly 400 years, for 'treason, contumacy and rebellion'. When after thirty days Becket failed to respond, the king had him charged with treason. He ordered the removal of Becket's bones, confiscated his treasures and removed his name from prayer books. For many years it was believed that Becket's bones had been burnt and scattered in the wind, but in 1881 workmen found a skeleton. Experts determined that it was that of a man of

Becket's age who had died from serious head wounds, but tests proved inconclusive.

The cathedral has been the setting for countless theological debates over the centuries. At the 2008 Lambeth Conference delegates discussed the row in the Anglican Communion over gay clergy.

Cranbrook

After 190 locals died of a plague in Cranbrook in 1598 the local vicar wrote in the parish register that it was a divine judgment for the town's sins, particularly for the 'vice of drunkenness which did abound here'.

Dartford

The Martyrs' Memorial located in an ancient churchyard above East Hill commemorates three Protestant Kentish martyrs burnt at the stake for their faith: Christopher Wade (burnt at Dartford 17 July 1555), Margaret Polley (burnt at Tonbridge 18 July 1555) and Nicholas Hall (Dartford the same day).

Wade, a Dartford linen-weaver, was convicted for refusing to give up his faith and convert to Catholicism. When the bishop asked Wade if he would be obedient to Mother Church, he replied that the phrase did not appear in the Bible. He was burnt in a local gravel pit, the Brimpt, wearing a white wedding shirt his wife gave him (Protestant martyrs saw their martyrdom as a marriage – a marriage to Christ). Wade's wife seeing him waiting to die cried out: 'You may rejoice, Wade, to see such a company gathered to celebrate your marriage this day.' Before the flames went up Wade called on those watching to beware of the 'whore of Babylon' (the Pope) and to stay true to the religion of Edward VI, which caused the sheriff to retort: 'Be quiet, Wade, and die patiently.'

That wasn't the end of religious controversy in the Thames-side town. Opponents of John Denn, vicar of Dartford, described him as a 'common alehouse and tavern haunter, commonly drunk on the Sabbath day [who] used to sit till twelve at night sending for bottles of wine', so it came as little surprise when the Church authorities removed him from his post in 1643. And in the eighteenth century a Doctor Vane was accused of 'pernicious and popish doctrine' after preaching at Holy Trinity church.

→ Burnings at Smithfield, p. 33

HIGHFIELD ROAD BAPTIST CHURCH

The church's vicar, the Revd David Parsons, led the protests against the BBC's screening of the allegedly blasphemous show *Jerry Springer: The Opera*, in January 2005. The musical had opened at the National Theatre in 2003, and despite protests outside Broadcasting House by Christian and Muslim groups who symbolically burnt TV licences, the BBC went ahead with the broadcast of the programme. According to the Revd Parsons: '*Jerry Springer: The Opera* is more than an attack on Christianity. It's an attack on decent standards of society generally. It depicts the characters of Jesus, Mary and God as self-centred sexual deviants who give and receive extreme verbal abuse and a horrific series of blasphemies all in the name of comedy.'

The BBC explained that the show was 'not to be taken literally'. Nevertheless the prayer group Christian Voice tried to bring a private prosecution against the Corporation. According to Christian Voice's national director Stephen Green: 'If *Jerry Springer: The Opera* isn't blasphemous then nothing in Britain is sacred. [Jesus] proclaims he is a bit gay, he has this shouting match with the devil – it's just foul-mouthed tirades against the devil and against his blessed mother. The damage that must have done to impressionable young people is incalculable.' Nevertheless Magistrates refused to issue a summons, a decision later upheld by the High Court of Justice.

→ Sikh protests force play to close, p. 155

Dover

After Pope Innocent III excommunicated King John in 1205 in a row over the appointment of a cardinal, Christianity in England fell into disarray. Seven years later, on 15 May 1212, near Dover, John handed over the kingdoms of England and Ireland to the Pope, immediately receiving them back in exchange for an annual payment. In 1670 Charles II signed a secret treaty at Dover with the French king, Louis XIV, allowing him to adopt Catholicism 'as soon as his country's affairs permit'. In return Louis was to pay £150,000 and provide 6,000 troops to quell any civil disturbance that might ensue once the news was known. Matthew Arnold's much-loved 1867 poem 'Dover Beach' bemoans the loss of faith in the newly industrialised world.

Gillingham

JEZREEL TOWER, **Canterbury Street**

A breakaway movement of the Christian Israelites founded by Clarissa Rogers and James White built an ungainly 95-foot high temple in Gillingham in the 1870s. It was supposed to contain an assembly hall, bakery, dairy, printing firm and smithy, but ended up an incomplete folly.

Rogers and White changed their names. She became 'Queen

Esther' and he 'James Jezreel, the Sixth Messenger of God', a line taken from the Book of Hosea. They forced their followers, recognisable by their long hair tucked into violet caps, into making compulsory 'donations' to remain in the group. They also prepared them to be among the 144,000 they claimed would be saved in the 'final gathering of AD 2000'.

In his book *The Flying Scroll*, White argued that he was Shiloh, the messianic figure from Genesis 49 and the Book of Revelation. He explained that during Creation Satan rebelled, together with some spirits now present on earth. Because Eve had seduced Adam into evil he would seduce women into good, around 72,000 of them – half the 144,000 earmarked for salvation. It is not known whether he was entirely successful. White also spent much time preaching abstinence, which only made it the more surprising when he later died of alcoholism.

After the deaths of Rogers and White the community fell apart and funds ran out. However, branches were successfully founded in America. For instance, in 1903 a Benjamin Purnell founded the House of David in Benton Harbor, Michigan, which later came to have its own orchestra and baseball team. Things went awry there in 1926 when Purnell was arrested, and the colony was officially declared a public nuisance.

The Gillingham tower in its incomplete state was demolished in 1961, by which time the sect had been defunct for forty years.

→ James Wroe, Christian Israelite leader in Ashton-under-Lyne, p. 216

Lamberhurst

SCOTNEY CASTLE

The Jesuit priest Richard Blount made fourteenth-century Scotney Castle, traditional home of the Darrell family on the

Kent–Sussex border, his secret hideaway from 1591-8, a time when Romish beliefs were illegal.

One Christmas at the end of the sixteenth-century priest-hunters seized the castle looking for Blount. He fled into a recess behind a solid stone wall but caught his clothes in the doorway. Fortunately for him an ally spotted the revealing cloth and cut it away, but Blount was unable to get rid of it all. A piece of the incriminating garment remained stubbornly visible, and the friend had to call out to the priest to tug the scrap from his hideaway. The priest-hunters heard voices, ran to the area, and began to hammer on the walls. On the other side were Blount and his allies, pushing their weight against the pursuers to keep them from opening the door. It was a rainy night and the priest-hunters decided to postpone the chase until the following day, by which time Blount had escaped over the walls.

During another raid Blount hid in a secret hole in the castle walls. While the search was taking place Mrs Darrell, the lady of the house, noticed that a length of cord from Blount's cassock was protruding. Somehow she managed to alert him and he quickly pulled the cord in. Alas one of the guards saw the woman talking to a blank wall and began to attack it until the arrival of heavy rain again saved Blount. The priest hid at Scotney for seven years before he was discovered.

Rochester

John Fisher, Bishop of Rochester during the turbulent years of Henry VIII's reign and the dissolution of the monasteries, became the only member of the College of Cardinals to be executed for his beliefs. Accused of treason for opposing Henry's divorce from Catherine of Aragon, Fisher was sent to the Tower of London, and as he had been removed from his position was treated as a commoner. He was found guilty, and sentenced to be hanged, drawn and quartered at Tyburn in 1535.

The public was dismayed. Some likened Fisher's fate to that of John the Baptist, executed by King Herod for challenging the latter's marriage to his brother's widow. So Henry VIII magnanimously commuted the sentence to beheading on Tower Hill which took place on 22 June 1535 (→ Tower Hill, p. 52).

In a separate drama, after Fisher first rowed with the king, several of the bishop's servants were taken ill with food poisoning. Two of them died and many suspected foul play, possibly an attempt on the bishop's life, although fortunately Fisher had not eaten the food. The culprit was Richard Roose, Fisher's cook, who admitted, probably under torture, that he had indeed added the poison – as a 'jest' with no harm intended. Henry was mortified and promulgated a special Act of Parliament whereby poisoning was adjudged to be high treason, the penalty for which was being boiled to death.

In 2006 the Bishop of Rochester, the Right Revd Dr Michael Nazir-Ali, made headlines by claiming that some places in Britain were no-go areas for non-Muslims. He criticised what he called the 'dual psychology' of Muslims who sought 'victimhood and domination . . . their complaint often boils down to the position that it is always right to intervene when Muslims are victims, and always wrong when Muslims are the oppressors or terrorists'.

SURREY

Chertsey

CHERTSEY ABBEY, **Abbey Gardens**

Church leaders led by Thomas Cranmer, Archbishop of Canterbury, met at Chertsey and later Windsor in 1548 to create that cornerstone of English Protestantism, The Book of Common Prayer. It was the first liturgical work to contain in one volume the form of service for daily and Sunday worship in English.

A revised edition appeared in 1552 but was never used, for when the Protestant Edward VI died his Catholic half-sister, Mary Tudor, took the throne and Cranmer's life was now in jeopardy. He was punished for his work and beliefs, and burnt at the stake in Oxford in March 1556.

Mary's successor, Elizabeth, was more ambiguous in religious matters and published a modified version of the 1552 edition. This time controversy centred around the wearing of vestments, which was now allowed again. Elizabeth also passed a law that forbade subjects from criticising the prayer book or forcing the clergy to use any other form of liturgy. The punishment for disobeying this law was a fine of 100 marks, followed by a fine of 400 marks for a second offence, and if that didn't work, the sanction would be life imprisonment.

The Cranmer prayer book lasted for around a hundred years until the Puritan revolution. The 1662 version, produced on the restoration of Charles II to the throne, has since remained the official prayer book of the Church of England, although there is now an alternative, Common Worship, which has replaced the Book of Common Prayer in many parishes.

Walton-on-Thames

ST MARY, Church Street

To the amazement of St Mary's congregation, six soldiers entered the church in March 1649, two months into Oliver Cromwell's monarch-free Commonwealth, led worshippers outside and informed them that the Sabbath had been abolished as 'unnecessary, Jewish and ceremonial'. They also claimed that church ministers were 'anti-Christian' and of no use now that Christ had 'descended into the hearts of his saints'. Their leader then pulled out a Bible and showed it to the crowd. 'Here is a book you have in great veneration, consisting of two parts, the Old and the New Testament. I must tell you it is abolished. It containeth beggarly rudiments, milk for Babes.'

On 1 April that year Gerard Winstanley, a local tradesman, led a band of disciples into creating a proto-communist settlement at St George's Hill, a mile west of Walton. Winstanley was convinced that a new age had dawned with the execution of Charles I that would restore humanity to a state similar to Adam's perfection before the Fall. His group came to be known as the Diggers, as they blatantly dug up the land to provide themselves with food.

Winstanley advocated a form of Christian communism based on Acts 2 which argued that 'in the beginning of time God made the earth. Not one word was spoken at the beginning that one branch of mankind should rule over another, but selfish imaginations did set up one man to teach and rule over another.' Violent attacks from local landowners and clergymen soon forced the Diggers to flee. They ended up a few miles away in Cobham, where their settlement collapsed in April 1650. Winstanley later published a manifesto, *The True Law of Freedom* (1652), in which he outlined his Utopian dreams of a classless agrarian society.

→ Cromwell bans Christmas, p. 109

Sussex

Chichester

The strangely named John Hogsflesh was forced to parade through the streets of Chichester on 14 November 1534 at market time wearing only a strip of linen around his waist. He was carrying a faggot, a bundle of sticks that showed he was a heretic and that he might be about to be burnt at the stake. Hogsflesh was being punished as the authorities had discovered he didn't believe in the Virgin Mary, nor that the body of Christ was present in the Eucharist.

Once Hogsflesh arrived at the marketplace, he was forced to climb on to a small platform and read out a statement explaining that he had been convicted of heresy but had now renounced his unfortunate beliefs: 'I do this penance here this day, beseeching you all and every one of you to take no example of any of my misdoing or saying, but that this my punishment may be a warning unto you to abstain from all such and other heresies and prohibited opinions at all times.' He was forced to repeat this invocation in November at Midhurst market and Lewes market. His last humiliation was on Sunday 22 November, when he joined a procession at Chichester Cathedral, still carrying the faggot.

Two decades later, on 13 October 1555, Richard Hook was executed in the town for his Protestant beliefs. Though he was not a well-known figure, his was a significant martyrdom on account of the vehemence with which the authorities condemned him. The public record states that Hook was a

child and nursling of devilish iniquity, on account of his manifest wicked errors, detestable heresies, and damnable opinions opposed and repugnant to the Catholic faith. Since Holy Mother Church can do nothing further against such a putrid member, we have handed over to your Royal Highnesses and the power of the secular arm the said Richard Hook to be punished and broken.

In the mid-seventeenth century, during the reign of Charles I, the Bishop of Chichester was Richard Montague, one of the most controversial pamphleteers of the age. Montague abhorred both Catholicism and its diametric Christian opposite, Puritanism. He equated Catholicism with tyranny and superstition, and Puritanism with anarchy. In 1619 Montague had clashed with

Catholics in his parish, and in 1623 he was attacked in a publication called *The Gagg of the Reformed Gospell.* He replied the following year with the wonderfully titled *A Gagg for the New Gospell? No. A New Gagg for an Old Goose.*

Lewes

A centre for fierce anti-popery over the last few centuries, Lewes hosts Gunpowder Plot celebrations every 5 November in which locals stage a procession that climaxes in not just the burning of an effigy of Guy Fawkes but the torching of the 'Pope', cheered on by rabble-rousers dressed as Vikings, smugglers and Zulus – all watched over by police in riot gear.

Yet Lewes was once hostile to Protestantism and the setting for executions of those who embraced reformed Christianity. Deryk Carver was the first Protestant martyr executed in Lewes, burnt at the stake on 22 July 1555. A brewer in Brighton, he was caught reciting the service in English, 'as set forth in the time of Edward VI' in his own house during Mary Tudor's Catholic reign.

The sheriff sent Carver to London to be questioned. Carver refuted the notion of transubstantiation and confession, and claimed the Latin Mass was 'unprofitable', adding that the Catholic doctrine was 'poison and sorcery. If Christ were here you would put him to a worse death than he was put to before. You say that you can make a God. Ye can make a pudding as well. Your ceremonies in Church be beggary and poison.'

A stake was built for him in Chichester by the Sign of the Star inn and his Bible (it was in English and therefore unacceptable to the Catholics) thrown into a barrel. Carver stepped into the barrel and threw the Bible out. The sheriff ordered it to be thrown back in immediately and Carver then uttered his last words:

Dear brethren and sisters, witness to you all, that I am come to seal with my blood Christ's Gospel, because I know that it is true. It is unknown unto all you, but that it hath been truly preached here in Lewes, and in all places in England, and now it is not. And for because I will not deny here God's Gospel, and be obedient to man's laws, I am condemned to die. And as many of you as do believe upon the Pope of Rome, or any of his laws which he sets forth in these days, you do believe to your utter condemnation, and except the great mercy of God, you shall burn in hell perpetually.

Understandably, the sheriff was not happy: 'If thou dost not believe the Pope thou art damned body and soul. Speak to thy God, that He may deliver thee now.' This had little effect on the accused, and the flames were soon upon him.

CHAPTER 4

THE MIDLANDS

It was in the Midlands in the 1370s that the first major translation of the Bible into English was begun. Behind the revolutionary move was the cleric John Wycliffe, based in Lutterworth, Leicestershire. He was already England's battering ram against papal excess. Now he was attempting to break the stranglehold priests had over the New Testament, which they allowed to be published only in Latin, understood by them and few others.

It was at Oxford that Wycliffe began to challenge papal authority, and it was in the great university town, with its long tradition of debate, that many of the most ferocious religious battles of the Middle Ages took place. Oxford became a great centre of Catholic opposition to the Church of England in the late sixteenth century. And it was in Oxford 300 years later that the Tractarians or Oxford Movement began a revival in traditional Catholic notions of Christianity that sparked the building of some of England's most striking churches (All Saints in London's West End and St Cross, Manchester).

Nowadays religious controversy in the Midlands is more likely to involve the religions of Asia. For instance, on 18 December 2004 the Birmingham Repertory Theatre had to cancel the opening night of the play *Behzti*, a black comedy about two Sikh women which contained a scene featuring a rape inside a temple, as hundreds of Sikh protesters gathered outside the theatre, resulting in some violence. Eventually, the company had to scrap the play altogether to appease the incensed Sikh community.

Key events

1382 **John Wycliffe, a Leicestershire rector, completes his revolutionary translation of the Bible into English.**

1427 **More than forty years after Wycliffe's death the Pope orders the Bible translator's corpse to be dug up and burnt, the ashes cast into the river, for crimes against papal authority.**

1555–6 **Three leading Protestant clerics, Thomas Cranmer (Archbishop of Canterbury), Hugh Latimer (Bishop of Worcester) and Nicholas Ridley (Archbishop of London), are burnt at the stake in Oxford's town ditch.**

1587 **Mary Queen of Scots is executed at Fotheringhay Castle for being involved in a Catholic plot to seize the throne from the Protestant queen, Elizabeth.**

1649 **Three leading Levellers, a mid-seventeenth-century politico-religious pressure group, are executed against the church wall at Burford on Oliver Cromwell's orders.**

1665 **The vicar of Eyam in Derbyshire selflessly closes off the village to prevent the plague spreading into the villages beyond.**

1678 **John Bunyan begins his great religious work, *The Pilgrim's Progress*, in Bedford county jail.**

1726 **Oxford student John Wesley begins to organise his life around a strict pattern of behaviour – what is later described as Methodism.**

1791 **Protestant rioters cause four days of violence in Birmingham while opposing the iconoclastic views of the scientist and theologian Joseph Priestley.**

1833 **John Keble launches the Anglo-Catholic Oxford Movement with his 'Assize Sermon' at St Mary's Oxford.**

2004 **An eleven-day Sikh protest forces the Birmingham Repertory Theatre to scrap a comedy about two Sikh women.**

BEDFORDSHIRE

Bedford

BEDFORD GAOL, **Silver Street**

John Bunyan began *The Pilgrim's Progress*, one of the first important works of English literature, while languishing in Bedford Gaol in 1675 for violating the Conventicle Act – holding a religious service run outside the guidelines of the Church of England. *The Pilgrim's Progress* is an allegory telling the story of Christian who makes his way from the 'City of Destruction' (earth) to the 'Celestial City' (heaven). It is peppered with imaginative place names (Slough of Despond, Valley of Humiliation) and memorable characters (Pliable, Obstinate, Mr Feeble Mind, Mr Stand Fast, Madam Bubble and a judge, Lord Hate-Good).

Bedford Gaol no longer stands but a stone set into the pavement marks the site. The local Bunyan Museum holds the door of the author's cell and the jug in which his blind daughter Mary brought him soup. Bunyan lived in a cottage at No. 17 St Cuthbert's Street, a building that stood until 1838. During its demolition a Deed of Gift with which Bunyan bequeathed his estate to his wife, Elizabeth, was found behind a brick in the chimney. He had hidden it there fearing arrest and the seizure of his assets.

→ John Wycliffe, Bible translator, p. 161

THE PANACEA SOCIETY, 12 Albany Road

After being released from an asylum in 1920 Mabel Barltrop, widow of an Anglican curate, formed the Panacea Society to promote the teachings of the early nineteenth-century false messiah Joanna Southcott. Barltrop and the Panacea Society campaigned to get the Church of England to open Southcott's famed box, which allegedly contained news about the end of the world and other important information, running their campaign under the slogan 'War, disease, crime and banditry will increase until the bishops open Joanna Southcott's box'.

A box *was* opened at Church House, Westminster, in 1927 but it yielded merely an assortment of ephemera and trivia. Southcott's supporters had an excellent riposte to those who mocked them. It wasn't *the* authentic Southcott box, and there had to be twenty-four bishops present at the opening rather than just the one who turned up. The Panacea Society now guards the right box at a secret location it will reveal only once all the necessary bishops agree to open it.

The society also owns the cot which Joanna prepared for the virgin birth of her messianic child, Shiloh, whose failure to arrive precipitated her death in 1814. This the Panaceans keep in the Haven, a twenty-room mansion at the corner of Castle Road and Newnham Road which they believe became earth's control centre when Shiloh was born in 2004, an occurrence which no non-members have confirmed.

→ Joanna Southcott's box, p. 80.

Elstow

ABBEY CHURCH OF ST MARY AND ST HELENA, Wilstead Road, Elstow

The village is the birthplace of *Pilgrim's Progress* author John Bunyan, Bedford's greatest son, who was baptised in St Mary and St Helena's font in 1628. Bunyan rang the church bells on Sundays, and he cast the belfry as Beelzebub's Tower in *The Pilgrim's Progress*. To the left of the central door is a smaller one with heavy iron hinges on which he modelled the book's Wicket Gate. To Bunyan these two doors were a parable of the broad and narrow ways of Matthew 7. The church windows have scenes from the book 'to remind all Christian people of the Holy War they should be engaged in on the side of Emmanuel'.

DERBYSHIRE

Derby

Henry Sacheverell became one of the most notorious preachers of the eighteenth century after railing against the Glorious Revolution in a speech at Derby Assizes in August 1709. The Whig government denounced him for making 'malicious, scandalous and seditious libels', banned him from preaching for three years and burnt his sermons outside London's Royal Exchange. This made him a martyr in many people's eyes, and led to Presbyterian and Dissenter places of worship being attacked in what became known as the Sacheverell Riots.

Eyam

ST LAWRENCE, Church Street

During a virulent attack of the Bubonic Plague in 1665 and 1666 St Lawrence's vicar, William Mompesson, selflessly closed off the village to prevent the plague spreading. The disease had been brought in in a parcel of damp cloth sent from London which was hung out in front of the fire to dry, releasing the fleas that carried the plague. On 7 September 1665 George Vicars was the first Eyam villager to fall victim. Mompesson's actions meant no one could leave Eyam, but the vicar realised correctly that those infected – around half the village – had no chance of escaping with their lives, so there was no point in letting them carry the infection into the villages beyond. Eyam has since been celebrated in history for its heroic act.

During restoration of the church in 1868 the solid oak chair used by Rev Mompesson disappeared. It turned up some years later in an antiques shop in Liverpool and was bought by a local man who returned it to its original home.

→ The Plague in London's East End, p. 41.

Chapter 4

Leicestershire

Dunton Bassett

The Family International religious cult, based in this Leicestershire village, used to be the better-known Children of God. Founded in California in 1968 by David Berg, the Children of God was briefly the most notorious religious cult in the West, a role later taken over by the Moonies and the Scientologists. Berg and his followers made great play of the Old Testament's first commandment, 'Be fruitful and multiply', sending out the most attractive female members, 'hookers for Jesus', as they came to be known, to entice gullible males into the cult. Their most famous devotee was the Fleetwood Mac guitarist Jeremy Spencer, who in 1971 left the band's San Francisco hotel mid tour, failed to return, and was later found among their followers. By then there were 130 Children of God communities in fifteen countries. The group curtailed its sexual activity following the findings about AIDS in the mid-1980s.

Lutterworth

ST MARY, Church Gate

John Wycliffe, the first important figure in religious history to attempt a translation of the Bible into English, was appointed rector of Lutterworth by Edward III in 1374. It was the king's way of thanking him for standing up to the Pope during delicate negotiations over the powers of Rome. In Lutterworth Wycliffe intensified his attacks on corruption in the Church. He began to argue that the Church had fallen into sin and that the clergy ought to live in complete poverty. Another controversial point was his argument that criminals who had taken sanctuary in a church should be arrested. It was here also that he began translating the Bible into English.

This was a revolutionary move as it threatened to break the stranglehold priests had over the New Testament, then available only in Latin, which few outside their closed circle could understand. Ironically, Wycliffe could deal only with the Latin, as he knew no Hebrew or Greek, the Bible's original languages. So how much of the translating he did himself and how much was performed by his assistant, John Purvey, is unknown. Either way, the whole thing would have been most painstaking, as each English Bible had to be individually bound.

Wycliffe also founded a group of lay preachers that became known as the Lollards (a Dutch word meaning 'mumbler'). They wanted to bring the word of God to people directly, orally, which was their only option in the days before the printing press was invented. The Lollards copied Wycliffe's sermons by hand and distributed them far and wide, but they were ridiculed by priests and monks for being ill-educated.

In 1382 the authorities banned all Wycliffe's writings. The Church was scared of the consequences of ordinary people understanding the Bible and made the teaching of his ideas punishable by death. Two years later Wycliffe received a summons to present himself before the Pope, Urban VI. Wycliffe knew that if he went to Rome he would not be allowed back to England. He apologised for turning down the invitation:

I am always glad to explain my faith to anyone, and above all to the Bishop of Rome, for I take it for granted that if he were orthodox he will confirm it. If it were erroneous he will correct it. I assume too, that as chief Vicar of Christ upon earth, the Bishop of Rome is of all moral men most bound to the law of Christ's gospel. Now, Christ, during His life upon earth, was of all men the poorest, casting from Him all worldly authority. I deduce from these premises as a simple counsel of my own that the pope should surrender all temporal authority to civil power and advise his clergy to do the same . . . I'm sorry that I cannot come, but the Lord Jesus Christ has further work for me to do for Him here.

The Pope's reaction is not known. On 29 December 1384 Wycliffe suffered a stroke at St Mary's altar. Attendants placed him in a chair and carried him into the rectory. Two days later he died. One person at least was pleased, the historian Thomas Walshingham, who wrote: 'John Wycliffe, that instrument of the devil, the enemy of the Church, the confusion of men, the idol of heresy, the mirror of hypocrisy, the nourisher of schism, was by the rightful doom of God smitten with a horrible paralysis [before he] breathed out his malicious spirit in to the abodes of hell.'

Wycliffe's death did not bring an end to the drama connected with him. In 1389, five years after the Bible translator's demise, William Courtenay, Archbishop of Canterbury, came to Lutterworth to preach Mass and excommunicate nine locals of uncertain identity whom he deemed Wycliffe supporters. Courtenay placed an interdict on the whole town until he discovered who the nine were.

But even that was not the end of the affair. In December 1427 the Pope ordered that Wycliffe's body be 'dug up and cast out of consecrated ground'. The corpse was exhumed from its grave in Lutterworth and burnt, the ashes cast into the nearby River Swift. Supporters later remarked that, since the Swift flows into the Avon, the Avon into the Severn, the Severn into the Bristol Channel, and the Bristol Channel into the Atlantic, the whole world would soon be washed with Wycliffe's remains. Indeed, the Church was unable to prevent the flow of Wycliffe's ideas, and Rome now permits the Bible to be translated into languages other than the (non-original) Latin.

St Mary's contains a number of Wycliffe memorials and mementoes. One from 1837 acknowledges that 'his whole life was one impetuous struggle against the corruptions and encroachments of the papal court, and the impostures of its devoted auxiliaries, the mendicant fraternities. His labours in the cause of scriptural truth were crowned by one immortal achievement, his translation of the Bible into the English tongue.'

→ Wycliffe's hearing at Blackfriars, p. 25

NORTHAMPTONSHIRE

Fotheringhay

FOTHERINGHAY CASTLE, **off the A605**

Mary Queen of Scots was executed at now long demolished Fotheringhay Castle on 8 February 1587 for being involved in a Catholic plot to seize the throne from the Protestant queen, Elizabeth.

Mary had endured a life riddled with intrigue and plot. She had become Queen of Scotland in 1542 when she was just six days old, and at the age of six months was briefly betrothed to Prince Edward, who four years later became Edward VI. The engagement was cancelled so that Scotland could form an alliance with France and in 1558 Mary married Francis, heir to the French throne.

Two years later Francis died and Mary, back in Scotland, married her cousin Henry Stuart, Lord Darnley. The marriage was a disaster. Darnley arranged the murder of Mary's secretary, David Rizzio, in 1566 in front of the queen herself, who was six months pregnant with the future James I. Darnley himself was strangled a year later and his house blown up. The chief suspect was the Earl of Bothwell, whom Mary had married, a move that outraged the people of Scotland who turned her out of the country.

In England Elizabeth I, her cousin, refused to help her, fearing that she was trying to raise Catholic support to capture the English throne, and kept Mary prisoner, mostly in Sheffield Castle. When Elizabeth's aides found letters Mary had sent to a

Catholic, Thomas Babington, outlining a plot to kill Elizabeth so that she could replace her, execution soon followed.

It took two strikes to remove Mary's head. The first blow missed her neck and the queen's lips were seen to mouth the words 'Sweet Jesus'. The second blow severed her neck, save for a small piece of sinew that the executioner cut away using the axe as a saw.

→ Mary Queen of Scots in Edinburgh, p. 268

Northampton

As James VI of Scotland made his way to London in 1603 to take the throne of England as James I he was met in Northamptonshire by a large delegation of Puritans, who presented him with their list of religious demands. This was the Millenary Petition, signed by 1,000 ministers objecting to the Anglican Church. Despite Queen Elizabeth's reforms they believed the Church was still too Romish, citing practices such as the signing of the cross during baptism, use of the ring in marriage, bowing at the name of Jesus and priests living in their churches. Although the new king rebutted many of the petitioners' demands, he did accede to the Hampton Court Conference (→ p. 2), out of which emerged a remarkable new English Bible – the Authorised or King James version.

NORTHAMPTON CASTLE, **St Andrews Road**

Thomas à Becket, one of the most famous martyrs in English history, was summoned to appear before Henry II at Northampton Castle in October 1164, two years after being appointed Archbishop of Canterbury, to answer charges of contempt of royal authority. After his conviction, he stormed out of the castle and fled the country. He was murdered six years later in Canterbury Cathedral by knights working for Henry II.

ST GILES

The church contains a memorial to Robert Browne, pioneer of Congregationalism. This late sixteenth-century movement not only rejected the notion of a vast hierarchical international church run from Rome but also the idea of a national church allied to the Crown (as in England) or even a local church body run by elders. Instead it sought to promote single stand-alone churches. The first Congregational church in England opened in 1581 in Norwich.

NOTTINGHAMSHIRE

Nottingham

ST MARY, High Pavement, Lacemarket

St Mary has a history of worshippers interrupting proceedings. In 1623 the vicar, Richard Taverner, sued a shoemaker, Robert Taylor, for 'obstructing the Divine Offices about to be celebrated and using malicious words against the vicar'.

Twenty-six years later George Fox, founder of the Quakers, recorded in his diary that, as he walked down the hill into Nottingham, he had seen a great 'Steeple House': St Mary. He was inspired to attend the service but, disagreeing with what was being preached, Fox interrupted and corrected the preacher. He was sent to prison for his pains. The sheriff, John Reckless, however, was convinced and converted to Fox's cause.

In 1724 an even more unusual incident occurred here. Lancelot Blackburne, the Archbishop of York, conducted a confirmation service in the church and then retired to the vestry, where he called for pipes and ale. However, on his return the vicar, John Disney, refused to allow the archbishop back in the church, so annoyed was he that St Mary was being turned into a 'tippling house'.

→ Archbishops of York, p. 209

Oxfordshire

Abingdon

Following the funeral of the Baptist leader John Pendarves at the Baptist burial ground in Ock Street in 1656, attended by mystics and religious extremists from across the country, three days of rioting erupted and troops had to be called in to quell it.

Burford

LEVELLERS' EXECUTION SITE, St John the Baptist, Church Green
Three leaders of the Levellers, a mid-seventeenth-century politico-religious pressure group, were executed against the church wall at Burford in May 1649, following an order given by the most powerful figure in the country, Oliver Cromwell.

The Levellers held themselves to be free-born Englishmen, entitled to protection by natural laws which originated in the will of God. They believed in religious tolerance and rejected executions, burnings, brandings and banishments that led to martyrdom. During the Civil War the Levellers had fought on Cromwell's side, seeing the parliamentarian leader as a liberator, and with Parliament in charge following the execution of Charles I they were impatient for greater democracy.

In May 1649 a number of troops in the parliamentary army

sympathetic to their aims mutinied at Salisbury. They marched north and swam across the Thames, joined up with other discontented soldiers at Oxford and arrived on 14 May in Burford. Cromwell rode into the town that night with 2,000 horsemen and captured 340 Levellers, imprisoning them in the church. There some carved their names in frustration. (Inside the font visitors can still read the inscription: 'Anthony Sedley 1649 Prisoner'). Three days later Cromwell ordered that three of the group, Private Church, Corporal Perkins and Cornet Thompson, be executed inside the church. The bullet holes can still be seen.

St John, begun *c.* 1175, has a slender and striking spire, and stands in a gorgeous setting by the river Windrush, though much of what can be seen today dates from major restoration in the late-medieval period. When the great Victorian polymath William Morris visited the church in 1876 he was horrified to see the vicar scraping off medieval wall-paintings, and even more horrified to hear him explain: 'This church, sir, is mine, and if I choose to, I shall stand on my head in it.' The incident inspired the illustrious aesthete to found the Society for the Protection of Ancient Buildings.

→ Cromwell devastates Ireland, p. 307

Chipping Norton

ST MARY, Church Street

Henry Joyce, St Mary's vicar, was hanged from the church tower in 1549 after leading a revolt against the imposition of the Protestant Book of Common Prayer. Yet Joyce was legally obliged to introduce this English work at the expense of the traditional Latin prayer book that few but the clergy understood. A year later the authorities insisted that the Church destroy the stone altars and replace them with wooden communion tables. The clergy cheated – slightly – by burying the altar in the churchyard rather than breaking it up, which proved convenient during the reign of the Catholic Mary Tudor, when it was reintroduced.

East Hendred

HENDRED HOUSE

Inside the Eystons' medieval house in this tiny village is the Saxon chapel of St Amand which troops attached to William of Orange, the Protestant prince invited to take the British throne at the expense of the Catholic James II in 1688, wrecked while marching through the village on their way to London. The soldiers weren't being destructive to make a religious point; they were celebrating the news that James had fled the capital and thrown the Great Seal (the king's symbol of authority) into the Thames to prevent Parliament being called in his name.

When the modern calendar, devised by Pope Gregory XIII, was adopted in England in 1752 the rector of East Hendred noted how people had shown great aversion to it; 'The common people don't like it, because it has something of popery in it they say; I wish we had no other reason but such as this to find fault with the Church of Rome.'

The Eyston family still owns two invaluable relics: Thomas More's drinking cup and the staff used by John Fisher, Bishop of Rochester, as he climbed to the scaffold at Tyburn to be executed.

Henley

STONOR HOUSE

Edward Campion, the mid-sixteenth-century Jesuit, secretly printed his controversial book *Decem Rationes* (*Ten Reasons*) or in full *Ten Reasons Proposed to his Adversaries for Disputation in the Name of the Faith and Presented to the Illustrious Members of our Universities*, a critique of the Anglican Church, on a samizdat press in Stonor House. For his pains he was later arrested in Lyford (see below) and executed at Tyburn in London.

→ Tyburn executions, p. 51.

Kirtlington

It was in the manor house of Kirtlington, a pretty village eight miles north of Oxford, that the Catholic martyr Father George Napper was arrested early in the morning of 19 July 1610, suspected of Romish practices. Napper was searched by a constable, who found his breviary, holy oils and a needle case with thread and thimble, and took him to Sir Francis Evers, the nearest Justice of the Peace.

Sir Francis evidently had some sympathy with Napper for he chose *not* to find the small bag of relics and the pyx containing two consecrated hosts which the Father had concealed in his clothing. Nevertheless Napper was accused of being a Catholic priest (then illegal) and incarcerated in Oxford Castle. At the trial the judge told the jury that if only Fr Napper were to say he was not a priest he would believe him. But Napper would not deny his calling, and when he refused to take the oath of allegiance which described papal power as being 'false, damnable and heretical', the authorities decided to execute him. The crowd was sympathetic and pulled on Napper's legs so that he would die before being disembowelled. Each of the four quarters of his body was then fixed to a gate of Oxford.

Lyford

Edmund Campion, the pioneering Jesuit, was captured here by the authorities on 14 July 1581 after preaching proscribed views. He was charged with 'in a certain room within the manor house of Great Coxwell being vested in alb and other vestments according to papist rites and ceremonies [he] did say and celebrate one private and detestable Mass in the Latin tongue, derogatory to the blood of Christ and contrary to his due allegiance'. At the time of his arrest Campion was on his way from Oxford to Norfolk and had left 400 copies of his controversial book *Decem Rationes* (*Ten Reasons*), a critique of the Anglican Church, on the benches of St Mary's, Oxford (→ p. 181). After his arrest Campion was taken to the Tower of London with his arms pinioned and wearing a hat inscribed: 'Campion, the Seditious Jesuit'. He was hanged, drawn and quartered in 1581.

Oxford

The great university city was at the centre of many of the fiercest religious controversies of the Middle Ages. For instance, it was here in the 1370s that the era's greatest Christian reformer, John Wycliffe, began to challenge papal authority. And it was here a generation later, in 1408, that the Constitutions of Oxford banned the translation of the Bible into English.

That law was drawn up by Thomas Arundel, Archbishop of

Canterbury, who, in a letter to the Pope sent in 1412, listed 267 heresies he had found in translations by Wycliffe, whom he colourfully described as 'a wretched and pestilent fellow, son of the Serpent, child of the Antichrist'. In Oxford itself Arundel thundered: 'This university which once was a juicy vine, and brought forth its branches for the glory of God and the advancement of his church, now brings forth wild grapes. It is a dangerous thing to translate the text of the Holy Scripture out of one tongue into another,' oblivious, it seems, to the 'dangers' of translating it from Hebrew into Latin in the first place. No man was now allowed to read such translations, Arundel concurred, and those who did would be 'accursed eating and drinking, walking and sitting, rowing and riding, laughing and weeping, in house and in field, on water and on land'.

When William Tyndale's later translation, the first published copies of the Bible in English, began arriving in England in 1526 Cardinal Wolsey, Henry VIII's leading minister, took charge of hunting down and burning these 'heretical' books. He ordered that Oxford be searched and had a number of men arrested, who were made to march in procession, each carrying a torch to light the English Bibles, which were destroyed in a large blaze. The men were then cast into a pit used for storing fish where four of them died during a six-month interment.

Oxford became a great centre of recusancy – Catholic refusal to comply with the established Church of England – in the late sixteenth century when Elizabeth was on the throne. The secret Catholics celebrated Mass illegally in Oxford inns such as the Mitre and the Star, and private houses such as Holywell Manor, which became a major refuge for Roman Catholic priests. Rowland Jenks, a stationer and bookbinder, distributed popish books. He was arrested in 1577, tried at the Black Assize, and punished by having his ears removed. Some recusants, however, were simply on the make. For instance, in 1591 John Allyn, an Oxford man, claimed to own a quantity of Christ's blood which he sold for £20 a drop to those who believed it would free them from ill fortune.

Catholicism declined in the city during the seventeenth century. In the Protestant fervour at the beginning of the Civil War Catholic books and pictures were burnt in the streets. At that time the town favoured Parliament, the university and the king; indeed Oxford became Charles I's headquarters.

In the mid-nineteenth century the city was at the centre of one of the century's most important evangelical campaigns: the Anglo-Catholic Oxford Movement or Tractarians, so called because they launched their campaign by producing 'Tracts for the Times' on theological issues. The members of the new group believed that England had forgotten the apostolic roots of its Church, so they set about to educate the English Church and the people, reintroducing Romish practices, such as candles, incense and the wearing of traditional vestments (→ St Mary's church, Oxford, p. 181).

Until 1871 it was a legal requirement that a religious test – receiving the sacrament according to the rites of the Church of England – had to be undertaken by Oxford University students hoping to be awarded a Masters' degree.

ALL SOULS COLLEGE OXFORD, Radcliffe Square

William Whittingham, an All Souls Fellow, was responsible for the finest English Bible yet, the Geneva Bible, in 1557. Whittingham, aided by Myles Coverdale, Thomas Sampson and others, produced from the Swiss city-state a small octavo volume of the New Testament based mostly on earlier translations by William Tyndale. The Geneva Bible was Puritan in outlook, easy to use, the first to be printed in Roman type, the first in which the text was divided into numbered verses, had a commentary in the margins, and even contained a preface by John Calvin, the great French theologian. His involvement made the Geneva Bible especially popular in Scotland, where a law passed in 1579 required every household that could afford it to buy it. The version remained popular for generations – it was the Bible Shakespeare used – and was the version that King James's scholars adopted as a template for their even greater Authorised Version (→ p. 250). Some US historians believe it was used at the signing of the Declaration of Independence due to Puritan influence in America at the time.

BOCARDO PRISON, **Cornmarket**

The Oxford Martyrs – Thomas Cranmer, Hugh Latimer, Nicholas Ridley (see below) – were imprisoned in the Bocardo before being burnt at the stake in the town ditch (now Broad Street) in 1555 and 1556. Their cell door can be seen in the tower of the nearby church of St Michael.

CATHERINE WHEEL INN, **Magdalen Street**

George Nichols, a teacher at St Paul's school in London, was arrested at the inn in May 1589 for being a Catholic priest. He and two laymen were sent to London's Bridewell Prison, where they were hanged from their hands to get them to betray their faith. When that didn't work, Nichols was thrown into a 20-foot pit in the Tower of London. At the end of June the men were sent back to Oxford for trial. They were all found guilty, and sentenced to be hanged, drawn and quartered. The authorities refused to allow Nichols to address the crowd, and after the execution the men's heads were displayed at the castle, and their quarters on the four city gates. The punishment must have worked as a warning to others for it was twenty years before another Catholic was executed in Oxford.

It was at the inn in January 1605 that some of the Gunpowder Plotters (→ p. 81), including Robert Catesby, met.

→ Matthew Parker, consecrated Archbishop of Canterbury at the Nag's Head, Cheapside, p. 138

CHRIST CHURCH CATHEDRAL, St Aldate's Street

The smallest cathedral in England and seat of the Bishop of Oxford was where Thomas Cranmer, the sixteenth-century Archbishop of Canterbury who produced the ground-breaking Book of Common Prayer, was ordained as a priest in 1523. Six years later Cranmer was advising Henry VIII on the legality of his marriage to Catherine of Aragon (he supported the king's divorce) and in 1532 was appointed Archbishop of Canterbury. But in 1556, with the Catholics now back in power, Cranmer was stripped of his vestments and burnt at the stake in Broad Street.

The bones of St Frideswide, patron saint of the university, were taken from Christ Church in 1558 and mixed with those of a former nun who had married an ex-monk, so that any future attempt to honour the saint by restoring the bones to a new shrine would be impossible.

Christ Church was where Charles I had his headquarters from 1642–6 during the Civil War. Both John and Charles Wesley, founders of Methodism in the 1720s, were ordained in the cathedral.

→ Exeter Cathedal, p. 239

CHRIST CHURCH COLLEGE

William Penn, who went on to found the American state of Pennsylvania, was expelled from the college (Charles I's headquarters in the Civil War) in 1662 for refusing to comply with the college's religious requirements, which included church worship. Six years later he was put in solitary confinement in the Tower of London for writing a blasphemous tract, *The Sandy Foundation Shaken*. The Bishop of London ordered Penn to be held indefinitely until he publicly recanted his views, but the Quaker retorted: 'My prison shall be my grave before I will budge a jot: for I owe my conscience to no mortal man.' He also produced another controversial paper, *No Cross, No Crown*, and unsurprisingly was refused an audience with the king (Charles II). He was released after eight months, and left the country for missionary work overseas. In the 1670s he suggested the Quakers leave Britain en masse for the American colonies. Charles II surprisingly granted him a huge estate of land south of New York, later named after him, in return for mining rights.

John Wesley, founder of Methodism, studied at Christ Church College in the 1720s. A contemporary, Samuel Badcock, described him as a 'very sensible and acute collegian, baffling every man by the subtleties of logic, and laughing at them for being so easily routed; a young fellow of the finest classical taste, of the most liberal and manly sentiments'.

KEBLE COLLEGE, Parks Road

Many Oxford colleges began as houses of study for those who wished to become priests. Exeter College, for instance was founded in 1314 to train priests for the diocese of Exeter. Not so Keble. It was a late starter, founded in 1870 in memory of John Keble, one of the instigators of the Oxford Movement (see below). The college buildings were designed by William Butterfield, the Oxford Movement's greatest architect, who was also responsible for the remarkable All Saints, Margaret Street in London's West End (→ p. 70). At first only members of the Church of England were admitted to the college, but the religious requirement has long been dropped.

LINCOLN COLLEGE, Turl Street

After being elected to a Fellowship in 1726 John Wesley, founder of Methodism, began to organise his time according to a strict pattern: Mondays and Tuesdays he used for studying Latin and Greek; Wednesdays, logic and ethics; Thursdays, Hebrew and Arabic; Fridays, metaphysics and natural philosophy; Saturdays, rhetoric and poetics; and Sundays, theology.

Wesley became obsessive about his methods. He dismissed

sleep as self-indulgent and set his alarm for 4 a.m. In his journal he began to record concepts and reactions: 'Whenever you are to do an action, consider how God did or would do the like, and do you imitate his example?' Under General Rules of Employing Time, Wesley wrote:

> Begin and end every day with God.
> Be diligent in your calling.
> Employ all spare hours in religion, as able.
> Examine yourself every night.
> Avoid idleness.
> Resist the very beginnings of lust.
> In every act reflect on the end.

Wesley and his associates became well known for their religious observance, fasting twice a week and spending part of each day in meditation. Detractors nicknamed them the Holy Club, the Godly Club, Bible Moths and Methodists, a name that stuck in 1732. Later John Wesley remembered how at Oxford: 'I lived almost like a hermit. I saw not how any busy man could be saved. God taught me better by my own experience.'

MAGDALEN COLLEGE, High Street

In a provocative move in 1687, the Catholic king, James II, proposed his own Catholic nominee, Anthony Farmer, as president of the college – against the wishes of the Magdalen Fellows. When they refused to accept Farmer, something of a playboy who had been sacked from Trinity College, Cambridge, and elected their own man, a Dr Hough, instead, the king ordered one of his minions to break open the college door and take over the presidency, expelling the disobedient Fellows at sword point and replacing them with Catholics.

MARTYRS' MEMORIAL, Broad Street

The Martyrs' Memorial commemorates three leading sixteenth-century Protestant clerics, Thomas Cranmer (Archbishop of

Canterbury), Hugh Latimer (Bishop of Worcester) and Nicholas Ridley (Archbishop of London), who in the 1550s were burnt at the stake in the town ditch, a site now covered by the modern-day Broad Street, for Protestant heresy.

The three clerics knew their survival was in jeopardy the moment the Catholic queen, Mary Tudor, came to the throne in 1553. Mary summoned them to appear before a commission at the Oxford church of St Mary the Virgin so that they could be questioned about their beliefs. Asked about transubstantiation, the three men admitted to being non-believers in it and were duly found guilty of being Protestants.

Cranmer had been Henry VIII's Archbishop of Canterbury and had defended Henry when the king annulled his marriage to Catherine of Aragon, which led to England's break with the Rome Church. Cranmer was particularly troubled by Mary's regime for he believed that a Christian's duty was to obey the monarch; with Mary on the throne, commanding him to obey Rome's will, he was in a quandary. Five times he tried to write a letter to the Pope, Paul IV, to seek clarification and four times tore it up. At his trial in Oxford Cranmer was cross-examined by Thomas Martin, an expert in Roman civil law, who questioned him about his marriage to 'Black Joan of the Dolphin' in Cambridge forty years earlier, about another marriage in Germany, and conflicting opinions he had held over the previous two decades as to whether Christ was present in the sacramental bread and wine. Cranmer found himself unable to cope with the intense interrogation, but still refused to recant.

Latimer and Ridley met their fate on 16 October 1555, burnt at the stake next to Balliol College. Latimer's last words were: 'Be of good cheer, Master Ridley, and play the man, for we shall this day light such a candle in England as I trust by God's grace shall never be put out.' For Ridley the fire burnt slowly, which meant that he suffered more. His legs were charred, but initially the flames would go no higher and so were not able to reach the gunpowder around his neck. An aide rushed forward to speed up death and reduce the martyr's torment, but to no avail. Ridley's legs had burnt off. However, he was still alive and cried out: 'For God's sake, let the fire come unto me! I cannot burn . . . Lord have mercy upon me.' Eventually he managed to hoist what was left of himself towards the flames. When they reached his neck there was an explosion and he died in that instant.

Cranmer was forced to watch his colleagues die their grim deaths. The authorities let him fester while they subjected him to personal abuse. But they also occasionally released him and allowed him to play bowls on the village green. After the Pope burnt Cranmer's effigy in Rome, he was sent back to Bocardo Gaol. Now he recanted, but even this failed to placate the Catholics. Cranmer then lost his integrity by agreeing to everything demanded of him. This should have been enough to earn a royal pardon but he was taken from the Bocardo on 21 March 1556 and burnt. He died a Protestant, angry with himself for recanting. 'I have sinned, in that I signed with my hand what I did not believe with my heart. When the flames are lit,' he vowed, 'this hand shall be the first to burn.' Once the fire was lit, Cranmer put his right hand in the flames until it was charred. He moved once as he met his end – to wipe the sweat from his forehead.

After the three deaths the Oxford bailiffs asked the Archbishop of Canterbury to pay for the costs incurred. Among the expenses relating to Cranmer was the purchase of wine, figs, oysters, veal and almonds, as well as of the hundred wood faggots which formed his pyre.

A cross to mark the event is set into a plaque in the wall of Balliol College. The cross is the 'gloomy and inauspicious' place where Jude meets Sue Brideshead in Thomas Hardy's *Jude the Obscure*. There is no memorial to four Catholic martyrs – Blessed Thomas Belson (a layman who had studied at Oxford's Exeter College), Blessed Humphrey Pritchard (also a layman), and the priests Blessed George Nichols and Richard Yaxley – who were hanged in what is now Broad Street on 5 July 1589.

→ Martyrs' Memorial church, Belfast, p. 287

MERTON COLLEGE, Merton Street

John Wycliffe, England's first great Christian reformer, studied at Merton. In the 1370s he began attacking the notion of transubstantiation – that the wine and wafer at Communion become the body of Christ. He also denounced Mass as satanic.

Should I once so far beguile the faithful of the Church, by the aid of Antichrist my vice-regent, as to persuade them to deny that this sacrament is bread, but merely looks like it, there will be nothing then which I will not bring them to receive, since there can be nothing more opposite to the Scriptures, or the common discernment.

While lecturing on the supposedly heretical nature of Mass in 1381, Wycliffe was interrupted by a messenger sent by the chancellor of the university, who warned that if he did not desist he would be imprisoned and excommunicated. That year a council of Oxford elders condemned his teachings and his 'many disciples in depravity, clad in long russet gowns of one pattern, going on foot, ventilating his errors among the people'.

Pope Gregory XI was particularly troubled by Wycliffe's teachings and issued a papal bull condemning the university for allowing Wycliffe to 'vomit' heresies. He also demanded that Wycliffe be thrown in jail. William Courtenay, the Archbishop of Canterbury, wanted to purge Oxford of Wycliffe and told Richard II: 'If we permit this heretic to appeal to the emotions of the people our destruction is inevitable. We must silence him.' In 1382 the synod meeting at Blackfriars, London, condemned Wycliffe on twenty-four counts of heresy.

OXFORD MOVEMENT BIRTHPLACE, University Church of St Mary the Virgin, High Street

Few parish churches have played so prominent a part in British religious life – and controversy – as the University Church of St Mary the Virgin. It was here in 1555 that the Oxford martyrs, Nicholas Ridley, Hugh Latimer and Thomas Cranmer, were tried for heresy. On the morning of his death, 21 March 1556, Cranmer, dressed in ragged clothes and a dunce's cap, was brought to St Mary's so that Dr Cole, Provost of Eton, could inform him of the reasons why the queen, Mary Tudor, felt he must die. Cranmer stood opposite the pulpit on a platform by a small shelf cut from a pillar now known as 'Cranmer's Pillar' and withdrew previous recantations of his Protestant beliefs. He also vowed that in the fire in which he would soon be cast, the hand he had used to sign those refutations would be the first to burn, which it was (see above).

Arthur Pitts, an Iffley rector and one of the so-called 'church papists' who practised Catholicism in private but publicly pretended to be devoutly Anglican, died in 1579 when entering St Mary's. Uncompromising Catholics who bemoaned his hypocrisy saw it as appropriate that he had been 'deprived by sudden death, or other obstacles, of sacramental confession'.

The late sixteenth-century Jesuit Edmund Campion left 400 copies of his *Decem Rationes* (*Ten Reasons*), a critique of the Anglican Church, which had been secretly printed in Henley, on the benches of St Mary's in June 1581. The incident and the book caused an outcry, and the authorities set up a search for the author. Campion was eventually captured in Berkshire and put to death at Tyburn that year.

John Wesley preached at St Mary's three times in the 1740s. On one occasion he attacked the moral laxity of the senior members of the university. 'I preached, I suppose for the last time, at St Mary's. Be it so. I am now clear of the blood of these men,' he wrote, accurately it turned out, for he was not invited back.

In the nineteenth century the church was central to the birth of the Oxford movement or Tractarians. This was a revival of Catholic ideas within the Church of England led by John Henry Newman, vicar here from 1823–43, and John Keble, whose 'Assize Sermon' at St Mary's on 14 July 1833 launched the movement. Between 1833 and 1841 Newman, Keble and Edward Pusey published a series of tracts (hence the other name for the group, Tractarians) arguing against the increasing secularisation of the Church of England and seeking a return to the early Catholic doctrines.

By 1843 Newman was disillusioned with Anglicanism. He resigned from St Mary's and later joined the Roman Catholic Church, despite having once denounced the religion as 'polytheistic, degrading and idolatrous'. Two decades later John William Burgon, Dean of St Mary's from 1863–75, savaged the local moves towards Catholicism. In 1869 he published *England and Rome: Three Letters to a Pervert*, the object of his ire a man, or 'designing Papist' as Burgon called him, who had suggested Burgon should convert to Rome. To Burgon, Catholicism had to answer a number of charges: 'idolatry, purgatory and indulgences; mariolatry; communion under one kind; superstition; legends of fabulous saints; the entire system of public worship; neglect of Scripture; exalting tradition to the level of Scripture; Papal infallibility; adding fresh articles to the Faith and Popery's political power'. From St Mary's on 12 December 1869 he denounced the Roman Catholic Church as the religious harlot of Revelation 17.

Burgon was a formidable biblical scholar. He toured European libraries, examined and collated New Testament manuscripts, and travelled to Mount Sinai to inspect documents. He made a number of startling discoveries about Mark 16. Examining one of the oldest texts, the *Codex Vaticanus* of the fourth century, he came upon after verse Eight, the only vacant column in the manuscript. Burgon concluded that the scribe had been instructed to leave something out and that the verses printed in existing Bibles, such as the definitive King James, were a spurious addition. 'Never was blank more intelligible! Never was silence more eloquent!' he roared.

The poet Matthew Arnold was impressed with the movement. 'Who could resist the charm of that spiritual apparition,' he once asked, 'gliding in the dim afternoon light through the aisles of St Mary's, rising into the pulpit, and then, in the most entrancing of voices breaking the silence with words and thoughts which were a religious movement, subtle, sweet, mournful?' George Orwell not so. He savaged the Oxford Movement in his cutting novel *A Clergyman's Daughter:*

'*. . . the old-fashioned High Anglicanism to which the Rector obstinately clung was of a kind to annoy all parties in the parish about equally. Nowadays, a clergyman who wants to keep his congregation has only two courses open to him. Either it must be Anglo-Catholicism pure and simple – or rather, pure and not simple; or he must be daringly modern and broad-minded and preach comforting sermons proving that there is no Hell and all good religions are the same. The Rector did neither. On the one hand, he had the deepest contempt for the Anglo-Catholic movement. It had passed over his head, leaving him absolutely untouched; 'Roman Fever' was his name for it.*

QUEEN'S COLLEGE, High Street

Nicholas Hereford, a college Fellow, began the first complete translation of the Bible into English under John Wycliffe's guidance here in 1384. He used the Latin vulgate rather than the original Old Testament Hebrew or New Testament Greek. It was painstaking work, hand-copying on to parchment bound between boards, but he received nothing but brickbats from the Catholic Church, which was opposed to the idea of the Bible being rendered into ordinary English that could be understood by the population as such a move would jeopardise the power of the priests. As the contemporary cleric Henry Knighton thundered:

'the gospel pearl is thrown before swine and trodden underfoot . . . and become a joke, and this precious gem of the clergy has been turned into the sport of the laity'.

ST EDMUND HALL, Queen's Lane

The college is named after Edmund Rich (St Edmund), thirteenth-century Archbishop of Canterbury. Walking in the fields around Abingdon at the age of twelve, Edmund had a vision of Jesus as a boy walking next to him. He studied in a building on this site which was later subsumed into the college, and became the first person to be described as a Master of Arts. At the bidding of Pope Innocent III, Edmund championed the Sixth Crusade of 1228 throughout England.

STAFFORDSHIRE

Gradbach

LUD'S CHURCH, near junction of A53 and A54

In a deep hidden gorge half a mile long near a medieval cross carved into a rock the Lollards, the first English Christian reformers, met in the fourteenth century to read the Bible in English. The Lollards wanted a Christianity without priests and rituals – the first recorded instance of such views. The barely penetrable site, set in a dark natural cleft riddled with damp moss, is also the Green Chapel where Sir Gawain battles with the Green Knight in the story of *Sir Gawain and the Green Knight*.

Chapter 4

Lichfield

'Field of the Dead' is the origin of the name of the ancient Midlands city best known for its cathedral and as the birthplace of Dr Samuel Johnson.

In April 1612 Edward Wightman was burnt at the stake in Lichfield after being convicted of heresy, mostly for believing that the baptising of infants was abominable, the last person to die so in England. But that was not the first time Wightman had gone to the flames. A few weeks previously he was at the stake, and as the fire started to take hold, he shouted out some barely comprehensible words which implied he was now ready to accept the faith of the Church of England. The sheriff released Wightman but he was soon preaching the same 'heresies', resulting in a fatal return to the pyre that April.

Lichfield was where George Fox, founder of the Quakers, walked barefoot through the Market Square one day in the winter of 1651 proclaiming: 'Woe to the bloody city of Lichfield!' He had not long been released in a weakened state from Derby gaol, where he had been serving a sentence for blasphemy. Fox later compared his position with the martyrdom of the thousand Christians in the time of the Roman emperor Diocletian, although his strange imprecation may have been connected with the martyrdom of Thomas Hayward, John Goreway and Joyce Lewis, burnt here at the stake during the mid-sixteenth-century reign of Mary Tudor.

LICHFIELD CATHEDRAL, The Close

Lady Eleanor Davis, a self-styled prophetess, went mad in the cathedral in 1625, defiling the altar hangings occupying the episcopal throne, while claiming she was Primate of All England and pouring hot tar and wheat paste over the altar. Lady Eleanor maintained that she had personally met the biblical hero prophet Daniel, who had urged her to preach the Last Judgment publicly. The government took action, arresting, fining and imprisoning

Davis, and burning her books. She was sent to Bedlam lunatic asylum for a couple of years and spent the last days of her life writing apocalyptic tracts. When Charles I was executed in 1649 Lady Eleanor claimed she had predicted the regicide and her circle of followers increased in number.

Mow Cop

The Primitive Methodists held their first meeting by this bleak, windswept rocky outcrop on 31 May 1807, as marked by an inscribed stone near the car park. The sect was led by Hugh Bourne and William Clowes, two manual workers from the Potteries, both charismatic figures, who felt that Methodism had become too respectable since John Wesley died. Bourne and Clowes were expelled from the main body of Methodists for holding open-air meetings, but their new group was a resounding success and soon attracted 100,000 members.

The Primitive Methodists' meetings lasted all day. They involved preaching and group prayer, and ended in a love feast – a religious meal closely related to the Eucharist. In February 1812 the group began to call themselves the 'Society of the Primitive Methodists', harking back to John Wesley's claim that the early Methodists embodied the 'Primitive' Christianity of the first century.

→ John Wesley's early days as a Methodist, p. 176

Chapter 4

WARWICKSHIRE

Job Throckmorton, a late sixteenth-century Warwickshire squire, is believed to have been responsible for a series of anonymous satirical tracts attacking the bishop system within the Anglican Church. They were distributed in 1588 and 1589 as the work of the pseudonymous Martin Marprelate, and were a riposte to Archbishop John Whitgift's 1586 decision to control all printing in the country. Queen Elizabeth was outraged and hired some of the best writers of the time, such as Thomas Nashe and Robert Greene, to produce counter-tracts, published as *An Admonition to the People of England* (1589). John Penry, the Welsh martyr, was charged with writing the tracts and was executed, but it was more likely that Throckmorton was the culprit.

Alcester

COUGHTON COURT, A435

This medieval mansion with its impressive Tudor gatehouse, home of the Throckmorton family since 1409, was caught up in the Gunpowder Plot of 1605. At that time it was a refuge for Catholic recusants – those who refused to attend Anglican services at the parish church.

Rebel worshippers would hold Mass in secret in the house's Tower Room from where they could see who approached. If they spotted anyone potentially hostile, they could quickly hide the priests in one of the turrets where they probably would not be discovered.

The Throckmortons also enabled priests to move across the country, away from the gaze of the authorities, and played a part in establishing colleges abroad to train priests for England. It was not so much that they wanted to break the religious law, which stood until 1792, but that they assumed Catholicism would soon be legal again and wanted to be sure they and the country were prepared for that day.

The family was gathered here in the early hours of 6 November 1605 when a colleague, Thomas Bates, arrived with news that the Gunpowder Plot, a plan devised by his master, Thomas Catesby, to blow up the Houses of Parliament and avenge wrongs against Catholics perpetrated by King James, had failed, and that those involved were now fleeing for their lives. One priest, Father Tesimond, left with Bates to join the conspirators and later fled to Europe. Another, Father Garnet, was implicated, captured at Hindlip House, Worcester, and executed.

Burton Dassett

ALL SAINTS, off B4100

The stained-glass window of this parish church supposedly contains a code revealing how to find some of the most sought-after of biblical treasures, such as the Breastplate of Judgment (see box, below) and the Ark of the Covenant containing the Ten Commandments. These treasures disappeared following the Babylonian invasion of Jerusalem in 597 BC, and conspiracy theorists believe they were brought to Warwickshire by local members of the Knights Templar, warrior monks whom Rome designated to look after pilgrims journeying to the Holy Land in medieval times, who came upon them when they searched the caverns and tunnels below Jerusalem.

In 1312 the Pope suppressed the order, and many Knights Templar went into hiding. One of these was a local man, Ralph de Sudeley, who, according to legend, had discovered the priceless hoard and removed it from the Holy Land for security reasons, in particular so that the Saracens couldn't seize it. The Elizabethan explorer Walter Raleigh visited Burton Dassett in 1600 after hearing that the Templars had hidden some treasure locally and spent months looking for it – unsuccessfully.

In the late nineteenth century the church was redecorated and some antique illustrations were found. They depicted two human figures wearing crowns, alongside some Latin inscriptions, and dated from about 1350, which was around the time the Templars built All Saints church. Jacob Cove-Jones, a wealthy local inhabitant, took up where Raleigh left off and armed with some arcane biblical and astronomical knowledge concluded that the Templars had left clues revealing the secret hiding place of the treasure – not that anyone has found anything yet.

The Breastplate of Judgment

Made from entwined golden linen and emblazoned with gems, the biblical Breastplate of Judgment was worn by the Levite high priest when a divine decision was needed to adjudicate on a matter. The high priest would recite the secret names of God – names only initiates knew – as revealed in Exodus 28 and the breastplate would then spark into life with its glowing jewels forming Hebrew letters.

West Midlands

Birmingham

DADLEY'S HOTEL, Temple Row

Lo! Priestley there, patriot, and saint, and sage,
Him, full of years, from his loved native land
Statesmen blood-stained and priests idolatrous
By dark lies maddening the blind multitude
Drove with vain hate.

Religious Musings, Samuel Taylor Coleridge, 1796

Anti-Dissenter Protestants caused four days of rioting in Birmingham in July 1791, beginning with an attack on this hotel. A local group booked Dadley's to host a banquet to commemorate the second anniversary of French Revolution and the storming of the Bastille. A few hours before the dinner they circulated a seditious handbill equating the British system with the repressive deposed French one, and called for a revolution. Far from being the work of radicals, the handbill was produced by their opponents just to cause trouble. It worked.

The mob's main target was Joseph Priestley, the leading theologian and scientist (he discovered oxygen), who was believed to be at the banquet. Priestley, controversially, saw the French Revolution in religious terms – he believed it presaged the Second Coming of Christ. However, his *History of the Corruptions of Christianity* had made him a pariah in some circles, and his *History of Early Opinions* had attacked the virgin birth and the Trinity.

When the crowd discovered Priestley wasn't at the hotel, they surged to his house. He and his family had fled, but the mob ransacked his library and laboratory, and destroyed his collection of scientific instruments. They then burnt down more than twenty other houses, several businesses and four chapels used by Dissenters (Protestants opposed to the official Church of England who did not enjoy the same civil rights as Anglicans at that time).

The authorities took little notice and mostly ignored the Dissenters' cries for help. It was later discovered that Birmingham town officials took part in planning the riots, which explains their reluctance to prosecute the ringleaders of the disturbances, only four of whom were eventually convicted. Even George III became involved, announcing: 'I cannot but feel better pleased that Priestley is the sufferer for the doctrines he and his party have instilled, and that the people see them in their true light.'

These were not the only religious disturbances in Birmingham that century. Locals claiming to be 'for Church and King' had attacked Dissenters' chapels in 1714 and 1715 during the London trial of the inflammatory preacher Henry Sacheverell. In the 1750s there were attacks on Quakers and Methodists in the city, and during the 1780 anti-Catholic Gordon Riots, a London phenomenon, crowds gathered in the town centre although no serious trouble ensued.

Walsall

Charles Wesley, the Methodist hymn-writer, preached from the steps of the Walsall market house in May 1743 as a mob roared, jeered and threw stones. Six months later Charles's brother, John, the founder of Methodism, angered the Walsall crowd with his preaching. As Wesley spoke, one man shouted: 'Knock his brains out; down with him! Kill him at once.' No one rallied to his call, but they did pull the Methodist leader's hair. He escaped over the fields – minus his coat.

Wednesbury

Some of the worst anti-Methodist riots of the mid-eighteenth century took place at Wednesbury in October 1743 in six days of violence. After preaching to a crowd at Wednesbury market, John Wesley left for a colleague's house, only to find a mob gathering outside shouting: 'Bring out the minister; we will have the minister.'

Wesley invited in the ringleader and managed to assuage him. He asked the man to collect some of the bitterest opponents to Methodism, and the man soon came back with a couple who 'were ready to swallow the ground with rage; but in two minutes they were as calm as he'. Wesley went outside and asked: 'What do any of you want with me?' They explained they wanted him to accompany them to the magistrate. 'That I will,' Wesley replied, 'with all my heart.' Finding the magistrate in bed, they complained to the magistrate's son: 'Why, an't please you, they sing psalms all day; nay, and make folks rise at five in the morning.'

→ John Wesley in Bolton, p. 220

Worcestershire

Hindlip

HINDLIP HOUSE, Pershore Lane

The priest-hole builder Nicholas Owen constructed a number of ingenious hiding places for Catholic clerics at Hindlip House in the sixteenth century at a time when it was illegal even to say Mass. Every room had a trap door, and every wall, well, those that weren't false, concealed a secret staircase. Chimneys had double flues, one for the smoke, one for the priest to hide in.

These priest's holes were at the centre of the dramatic search for the 1605 Gunpowder Plotters. The sheriff, Sir Henry Bromley, led a party looking for the conspirators, in particular the well-known Jesuit Father Henry Garnet, whom the authorities believed was instrumental in the plot. During a two-week hunt, masons and carpenters removed panelling and pulled up floors, and found eleven hidden Catholics including Garnet. They were fed by supporters through a small iron pipe that led from a bedroom to the chimney where they were hiding.

Sir Henry triumphantly wrote to King James's court, '. . . Wednesday, found a number of Popish trash hid under boards in three or four several places. Marmalade and other sweete meates were found there lying by them.' The hideout may have been useful at breakfast time but wasn't entirely homely. 'Now in regard, the place was so close, those customes of nature which of necessitie must be doone,' Sir Henry wrote, 'and in so long a time of continuaunce, was exceedingly offensive to the men themselves . . .'

CHAPTER 5

THE NORTH-EAST AND YORKSHIRE

York, the leading city in the region in religious terms, is second only to Canterbury in importance to the Church of England. The city has had to make do with second see status since 1071 following the ruling by Pope Alexander II. But York is not the only city with a strong religious history in the region. Whitby on the Yorkshire coast was where the date of Easter was determined in 664 at the now ruined abbey which still provides the town with an extraordinary skyline. Further north is Durham with its magnificent cathedral on a rocky outcrop overlooking the River Wear. It was here in 1569 that a Northern uprising against Queen Elizabeth began with the destruction of Protestant objects in the cathedral. The rebels tore up the new English prayer book and Bible, and demanded that the 'true and Catholic religion' be reinstated. It never was.

Key events

664 **The Whitby Synod fixes the date of Easter.**

735 **Pope Gregory III gives Ecgbert, Bishop of York, a papal cloak**

allowing him to run the Church in the North and become the first Archbishop of York.

735 **On his deathbed at Jarrow monastery Bede completes his translation of the Gospel of St John from the Latin.**

995 **Monks from Lindisfarne fleeing the Danes found Durham Cathedral.**

1569 **The North begins a rebellion against Queen Elizabeth to oppose the imposition of a new Protestant prayer book in English.**

1819 **The false messiah, John Wroe, has his first religious trances in his Bradford farmstead.**

DURHAM

DURHAM CATHEDRAL, The College

One of Britain's most spectacular religious buildings, Durham Cathedral is a masterpiece of medieval Gothic, and having been completed in only forty years exhibits more uniformity of style than most cathedrals of similar stature.

Monks from Lindisfarne fleeing the Danes founded the cathedral in 995. They brought with them the relics of St Cuthbert, patron saint of Northumberland, and built a church above a bend in the River Wear. Early in the twelfth century the nave was rebuilt by Bishop Ranulf Flambard, who had been imprisoned in the Tower of London in 1100 but escaped by climbing down a rope. When Flambard's successor, Geoffrey Rufus, died in 1141, the bishop's chaplain, William Cumin, claimed to be the new bishop, supporting his claim with documents supposedly issued by the Pope. The monks suspected they were forgeries and refused to accept him. Instead they sent a delegation to Rome to ask the Pope for clarification and the deception was soon uncovered.

A Northern uprising in 1569 against Queen Elizabeth erupted on 14 November with the destruction of Protestant objects in Durham Cathedral. The rebels, led by the Earls of Northumberland and Westmorland, tore up the new English prayer book and Bible, demanded that the 'true and Catholic religion' be reinstated, and celebrated Mass. Two days later at Darlington the rebels declared loyalty to the queen but tempered it with continued support for the Catholic monarch, Mary, Queen of Scots, whom they wanted to see married to the Catholic Duke of Norfolk. The rebellion collapsed after a month, and some 800 men were executed for their part in the affair.

Unexpected religious controversy surrounded Durham in the 1980s when the cathedral's bishop, David Jenkins, voiced his scepticism about the literal interpretation of the Scriptures and then angered the press by daring to criticise the policies of the prime minister, Margaret Thatcher. A few days after Jenkins's inauguration, one of the transepts of Durham Cathedral was gutted by fire, possibly through the same sort of act of God that brought about an earthquake at Blackfriars monastery in 1382 during the hearings into John Wycliffe's alleged heresies.

→ John Wycliffe at Blackfriars, p. 25

NORTHUMBERLAND

Farne Islands

St Cuthbert, an English monk, moved to the Farne Islands in 676 after finding the almost deserted nearby island of Lindisfarne too crowded for his liking. According to Bede, the major religious chronicler of the time, Cuthbert prayed at night in the cold sea and once had his feet warmed on the sand by two seals. Bede also told the story of how Cuthbert in his youth was once navigating the River Tyne on five rafts filled with monks when it looked as if they might be swept out to sea. People on the banks of the river began jeering, and when Cuthbert protested the mockers responded: 'Let no man pray for them, and may God have no mercy on any one of them for they have robbed men of their old ways of worship, and how the new worship is to be conducted nobody knows.' In other words, these Christian figures were responsible for the decline of the old English pagan religions and were therefore not to be taken too seriously.

Shortly before his death in 687 Cuthbert found himself cut off from the mainland by a storm with just five onions for nourishment. When his fellow monks reached him they found four of the onions untouched. Cuthbert was buried with a large ivory comb, a portable altar and a cross with a shell from the Indian Ocean. An autopsy carried out in 1827 after the discovery of the body revealed that he had been riddled with TB and ulcers.

Jarrow

Bede, England's first major historian, completed his translation of the Gospel of St John from the Vetus Italica, the old Latin Bible, on his deathbed at Jarrow monastery in May 735. Unusually for the time, Bede believed that the holy book should be available to the uneducated in their own language. Earlier he had written to Ecgbert, Archbishop of York: 'Do you cause them [the Scriptures] to be known and constantly repeated in their own tongue by those that are unlearned, that is, by them who have knowledge only of their proper tongue?' Jarrow has the church with the oldest dedication in England – it dates from 685 – and survives as the chancel of the parish church, St Paul's.

Lindisfarne

The Lindisfarne Gospels, illuminated manuscripts of the books of Matthew, Mark, Luke and John, were produced early in the eighth century from this tiny island which is connected to the mainland by the Pilgrims Way during low tide. They were to be used at the ceremonies celebrating the life of St Cuthbert, who was buried on the island in 687, fifty years after St Aidan, an Irishman, founded its monastery.

On the eleventh anniversary of Cuthbert's death the coffin was opened. To their amazement, the monks, found the body complete and undecayed – a sure sign of sainthood, they claimed.

Pilgrims began to flock to Lindisfarne until the year 793, when the Vikings raided the island, captured several monks and used them as slaves. Some islanders fled, taking with them the body of Cuthbert, who is now buried in Durham Cathedral.

In the late tenth century Aldred, a Lindisfarne monk, rendered the Gospels into the English of the period. They are the oldest surviving copies of the Scriptures in Old English. After the Norman Conquest the priory became a Benedictine house, famous for the production of mead, which the monks believed should be drunk to ensure the soul remained in God's keeping. The monastery was dissolved under Henry VIII in 1536 and survives only as ruins.

Lindisfarne has recently emerged as a centre for the revival of Celtic Christianity.

Chapter 5

Tyne & Wear

Newcastle

ST NICHOLAS, St Nicholas Churchyard

John Knox, best known as the leader of the Protestant reformation in Scotland in the sixteenth century, became preacher of St Nicholas in 1550. The following October he became embroiled in controversy when from the pulpit he condemned John Dudley, 1st Duke of Northumberland, for ousting Edward Seymour as regent for the new young monarch, Edward VI.

Dudley visited the city to hear Knox speak and invited the fiery preacher to address the royal court. There Knox railed against the requirement that worshippers had to kneel during communion, which he found idolatrous. Knox won a concession for a new edition of the prayer book and was also offered the bishopric of Rochester by Dudley but he turned it down and returned to Newcastle.

When Mary Tudor, Edward's Catholic successor, reintroduced Mass, Knox fled to the continent. 'Sometime I have thought that impossible it had been so to have removed my affection from the realm of Scotland that any realm or nation could have been equally dear to me,' he wrote, 'but God I take to record in my conscience that the troubles in the realm of England are double more dolorous unto my heart than ever were the troubles in Scotland.'

→ John Knox in Edinburgh, p. 268

Yorkshire

Bradford

When Samuel Walker, a Bradford fortune-teller, died in 1838 many locals blamed the false messiah John Wroe, recalling that he had placed a curse on Walker after the latter had accused him of sexual abuse. Wroe had in turn derided Walker for committing 'whoredom' and raged: 'I will prove him before the whole house of Israel, by his flesh pining from his bones; I will make him a sign to the four winds, that his name may be carried into many nations; and I will punish their souls during the life of their bodies by a grievous punishment.'

JOHN WROE'S ADDRESS (LATE EIGHTEENTH CENTURY),

Street House, Tong Street

One of the most fascinating of the English false messiahs, John Wroe had his first religious trances at this farmstead in November 1819 after recovering from a fever that left him looking like a skeleton. 'I saw numbers of persons who were bearing the cross of Christ,' he later wrote, 'and I saw angels ascending and descending. There appeared a great altar, and I looked up and beheld, as it were, the Son of God . . .'

Wroe continued to have extraordinary visions, often seeing Moses, Aaron, various angels and Christ on the cross. Eventually some locals were invited in to witness Wroe in one of his trances – as long as they agreed to place some money in a basket at the foot of the bed first. The neighbours were suspicious, however. One man broke into the house after Mrs Wroe had gone out and found Wroe sitting up in bed indulging in a meal of beefsteak, pickled cabbage and oatcake – evidently not in a trance.

When Wroe returned to Bradford in Easter 1831, after provoking considerable controversy in Ashton-under-Lyne (→ p. 216), there were severe disturbances. A mob burst into the meeting room run by his Christian Israelite sect, destroyed the premises, dragged out Wroe himself by the hair, while pulling out chunks of his beard. Some of the aggressors cried out: 'Murder him,' and even one of the constables joined in, shouting: 'Throw him into the beck! If he cannot divide the water, let him sink or swim.' They propelled the prophet along the street with the intention of testing out the constable's cry until a shopkeeper took pity on Wroe and seized him, locking the door behind him.

→ Wroe in Ashton, p. 216

Idle Thorpe

John Wroe, the charismatic and controversial early nineteenth century false messiah, was baptised at Idle Thorpe on 29 February 1824 before 30,000 people, enticed there by the handbills distributed by Wroe advertising the event:

> The public are respectfully informed
> That
> JOHN WROE
> The Prophet of the Lord
> Will be
> Publicly Baptised
> In the River Aire'

To prove he possessed divine powers, Wroe claimed he would walk across the River Aire, which would part for him as the Red Sea had done for Moses in the Book of Exodus. It didn't, so the crowd pelted him with mud and stones, and threw him back in the river.

→ Mr Wroe's virgins, p. 215

Knaresborough

The spa town was the 1488 birthplace of the late-medieval-soothsayer and prophetess Ursula Sonthiel, better known as Mother Shipton. She was born in a cave (now known as Mother Shipton's Cave) and throughout her childhood was supposedly blessed with telekinetic powers – furniture would move through the house by itself and crockery fly around the room.

Sonthiel's best-known prophecies involved the dissolution of the monasteries, victory over the Spanish Armada and the outbreak of the Civil War. When the Fire of London broke out Prince Rupert, Charles I's nephew, remarked: 'Now Shipton's Prophecy is out.' She was not, however, the only figure to predict a major blaze for that year (→ p. 18) and was less successful with her prediction of the date for the end of the world: 1881. As with Nostradamus, her supporters are wont to cite her rantings to prove any event they choose. Recent research has suggested that the majority of her prophecies were composed by others after her death.

Pudsey

It was in this bleak hillside town near Leeds in 1743 that Count Nikolaus Ludwig von Zinzendorf founded Fulneck, a Moravian community. Members, or 'assistants to the Holy Spirit' as they were known, concentrated on prayers and patience, but they also opened a clothing business, glove factory, farm, bakery, inn and general store.

The group's strict moral code meant that elders decided who could court whom and settled controversial matters by lot. Each member had to carry about them a little green book with detachable leaves, inscribed with biblical texts that they could consult at times of difficulty, and all business was conducted for the benefit of the whole congregation, that is until 1752 when the finances went awry. The community had invested £67,000 with a Portuguese financier who suddenly stopped releasing funds. Nevertheless the sect went on to establish other communities at Ockbrook, Derby; Gracehill, Ireland; and Fairfield near Manchester.

John Wesley, founder of Methodism, was impressed. When he visited he found 'above a hundred young men, above fifty young women, many widows, and above a hundred married persons, all of whom are employed from morning to night, without any intermission, in various kinds of manufactures, not for journeymen's wages, but for no wages at all, save a little very plain food and raiment'.

→William Blake's vision, p. 63

Scarborough

SCARBOROUGH CASTLE, Castle Road

George Fox, founder of the Quakers, was incarcerated in the seaside town's castle from April 1665 to September 1666 for his religious ideas, which included the notion that the Holy Spirit bestows qualification for ministry, and that anyone has the right to minister with the proper guidance, even women and children.

Although this meant Fox was absent from London during the Bubonic Plague and Fire, he still suffered as his cell had 'neither chimney nor firehearth', and he was subjected to the rain that poured in through the castle's open windows leaving him 'numbed with cold, my fingers swelled, that one was grown as big as two'. This being the seaside, the wind drove the rain so forcefully that water came up over his bed 'and ran about the room that I was fain to skim it up with a platter'.

Stapleton

The Brotherhood Church, a Christian anarchist colony founded in 1887 and based here since 1921, has regularly clashed with the authorities. Behind the group's genesis was a pacifist Ulster-born preacher, John Bruce Wallace, who was greatly influenced by Tolstoy's views on war and economic slavery. He styled the Church as a body of Christian pacifists living according to the ideas Jesus preached at the Sermon on the Mount ('Blessed are the meek: for they shall inherit the earth . . . Blessed are the peacemakers: for they shall be called the children of God . . .').

Wallace moved to London in 1891 and took over a derelict building in Dalston, east London, that became the Brotherhood Church. It was where many of the early Bolsheviks, including Lenin and Trotsky, held their 1907 congress. During the First World War the Brotherhood were conscientious objectors, and in the Second World War they refused to register on the grounds that by doing so they would be accepting the right of the government to introduce conscription. They also failed to cooperate with the local war effort and ignored rationing (as best they could).

Since the war the Church has built dwellings without permission, and rebuilt them as soon as the council's demolition team tears them down. They refuse to register the birth of their children, whom they keep out of state schools, and ignore census forms and council tax bills.

Whitby

The dilapidated abbey with its dramatic clifftop position just south of the old whaling town was the setting for a synod in the year 664 that stands as one of the defining moments in the Christian history of England.

One of the main topics discussed at the conference was how to determine the date of Easter. This was a notoriously thorny issue complicated by the Church's insistence on using astronomical events to set it rather than staying faithful to its origins in the Jewish Passover, which occurs on the same (Jewish) date every year. In the years leading up to the synod Christians, farcically, had two different Easters: one was the Ionian version, set according to the 325 Council of Nicaea and used in the Hebrides and Ireland; the other was that used by Rome which King Oswy of Northumbria backed, and was the one adopted at the Whitby Synod.

Whitby Abbey was destroyed by the Vikings in the ninth century. It was rebuilt 400 years later and unusually admitted worshippers of both sexes.

Wrenthorpe

MELBOURNE HOUSE, Brandy Carr Road

John Wroe, the millennial prophet chased out of Ashton-under-Lyne in the 1820s for debauching local virgins, came to Yorkshire in 1853 to build what he called 'Prophet Wroe's Temple'.

The idea for the temple had been revealed to him by God in a dream, and the money came from funds raised on a tour of Australia. Without a clear design in mind for the building, Wroe settled for a replica of Melbourne Town Hall, albeit made of Yorkshire millstone grit. It opened on Whit Sunday 1857, when about 250 followers gathered from America, Germany and Australia dressed as elders in white robes and marched around the site.

Wroe was a Christian Israelite, a group that believed the lost tribes of Israel had ended up in Britain. They claimed that full salvation of body, soul and spirit would reach only the chosen few

– some 144,000 individuals they estimated – all descendants of Abraham, who would bcome immortal and jointly rule with God an eternal kingdom that would soon be established.

In 1859 Wroe was challenged by an American member of the Christian Israelites, a Daniel Milton, who journeyed over from New York to claim Melbourne House as his rightful inheritance. By the time Milton arrived in Yorkshire he had only a farthing left in his pocket, which probably explains why Wroe was unwilling to see him. The usurper was not easily dissuaded, however, and reappeared a year later, preaching from an open cart and causing trouble. He failed in his mission but caused something of a furore in the community and even in the pages of the *Manchester Guardian*, which extensively described Milton's diet: 'For breakfast I generally have boiled beans and toast. For dinner I have pea flour. My third and last meal is supper – sometimes bread and water, sometimes pea-flour.'

Wroe passed away in Australia in 1864. His followers were furious for he had promised them he would never die., and just to be on the safe side, they kept his slippers and suit ready in a room in Melbourne House, Wakefield, lest he should return. The house remained with Wroe's descendants until the 1930s, by which time he hadn't managed a resurrection, and is now offices for a telecommunications company.

→ John Wroe worries Ashton, p. 216

York

Second in importance only to Canterbury and home to the Archbishop of York, the town became a bishopric in 735 when Pope Gregory III gave Ecgbert, Bishop of York, the pallum, a papal cloak, allowing him to take control of much of the North.

York has since had a chequered religious history dominated by anti-Semitism and rebellion. Hundreds of Jews died in horrific circumstances in 1190 after taking refuge in the castle keep. Nearly four centuries later, in 1536, worshippers who staunchly opposed Henry VIII's break with Rome took the king's tax commissioners hostage and marched on the city to reinstal expelled monks and nuns in what became known as the Pilgrimage of Grace. They demanded a return to papal rule and the establishment of a Parliament without a king, neither of which happened. The main rebels, led by Robert Aske, were arrested and hanged at York Castle.

On arriving at York on his way to claim the English throne in 1603, James VI of Scotland was presented with a petition on behalf of English Catholics by a 'gentleman' urging him to repeal the penal laws that discriminated against them. However, the petition contained a tactless biblical reference that made it look as if the mystery petitioner was threatening the king. The anonymous 'gentleman' was soon unmasked as a Catholic priest, Father Hill, and he was clapped in jail.

CLIFFORD'S TOWER, Tower Street

York's medieval Jewish community burnt to death on 16 March 1190 while sheltering from the mob in Clifford's Tower, the castle keep. The Jews' troubles had started in London at the coronation of Richard I a year previously. Flushed with patriotism which quickly escalated to xenophobia that day, a mob turned on the Jews who had brought the new king gifts at Westminster Abbey. In the violence that ensued many were killed. One man who escaped with his life was Benedict of York and that was only because he converted to Christianity on the spot and agreed to be immediately baptised at a nearby church. Benedict later appealed to the king, who allowed him to recant, but many claimed this was against the law. He died a few months later, neither Jew nor Christian (officially) and so could not be buried in the cemetery of either faith.

Early in March 1190 a group of men broke into the house where Benedict had lived, and killed his widow and children. York's Jews were now in fear of their lives, and took refuge in Clifford's Tower. Every morning during their stay there a monk in white robes celebrated Mass in front of the tower . . . until a stone fell and killed him. That infuriated the mob all the more, and they surrounded Clifford's Tower.

The Jews' leader, Yom-Tov of Joigny, urged his followers to kill themselves rather than surrender. Those who did not want to commit suicide were allowed to leave. The rest set fire to their clothes and goods so that they would not fall into the hands of the mob. Joce, one of the Jews' leaders, cut his wife's throat with a knife used in animal slaughtering. Yom-Tov killed Joce and then stabbed himself. Others died in the flames they had lit, while those who surrendered were murdered. Soon the entire community of around 150 was wiped out.

William de Longchamp, who was in charge of the kingdom in Richard's absence, was horrified as the Jews were supposedly under the king's protection. He marched to York and imposed heavy fines on leading citizens.

→ Anti-Semitism in Lincoln, p. 217

YORK CASTLE, off Museum Street

Mary Bateman, 'the Yorkshire Witch' was hanged here in 1809 for poisoning a York woman. She was a follower of Joanna Southcott, the false messiah and self-styled 'woman clothed with the sun' of the Book of Revelation, and claimed her hens were laying eggs with the inscription 'Christ is coming!' She charged the curious a penny a go to view them and somehow managed to make quite a bit of money this way.

YORK MINSTER, Ogleforth

The seat of the Archbishop of York and one of the largest Gothic cathedrals in Europe started off as a wooden church in 627 built for the baptism of Edwin, King of Northumbria. The first Bishop of York was Paulinus, who had convinced Edwin to convert. Paulinus was a monk at St Andrew's Monastery, Rome, described by Bede, the great religious writer, as 'a man tall of stature, a little stooping, with black hair and a thin face, a hooked and thin nose, his aspect both venerable and awe-inspiring'.

The York church was extended in 630 and dedicated to St Peter, but was soon almost derelict. Major reconstruction took place in the mid-eighth century. The Danes destroyed the building in 1075 but it was again rebuilt. During the Reformation of the 1530s its treasure was looted.

The Archbishops of York

For a long time there was a tussle over whether York or Canterbury should take precedence as the main religious seat of England. In 1071 Thomas of Bayeux, Archbishop of York, and Lanfranc, Archbishop of Canterbury, sought guidance from Pope Alexander II. The Pope chose Canterbury. In future the Archbishops of York would have to swear allegiance to the Archbishop of Canterbury, a position ratified by the Winchester Accord of 1072.

Not all Archbishops of York were happy to do so. In 1119 Thurstan, Archbishop-Elect, refused to acknowledge Canterbury's superior status. Consequently, Ralph d'Escures, Archbishop of Canterbury, refused to consecrate Thurstan, who appealed to Rome where Pope Callixtus II personally consecrated him and issued a papal bull revoking the supremacy of Canterbury. The matter wasn't resolved until the fourteenth century, by Pope Innocent VI. Despite the Reformation and break from Rome, Innocent's ruling still stands: the Archbishop of Canterbury is the

Primate of All England and the Archbishop of York simply the Primate of England.

Archbishops of York include:

• **Ecgbert** (732–66)
In 735 the Pope elevated York from bishopric to archbishopric. He gave Ecgbert, Bishop of York, the pallium or holy woollen cloak.

• **William Fitzherbert** (1143–7, 53–4)
Fitzherbert had the strange honour of being Archbishop of York twice. He secured the post through the efforts of his relative, King Stephen, but the Cistercians managed to have him removed from office. When his replacement, Murdac, died, he was restored to office, but he was soon fatally poisoned. Miracles were witnessed at his tomb, it was claimed, and he was canonised in 1226.

• **Geoffrey Plantagenet** (1191–1212)
An illegitimate son of Henry II, Geoffrey suffered the ignominy of being abducted by opponents on his return to England for the first time as Archbishop of York in 1191. Geoffrey landed at Dover but was apprehended by agents working for the Lord Chancellor. He took refuge in St Martin's priory but was dragged out and briefly imprisoned in Dover Castle. After another political altercation in 1207 he was forced to flee the country and died in exile.

• **Thomas Wolsey** (1514–30)
One of the most powerful politicians of Henry VIII's reign, Wolsey became Lord Chancellor and even a cardinal. In the 1520s he used his powers as papal legate to shut down thirty corrupt monasteries, including abbeys in Ipswich and Oxford, but he fell from grace when he failed to secure the annulment of the king's marriage to Catherine of Aragon in 1529. Stripped of most of his

positions, Wolsey was at least allowed to remain Archbishop of York, which city he now intended to visit for the first time. But he was apprehended along the way by the authorities, who accused him of treason and ordered him back to London. Wolsey died en route, at Leicester, on 29 November 1530. 'If I had served my God,' he noted wistfully towards the end, 'as diligently as I did my king, He would not have given me over in my grey hairs.'

• **Edward Lee** (1531–44)
The last Archbishop of York to mint coins, Lee assisted Henry VIII in his divorce from Catherine of Aragon. He disapproved of the king appointing himself head of the Church of England.

• **Nicholas Heath** (1555–9)
Heath refused to crown Elizabeth as queen in 1558 because she would not allow the elevation of the Host during the coronation service. He resisted Elizabeth's new religious laws and was consequently removed from his position in 1559, living out the rest of his life quietly.

• **Edwin Sandys** (1576–88)
Sandys was forced into preaching a sermon at Cambridge in 1553 supporting the accession of Lady Jane Grey to the throne. Once the noble claimant was removed after only nine days' reign, he was in trouble from the new monarch, Mary Tudor, who had him arrested. The queen sent Sandys to the Tower of London, but to his delight he was quickly transferred to more comfortable accommodation in Marshalsea Prison, from where he escaped to the continent. Only when Elizabeth succeeded to the throne was it safe for Sandys to return, and after becoming Bishop of Worcester, and then London, he was promoted to York, where he helped produce a new Bible, the Bishops' Bible.

• **Samuel Harsnett** (1629–31)
Heavily involved in religious debates about the diabolical subject of demons and witches, Harsnett was asked to write a paper condemning exorcisms. Shakespeare borrowed heavily from it in writing *King Lear*.

• **John Williams** (1641–50)
Williams was an adviser to King James and the last person ever to serve (at different times) as Archbishop of York and Lord Chancellor, then the most powerful political position in the country. His tolerance of Puritanism led to a clash with the Palace of Westminster's Star Chamber, which suspended him in 1636 and confined him to the Tower for four years. After a year as a free man Williams was sent back to jail by Parliament – despite being Archbishop of York. He spent little time in York.

• **Accepted Frewen** (1660–64)
When Oliver Cromwell ousted King Charles, Frewen lost his status as Bishop of Lichfield and was accused of treason. He fled to France, deciding it was safe to reappear in England only once Charles II had been restored to the throne, at which point he became Archbishop of York. One of his obituarists claimed that, having been born by cesarian section, Frewen decided to remain a bachelor and experienced 'discomfort in the presence of women'.

• **Thomas Lamplugh** (1688–91)
When William of Orange landed at Torbay to claim the British throne for the Protestants, Lamplugh urged people to remain faithful to the threatened Catholic King James II. James rewarded Lamplugh by appointing him Archbishop of York, a post which had been vacant for two years. James was not on the throne for much longer, but Lamplugh stayed in office, diplomatically officiating at William's coronation.

• **Lancelot Blackburne** (1724–43)
The only archbishop ever to have been described as a pirate – he sailed with a group of buccaneers in the West Indies in the 1680s after graduating – Blackburne earned a mention in the *Dictionary of National Biography* as having a 'reputation for carnality'. He was once thrown out of St Mary's, Nottingham (→ p. 166) for asking for his pipe and a tankard of beer after a service. Blackburne secretly married George I to his mistress.

• **Cosmo Lang** (1908–28)
When studying to become a barrister Lang heard, an inner voice, a question tugging at his conscience, asking him: 'Why shouldn't *you* be ordained?' Later at evensong the voice insisted: 'You are wanted. You are called. You must obey.' He became the first archbishop since the Reformation to wear a mitre, which previous incumbents considered too Catholic.

• **William Temple** (1929–40)
One of the great theologians of the twentieth century, Temple founded the Council of Christians and Jews with Chief Rabbi Joseph Hertz in 1942 to counter bigotry. He coined the memorable saying 'The Church is the only society that exists for the benefit of those who are not its members.' Controversially, Temple refused to condemn the Allied blanket bombing of Germany, explaining that he was 'not only non-pacifist but anti-pacifist'.

• **John Sentamu** (2005–)
One of thirteen children, the early twenty-first-century archbishop was once imprisoned in his native Uganda by the deranged dictator Idi Amin, and in jail was 'kicked around like a football and beaten terribly'. He fled to Britain in 1974, read theology at Cambridge, and became a priest in 1979. He played African drums when enthroned at York Minster in 2005.

CHAPTER 6

THE NORTH WEST

Little of the turmoil that has characterised religious history in age-old cities such as London, York or Canterbury has hit the North West. For here the main centres of population, such as Liverpool and Manchester, are relatively new. Consequently they were not significant enough when religious turmoil was at it height in England, in the sixteenth and seventeenth centuries, to feature among the most dramatic stories.

In Liverpool religious history has mostly involved low-level clashes between Catholics and Protestants – a spin-off from the greater conflict taking place nearby geographically in Ulster. Here the battle of the denominations was played out farcically for much of the twentieth century in the long-drawn-out sagas over the building of the two Liverpool cathedrals.

In Manchester, a city with a long record of tolerance towards those of different faiths, there have been few religious flashpoints. It was however in the city's cathedral, in its earlier guise as a collegiate church, that the Nonconformist cult that became the Shakers made its first public appearance when the movement's founder, Ann Lee, disrupted a service in 1773.

To the east of Manchester is Ashton-under-Lyne. It was in this unlikely setting that the extraordinary nineteenth-century false messiah John Wroe set up his Christian Israelite Church in 1825. The drab mill town would now become the holy city, the New Jerusalem, and Wroe built four 'holy' gateways while awaiting the imminent return of Jesus Christ presumably through one of them. He was still waiting when he died in 1863. It is not known whether Jesus did ever appear in Ashton.

Key events

1652 **George Fox has a vision on Pendle Hill, Lancashire. He later founds a new Christian movement: the Society of Friends or Quakers.**

1773 **Ann Lee interrupts the service at Manchester's Collegiate Church (now the cathedral) and soon after establishes the Shakers.**

1794 **St Mary's, the first Catholic church to be built in England since the Reformation, is erected in Manchester. The building lasts until 1835 when the roof falls in. It is later rebuilt on the same site.**

1825 **The false messiah John Wroe moves to Ashton-under-Lyne. Here he attempts unsuccessfully to build the New Jerusalem.**

1853 **The commission to build a Catholic cathedral in Liverpool is handed to E. W. Pugin. It doesn't open until 1967.**

1902 **Work begins on Liverpool's Anglican cathedral, the fifth largest in the world. It is not completed until 1980.**

1968 **A Roman acrostic is found during an archaeological dig in Manchester. It turns out to be one of the oldest known Christian relics in Britain.**

CHESHIRE

Tarvin

An infamous early seventeenth-century puritan was Squire Bruen of the Cheshire village of Tarvin. According to contemporary reports Bruen rose every day at 5 a.m. and spent his first waking moments meditating upon the Bible or writing out a sermon he had heard in church. When the squire deemed the household to be ready to rise he would ring a bell so that they knew prayers were about to begin. One day Bruen caught a guest playing cards. He later entered the man's room and took the jacks out the pack. Bruen also removed the stained glass from his local church as he considered it to be too papist in spirit.

GREATER MANCHESTER

Ashton-under-Lyne

Walter Carver, a member of the Primitive Methodists, was attacked as he preached at the marketplace cross on 8 July 1821. As he began speaking a constable took down his name and assaulted him – on the orders of the local vicar, the Revd George Chetwode, who himself was in the pay of the Ashton area landowner, the Earl of Stamford, his uncle.

The would-be messiah John Wroe announced in 1825 that this grim mill town to the east of Manchester would become a holy city, the New Jerusalem, and moved his Christian Israelite Church here. The Christian Israelites believed they were the descendants of the lost tribes of Israel. On Christmas Day 1825 Wroe opened a miniature version of Solomon's Temple, the Sanctuary, on Ashton's Church Street. Over the entrances were stone slabs, one

ABOVE John Wesley, founder of Methodism, toured the country in the late 18th century preaching but was constantly harassed and chased out of town by opponents.

BELOW Mary, Queen of Scots, lost her head at Fotheringhay Castle in 1587 after one too many Catholic plots to seize the throne from the Protestant Queen, Elizabeth.

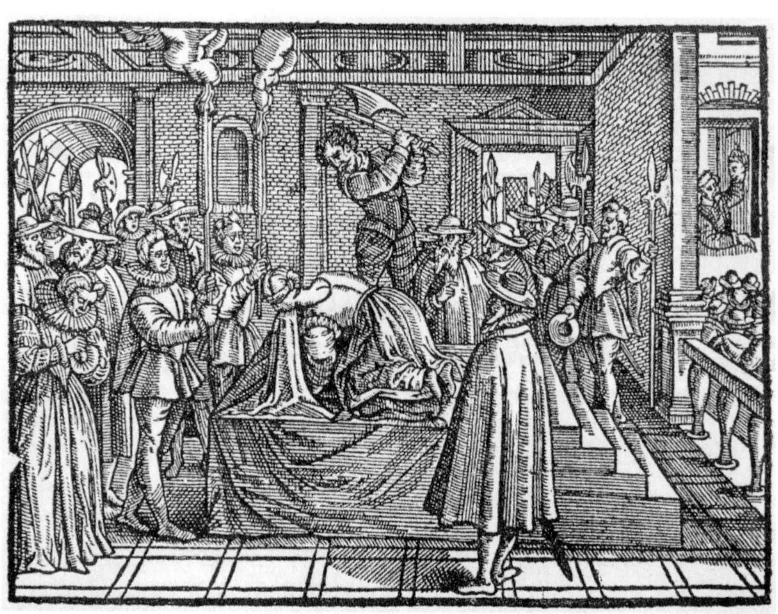

ABOVE LEFT The ancient York structure of Clifford Tower was where the town's Jews burned to death in 1190 while sheltering from the mob.

LEFT The dramatic clifftop remains of Whitby Abbey give little indication that this was where the date of Easter was fixed in the year 664.

ABOVE Lichfield Cathedral was defiled in 1625 by Lady Eleanor Davis, a self-styled prophetess who claimed she was Primate of all England and poured hot tar and wheat paste over the altar.

ABOVE The late mediaeval soothsayer Mother Shipton was supposedly blessed with telekinetic powers, for furniture would move through the house by itself and crockery fly around the room at her say-so.

ABOVE RIGHT It was on Glastonbury Tor that Richard Whiting, the last abbot of Glastonbury, was hanged alongside two of his monks for taking part in earth and fertility rites in 1539.

RIGHT Avebury's ancient stones in Wiltshire may have been used as a pagan sun temple around the year 2000 BC. They rival Stonehenge as a centre of ancient British mysticism.

LEFT The once obscure Scottish chapel of Rosslyn has become a major tourist draw since the publication of the mystical thriller *The Da Vinci Code*. Conspiracy theorists believe that the Holy Grail may be buried here.

BELOW The Dutch prince William of Orange crossing Ireland's River Boyne during the 1689 Battle of the Boyne in which he routed England's Catholic king James II.

RIGHT A chilling Northern Ireland mural in favour of the ultra-Loyalist Ulster Volunteer Force.

ABOVE Iona Abbey was founded on the isle where Christianity first arrived in the year 563.

depicting the Star of David, the other inscribed with the words 'Israelite Society' in Hebrew characters. Though stark on the outside, it was so lavishly decorated within that the budget was greater than the sum spent on the town hall. Wroe also drew up plans to build four 'holy' gateways into Ashton and, while awaiting the imminent return of Jesus Christ, underwent a public baptism in the River Medlock.

Wroe made his Christian Israelites adopt some tenets of Judaism. Males had to be circumcised, meat kosher, the Sabbath rigorously observed and there was to be no shaving or cutting of hair. Any follower who broke these rules could expect a beating. Only those members who had regularly to attend the Manchester Stock Exchange were allowed to shave their beards for reasons of commercial expediency.

Less controversially, the sect opened stores they called Israelite shops in which men with long straggly beards and tall felt hats mocked by locals as 'Joannas' (after the earlier false prophetess Joanna Southcott) sold groceries with stricter conditions about true weights and measures than most stores then used. However these Israelite shops closed for twenty-four hours from 6 p.m. on Fridays so that the group could keep the Sabbath, which they believed fell on Saturdays in the Jewish manner rather than on the Christian Sunday.

There was a darker side to the Israelites' activities. An infant circumcised by a disciple called Henry Lees bled to death and Lees was subsequently convicted of manslaughter, Wroe disappeared from the public eye for a fortnight. But the tragic incident didn't stop Wroe himself from being publicly circumcised in rooms on Oldham Road. After the ceremony he declared that on the following day a light would emanate from an adjacent field to illuminate the town. Nothing of the sort happened – although the town gas works were later built on the site.

By 1830 Wroe was receiving messages from heaven. One of them told him to 'take seven virgins to cherish and comfort him'.

Three local families helpfully provided the required maidens who, according to *Bell's Life in London*, 'were to live with him in a state of innocence, and thus display a pattern of purity to the whole people'. Wroe left with them to go on a preaching tour, but by the time the party returned to Ashton one of the girls, Sarah Lees, was pregnant. *Wheeler's Manchester Chronicle* explained how it had happened.

The appointment of the seven to this holy calling took place on the feat of the full moon when the high priest delivered a disclosure on the coming of Shiloh and his reign upon earth . . . The ladies were entrusted by the committee to the prophet who was to take care that they were kept free from the world and its impurities . . .

The town was scandalised, and barely placated by assurances that the newborn would be the messianic child, Shiloh, as outlined in the biblical Book of Revelation. A child was born, but it was a girl, and therefore unlikely to be the messiah, critics claimed. Wroe, humiliated, was forced to leave Ashton, and was deserted by a number of his disciples, even Henry Lees, the overenthusiastic circumciser. When he revisited the town in Easter 1831 there was uproar. The congregation at the Sanctuary had to lock the doors to keep out the mob who wanted to tear Wroe limb from limb, and they all had to escape through a tunnel that led to a nearby house.

Wroe eventually resurfaced at Wrenthorpe, Yorkshire (→ p. 205), where he forecast that the millennium would begin in 1863. He died that February in Australia after breaking his collar bone. One section of the group then gathered around John Ward, an Irish cobbler, who believed the Scriptures were not history but prophecies. Ward decided that as he had been born on Christmas Day to a woman named Mary he was Jesus. He escaped from the poorhouse where he had been incarcerated and roamed the countryside preaching against landlords, the government, and the Church until he died of a stroke in 1837.

• The house where the female Shiloh was born in 1824 has since been replaced by Tameside Magistrates Court, where the mass murderer Doctor Harold Shipman was tried in 1998.

→John Wroe in Bradford, p. 200

ODD WHIM PUB, Mossley Road

A plaque recording the remarkable local tale of the false messiah John Wroe (see above) can be found on the wall of what was until recently the Odd Whim pub. Wroe scheduled this building as one of his gateways into the holy city (Ashton-under-Lyne), but he was tried here in 1830 after impregnating one of his chosen 'virgins'. At the end of the hearing the verdict was inconclusive, but the judge announced: 'I say as Pilate said to the Jews of old, when our Lord was before him: I wash my hands from the blood of this man.' Nevertheless Wroe's most vociferous opponents then began distributing handbills around Ashton explaining how 'John Wore, alias Asrael Wroe, stands charged with acts of indecency, immorality and perjury, of the most offensive and disgusting nature . . .' A year later Wroe's supporters made a symbolic return to the gateway where his trial had taken place, singing the Lord's Prayer in Hebrew, a most unusual occurrence given that it had never been a Hebrew prayer.

• The other Wroe gateways were Moss Lodge on Moss Close off Manchester Road, demolished in the 1990s to build the M60; Taunton Lodge, Taunton Road, demolished 1890; and a gatehouse near Dukinfield Hall in a small area known as Jerusalem. The Odd Whim pub has since been converted into flats.

ST ANN'S, Burlington Street

What became known as the Murphy Riots broke out in Ashton in 1868. They took their name from William Murphy, a fiercely anti-Catholic orator once described as having 'matchless effrontery' and being 'intolerant, devoid of conscience, callous and unscrupulous to the last degree'. A year previously Murphy had incited trouble in Birmingham where he had called the Pope a 'rag and bone gatherer'. This time Murphy led a mob on an anti-Catholic rampage through Ashton on 10 May 1868 during which more than a hundred Catholic homes were gutted. The rioters then made their way to St Ann's Church and Presbytery while the Sunday evening service was taking place. The priest just had enough time to send the congregation home before the windows were smashed. Murphy continued to tour the country making inflammatory speeches against Catholics, that is until he was thrown downstairs by some miners in Whitehaven in 1871. He never recovered and died a year later.

Bolton

When John Wesley first came to this depressed mill town in August 1748 he was stoned by a mob. In his journals he described how

I went to the cross in Bolton. There was a vast number of people, but many of them utterly wild. As soon as I began speaking, they began thrusting to and fro; endeavouring to throw me down from the steps on which I stood. They did so once or twice; but I went up again and continued my discourse. They then began to throw stones; at the same time some got upon the cross, behind me, to push me down; on which I could not but observe how God over-rules even the minutest circumstances . . . such rage and bitterness I scarce ever saw before in any creatures that bore the form of men.

Manchester

One of the oldest known Christian relics in Britain is a word square, or acrostic, dating back to around AD 170 which was found during an archaeological dig in Manchester in 1968. The acrostic is inscribed in Latin 'Sator, Arepo, Tenet, Opera, Rotas' (Arepo the great sower holds the wheel with force), which reads the same across, down and backwards. The twenty-five letters can be rearranged as Apaternostero, a word containing the opening of the Lord's Prayer (*Pater Noster* – Our Father), the 'a' representing alpha and the 'o' omega, the first and last letters of the Greek alphabet, signifying Christ at the beginning and at the end. The acrostic is one of only six in the world and is believed to have been used by Christians for secretly communicating with each other before the religion was adopted by Rome.

Manchester has long boasted the second biggest Jewish community in Britain, but it was only as recently as 1788 that the first Jewish presence in the city was recorded: Hamilton Levi, a flower dealer of Long Millgate, then the main street in the growing town, listed in that year's trade directory. Manchester's first Jewish community settled around the parish church (now the cathedral) and at first consisted mostly of German hawkers and peddlers. There was a synagogue on Garden Street from 1794 and a burial ground paid for by Samuel Solomon, a well-known quack doctor responsible for the supposed cure-all 'Balm of Gilead' which was mostly intended to discourage masturbation.

A regular visitor to Manchester early in the ninteenth century was the false prophet of Ashton-under-Lyne, John Wroe, leader of the so-called Christian Israelites. Indeed, religious Manchester Jews with their long beards and antiquated clothing were often mistaken for Wroe and his Christian Israelites on the streets of Manchester at that time. Even Friedrich Engels, the pioneer of communism (who was not Jewish), was once accused of being a follower of Wroe simply because he had a beard.

Wroe visited a watchmaker's on Shudehill in summer 1820, where he met two Jewish men. He explained to them that the God of Israel had chosen him as a prophet to tell the Jewish people that God would 'set his hand the second time to the covenant which he made with Abraham and he would cause those which were joined amongst the Gentiles to come and join them'. The men laughed at Wroe and told him if he were that keen on helping the Jews they could arrange for him to be circumcised. Wroe quickly left the shop.

As Manchester's Jews prospered economically they moved north, away from medieval Manchester, first to Cheetham Hill, and later to Prestwich and Whitefield.

CHURCH OF THE HOLY NAME OF JESUS, Oxford Road, Chorlton-on-Medlock

This imposing Gothic church by Manchester University was built from 1869–71 by Joseph Aloysius Hansom, best known for designing the Hansom cab. The young Anthony Burgess, the *Clockwork Orange* novelist, who attended the Holy Name in the 1920s, portrayed the priests as 'steely-eyed and blue-jawed' and later described the church as 'a stronghold of the British Jesuit [which] would soon have to be deconsecrated for a lack of sufficient congregation. Islam was growing, Irish Catholicism disappearing.' Burgess's father once entered the building for a service still absent-mindedly wearing his bowler hat and smoking a Three Castles roll-up. A priest doused the cigarette with a spray of holy water but took more offence to the bowler, hissing at Burgess Snr: 'This is not a synagogue.'

→ George Orwell's Ministry of Love, p. 70

CROSS STREET CHAPEL, Cross Street

Manchester's main Nonconformist place of worship, now in its fourth building on the site, was originally the Dissenters' Meeting House, built for the Revd Henry Newcome in 1694, five years after the Toleration Act allowed non-Anglican Protestant places of worship.

During the eighteenth century Cross Street Chapel became a

centre of support for the Hanoverian line to the throne while their opponents, the Jacobites, who wanted the crown to go to the Catholic Stuarts, worshipped at the nearby Collegiate Church (now Manchester Cathedral). Simmering tension between the two groups boiled over in June 1715 when a Jacobite mob led by blacksmith Thomas Syddall smashed through the doors of the chapel and overturned the pews. Syddall was hanged a year later for a different crime. Thirty years on his son, also Thomas, was hanged for his part in the 1745 Jacobite uprising, his head displayed at Manchester's Market Cross.

→ Pope burning in Lewes, p. 153

JOHN RYLANDS LIBRARY, Deansgate at Wood Street

One of the world's greatest libraries, free and open to the public, is housed in a cathedral-like Gothic structure built in the 1890s with funds from the huge will left by the multi-millionaire Victorian cotton magnate John Rylands. The collection began as Rylands's own library of theological works but has since expanded to become a barely rivalled treasury containing such rarities as the second-century St John Fragment, the oldest existing edition of the New Testament. There are Bibles in more than 400 languages, nearly a hundred editions of the Latin Vulgate printed before 1500, and collections of the private papers of obscure but fascinating religious extremists such as William Clowes, the early nineteenth-century co-founder of the Primitive Methodists.

Since 1972 the library has been owned by Manchester University.

→ John Wycliffe translates the Bible, p. 60

ST MARY (THE HIDDEN GEM), Mulberry Street

Central Manchester's only Catholic church, built in 1794 to cater for local Irish immigrants, was the first erected in England since the Reformation. It acquired its popular name, 'the Hidden Gem' when Herbert Vaughan, Bishop of Salford, was moved to comment after a visit: 'No matter on what side you look, you behold a hidden gem.' In 1835 the roof collapsed, having been badly put up by volunteers hired by the local parish priest, Father Henry Gillow. The new building with its odd Spanish and Byzantine features aroused fury in the great Catholic architect Pugin, who raged that 'it shows to what depths of error even good men fall when they abandon the true thing and go whoring after strange styles'. St Mary still has one of the largest congregations in the North West and is home to Norman Adams's remarkable series of expressionist paintings 'The Stations of the Cross'.

→ Ian Paisley's Martyrs Memorial Church, Belfast, p. 287

SHAKERS' BIRTHPLACE, Victoria Station Approach

The Shakers, officially the United Society of Believers in Christ's Second Coming, are now one of America's most famous cult movements but they had their origins in the mid-eighteenth century. Ann Lee, a cook at Manchester Infirmary, who lived on what is now the approach route to Victoria station, had suffered the deaths of four of her children in infancy and was convinced that God was punishing her. To seek forgiveness Lee became celibate and founded a group of worshippers whose trembling in church in fear of the supposed imminent Second Coming of Christ earned them the name 'Shaking Quakers' or 'Shakers'.

Lee herself came to be nicknamed 'the woman clothed with the sun', as described in the Book of Revelation. After she was imprisoned for disrupting a service in Manchester's Collegiate Church (now Manchester Cathedral) in 1773, she and her followers emigrated to America. Their ship nearly sank during the rough voyage, but eventually they landed in upstate New York where they were branded as spies (these were the days leading up to the American War of Independence).

Unperturbed, the Shakers stood firm on their beliefs: the cult of the Messiah, common ownership of property, the sanctity of labour and isolation from the everyday world. To supplement their incomes they began making furniture, in an austere style, which is what they are now best known for. Ann Lee died in 1784, by which time she had established what her modern-day biographer, Richard Francis, has called 'a community of around a thousand souls'. The Shakers' support for celibacy has curtailed their number.

→ The Muggletonians, p. 23

LANCASHIRE

Baycliff

In 1652 James Milner, a seventeenth-century Quaker, was so overcome with apocalyptic dreams of the Judgment that he claimed to be none other than Jesus Christ and tried to set up the New Jerusalem in Baycliff by the Furness coast. That November Milner began fasting strictly to save the souls of two local women. He also proclaimed that Wednesday 1 December 1652 would be the Day of Judgment and the next day the start of the new Creation. He was wrong on both counts. Quaker leaders condemned him, and Milner later apologised for bringing dishonour on the movement.

→ John Nichols Thom, nineteenth century false messiah p. 133

Clitheroe

PENDLE HILL

It was on this east Lancastrian hill near Burnley, famous for the legend of the Pendle Witches, that George Fox, a Lincolnshire man, had a vision in 1652. He claimed that God inspired him to pioneer a new Christian movement: the Society of Friends or Quakers, so called because they quaked when moved by the spirit of God.

Fox refreshed himself at a spring and travelled to Sedbergh in the Yorkshire Dales, where he addressed a large crowd on Firbank Fell. However, his followers soon began to be persecuted in the local towns. For instance, in 1655 George Bland, a Fox acolyte, and two other men were beaten in Bentham. A year later Robert Barras was battered to death, and in 1657 Robert Burrough spoke out at a church and was stoned to death. Quakers were brought to trial for not attending church and engaging in unlawful assembly, and a Marmaduke Tatham and 269 associates were sentenced to have their tongues torn out, although they managed to escape punishment.

Fox was reluctant to create a new sect. He simply wanted to adapt existing structures to follow Christ more faithfully, as he saw it. Believing that the seventeenth-century Church had lost its way, Fox looked to Acts 2 and 3 from the New Testament. He sought ways of establishing an egalitarian Christianity and challenged the Church's hierarchy to emphasise the personal relationship of an individual with Christ. His followers refused to bow or take off their hats to those of supposedly superior social status, believing all men equal under God. They also refused to swear the oath of loyalty to the king on the grounds that Jesus forbade swearing, in Matthew 5:34.

Fox's vision on Pendle Hill

As we travelled we came near a very great hill, called Pendle Hill, and I was moved of the Lord to go up to the top of it; which I did with difficulty, it was so very steep and high. When I was come to the top, I saw the sea bordering upon Lancashire. From the top of this hill the Lord let me see in what places he had a great people to be gathered. As I went down, I found a spring of water in the side of the hill, with which I refreshed myself, having eaten or drunk but little for several days before.

At night we came to an inn, and declared truth to the man of the house, and wrote a paper to the priests and professors, declaring the day of the Lord, and that Christ was come to teach people Himself, by His power and Spirit in their hearts, and to bring people off from all the world's ways and teachers, to His own free teaching, who had bought them, and was the Saviour of all them that believed in Him. The man of the house spread the paper abroad, and was mightily affected with the truth. Here the Lord opened unto me, and let me see a great people in white raiment by a river side, coming to the Lord; and the place that I saw them in was about Wensleydale and Sedbergh.

Lancaster

LANCASTER CASTLE, Castle Parade
After the unsuccessful *coup d'état* staged by the Fifth Monarchists in January 1661, the state was keen to clamp down on all sects. As a result George Fox, founder of the Quakers, was imprisoned here on charges of blasphemy in 1664. He was released, but was soon sent back, accused of being 'the king's enemy'. During his time inside, Fox wrote to Charles II, urging him to desist from 'war and

taking oaths'. Charles took some notice: he released around 700 Quakers imprisoned under the previous regime of Richard Cromwell. When Fox was freed again after a couple of months, he was unable to stand and had to be lifted on to his horse.

→The Fifth Monarchists, p. 14

MERSEYSIDE

Birkenhead

CLAUGHTON MUSIC HALL, **Claughton Road**

John Kensit, a Protestant extremist, died in September 1902 a week after hosting an anti-Catholic rally at this venue. Kensit was the founder of the Protestant Truth Society, set up to challenge the newly formed Anglo-Catholic Oxford Movement and its Romish practices. Some saw him as a defender of evangelical Protestantism, others as a rabblerouser. In 1902 he went to Liverpool to secure the release of his son, John A. Kensit, from prison, where he had been sent for organising open-air religious meetings. As he boarded the Mersey ferry after the rally Kensit Snr was struck on the head by an iron bar thrown by a protester.

→Anglo-Catholic Movement, p. 56

Liverpool

LIVERPOOL ANGLICAN CATHEDRAL, Cathedral Close

The fifth largest cathedral in the world was designed in 1902 by the 22-year-old student Giles Gilbert Scott in what was his first commission, a remarkable achievement considering not just his age but the fact that he was a Roman Catholic. It was 1980, however, with Scott long dead, before the work was completed. By then the Bishop of Liverpool was David Sheppard, the former England cricket captain. During the riots that tore apart the city the following year he and Liverpool's Catholic Archbishop, Derek Worlock, were approached by leaders of the black community asking for megaphones so that they could urge the ringleaders to call off the disturbances. The police were not enthusiastic initially but eventually handed the bishops the megaphones, which they carried under their coats to the main trouble spot where they found a boy willing to take them to the ringleaders. The violence soon abated.

LIVERPOOL METROPOLITAN CATHEDRAL OF CHRIST THE KING, Mount Pleasant

The city's Roman Catholic cathedral, irreverently dubbed 'Paddy's Wigwam' on account of its uncompromising shape, was over a hundred years in the making. The commission to design the building was granted in 1853 to E. W. Pugin, the noted Gothic stylist, but only the Lady Chapel was constructed. It stood in the grounds of St Edward's College, Everton, for more than a century as the local parish church until it was demolished for being unsafe.

Years passed before the idea of building a Catholic cathedral in Liverpool resurfaced. A new site by the city centre, near the Anglican cathedral, was found, money was raised and Edwin Lutyens, one of the most formidable architects of the era, a doyen of major commissions, drew up a design for a Byzantine structure that would have been the second largest church in the world. As detractors predicted, the scheme foundered and so Adrian Gilbert Scott, brother of the architect of the Anglican cathedral, was commissioned to scale down Lutyens's plans, but his ideas were not well received. A competition was then held to meet a more realistic budget, which resulted in Frederick Gibberd's unusual tepee-like creation, finished in 1967.

→ Church of the Holy Name of Jesus, Manchester, p. 222

CHAPTER 7

WESSEX AND THE SOUTH-WEST

The West Country has long been the spiritual heartland of the country thanks to the mysterious ancient sites of Stonehenge and Avebury, and the myths surrounding Glastonbury, capital of 'alternative' Britain and non-establishment Christianity.

Glastonbury's revered status stems from the legend that some time around the year AD 30 Joseph of Arimathea, a merchant from the Holy Land and great-uncle of Jesus Christ, journeyed across the Mediterranean after Jesus' crucifixion with the Holy Grail, the vessel used by Jesus and the Apostles at the Last Supper, and preached the first Christian teachings heard in England in the town. Less well known is the story that ten years earlier Joseph landed in Cornwall on a tin-trading mission possibly with Christ Himself, prompting William Blake later to muse on how 'those feet in ancient time [did] walk upon England's mountains green'.

How fitting then that it was in the West Country, in the Gloucestershire village of Little Sodbury in the 1520s, that William Tyndale started working on the first publication of the Bible in English. This simple act fostered a spirit of independence that led to the English Church's break from Rome the following decade and the conversion of the country to Protestantism soon after.

Not that the region was always quick to welcome new forms of worship and new modes of belief. Rebellion greeted King Edward VI's insistence in the 1540s that Mass be performed in English rather than Latin. George Fox, founder of the Quakers, was sent to the town assizes in 1656 after preaching a series of controversial sermons – and because he insisted on wearing a hat – while John Wesley was nearly torn apart by the mob when he began expressing his new views on Christianity – Methodism – in Falmouth in 1745.

Key events

***c.* AD 20** **Joseph of Arimathea, a merchant from the Holy Land, lands in the West Country to trade tin. Legend has it his party includes his great-nephew, Jesus Christ.**

***c.* AD 30** **Joseph of Arimathea returns to England and ends up at Glastonbury, possibly with the Holy Grail, the vessel used by Jesus and the Apostles at the Last Supper, to preach the first Christian teachings heard in England.**

1520s **William Tyndale begins work in Little Sodbury, Gloucestershire on the first published version of the Bible in English.**

1531 **An unknown Protestant rebel fastens papers to the door of Exeter Cathedral naming the Pope as the Antichrist. It echoes the actions of the pioneering Protestant Martin Luther who famously posted his ninety-six theses on popish indulgences to the door of the church in Wittenberg, Germany, in 1517.**

1549 **Edward VI's new Protestant Book of Common Prayer is greeted with violentce in Devon and Cornwall.**

1620 **Christian exiles now known as the Pilgrim Fathers leave Plymouth for the New World. Landing in America, they name the spot Plymouth Rock and found the New Plymouth colony in what is now Massachusetts.**

1656 **George Fox, founder of the Quakers, is arrested in Launcestor for making controversial speeches and wearing a hat. He defends himself by citing pro-hat sentiments in the biblical Book of Daniel.**

1656 **James Nayler arrives in Bristol claiming to be the Messiah, imitating Christ's entry into Jerusalem on Palm Sunday. He is arrested and sent to London for trial on charges of blasphemy and of claiming divine status.**

1689 **William of Orange, the Protestant Dutch prince, lands in Torbay to take the throne at the expense of the Catholic James II.**

1745 **John Wesley, pioneer of Methodism, is besieged in a Cornish house as he prepares to preach.**

1830 **John Nelson Darby begins preaching in South Devon in 1830. His followers become the austere Plymouth Brethren.**

Cornwall

King Solomon, the legendary Old Testament king, sent traders from the Holy Land to Cornwall some time around the year 960 BC to buy tin from the Cornish miners. The traders included Jews and a number of Phoenicians (inhabitants of what is now the Gaza Strip) whose word for this island was 'Berat-Anach' –

'country of tin' – a word phonetically similar to 'Britain' whose etymology is uncertain.

More dramatically, a once popular legend, states that some time around the year AD 20, Joseph of Arimathea, a merchant from the Holy Land, journeyed across the Mediterranean, past the Straits of Gibraltar, and landed in Cornwall, also to trade tin. Allegedly travelling with him was his great-nephew, Jesus Christ.

Cornwall reacted violently to Edward VI's imposition of the Protestant Book of Common Prayer in 1549. The people rebelled not out of any particular reverence for Catholicism but because, already aggravated by high taxes they resented London foisting a foreign language – English – on long-standing customs. The Cornish opponents of the new measures summed up their grievances in what they called 'The Demands of the Western Rebels': 'And so we the Cornyshe men (whereof certen of us understande no Englysh) utterly refuse thys newe English.' Ironically, they had not objected to the holding of services in a dead foreign language: Latin.

During the violence that then swept through Cornwall and Devon rebels besieged St Michael's Mount Castle and burnt trusses of hay outside it. Order was eventually restored by royal forces composed mostly of German and Italian mercenaries, with considerable loss of life on both sides.

In June 2007 Bill Ind, the Anglican Bishop of Truro, apologised for the massacre carried out in the Anglican church's name during the Prayerbook Rebellion of 1549, calling it an 'enormous mistake which the Church should be ashamed of', before contradicting himself completely by adding: 'I don't think apologising for something that happened over 500 years ago helps, but I am sorry about what happened and I think it was an enormous mistake.'

→ Old Jewry, p. 24

Falmouth

It looked as if John Wesley, pioneer of Methodism, might be torn apart by the mob when he preached in the Cornish port on 4 July 1745. As soon as he arrived at the house of the woman he had arranged to visit, it was 'beset on all sides by an innumerable multitude of people', he wrote in his journals. 'The rabble roared with all their throats. "Bring out the Canorum" [a local insult for Methodists]. No answer being given, they quickly forced open the outer door, and filled the passage. I stepped forward into the midst of them and said, 'Here I am. Which of you has anything to say to me? To which of you have I done anything wrong?"'

Although Wesley suffered some blows and lost part of his clothes, the rabble soon calmed down and he escaped without serious injury. The Methodist leader left by boat a few hours later, watched by a number of the same mob '[who] could only revenge themselves with their tongues'. When Wesley turned to one man and bade him goodnight the man 'spake not nor moved hand or foot till I was on horseback. Then he said, "I wish you were in hell."'

→ Wesley in Bolton, p. 220

Launceston

George Fox, founder of the Quakers, was sent to the town assizes in 1656 after making a series of controversial speeches. The main bone of contention, though, seemed not to be Fox's theology but the fact that he wore a hat. The judge ordered him to remove his headwear but Fox refused, on biblical grounds. 'Thou mayest read in the third [Book] of Daniel,' he explained, 'that the three children were cast into the fiery furnace by Nebuchadnezzer's command, with their coats, their hose, and their hats on.' Fox and his two companions were jailed nonetheless.

When Oliver Cromwell, then ruling the country, heard about this farcical affair he ordered an investigation and told the authorities to release Fox as long as the Quaker leader desisted from preaching. Fox refused to do so, and continued to languish in jail until the authorities decided they wanted to rid themselves of these troublesome Quakers. On one occasion they even left the cell door open, but the Quakers refused to escape, saying they had been guilty of no crime. Fox and his companions were released without charge in September 1656.

Over the next thirty years more and more Quakers were imprisoned in Launceston jail for refusing to attend their parish church. James II granted them a general pardon in 1686, but they were barred from attending university or entering the professions until the 1830s.

→ Fox imprisoned in Scarborough Castle, p. 203

St Ives

The Cornish town of St Ives raged vehemently against John and Charles Wesley's new Methodist interpretation of Christianity in the mid-eighteenth century. When Charles Wesley visited in July 1743 a mob charged into the room where he was preaching, fists flying. Wesley remained calm, strode into the violent crowd, and tried to bring the most irate of the protesters up to the desk. He quietly subdued one man and even won over his fellow ruffians. When Wesley visited St Ives again the following April he found that the townsfolk had pulled down the venue, not out of religious spite but 'for joy that Admiral Matthews had beat the Spaniards [in a naval battle]'.

Chapter 7

Truro

GOLDEN HOUSE, Grampound

The late-medieval home of the Tregian family became a centre of secret Catholic worship in the 1570s. This was after Pope Pius V urged believers to rise up against Elizabeth I who had clamped down on Catholicism fearing a Rome-inspired insurrection.

On 24 April 1576 Golden House was visited by Cuthbert Mayne, who had just been ordained into the Catholic Church and was on an undercover trip to England. As a priest he was a likely target for the authorities' hostility, so once he arrived at the Tregian home he disguised himself as the family steward. Emboldened, he then began journeying across the county taking Mass and supporting the dispirited Catholic faithful.

A year later, on 8 June, Richard Grenville, the High Sheriff of Cornwall, sent a party of around a hundred men to Golden House to arrest Mayne. When Grenville came face to face with the priest and asked him: 'What art thou?', Mayne replied: 'I am a man.' The sheriff conducted a search of the property and found an Agnus Dei (lamb of God) case – a wax disc made from Easter candles imprinted with a relief of the paschal lamb which Parliament had banned under pain of death in 1571. Grenville also found a papal bull, which had been outlawed as well. He arrested Mayne and threw him into Launceston Castle.

Mayne was sentenced to death for high treason but was offered a way out: he would have to swear on the Bible that Elizabeth was the Supreme Head of the Church of England. Mayne simply restated his belief that England would soon once again be Catholic. He also dug his grave a bit deeper when he advocated that in the event of an invasion by a foreign Catholic power, English Catholics should rise up and help the invaders. He was executed in Launceston on 29 November 1577, his dying words being: 'the queen neither ever was, nor is, nor ever shall be, the head of the Church of England.'

→ Priest holes in Worcestershire, p. 192.

DEVON

Bradley Woods

A large steep limestone chasm by the River Lemon valley has been known as Puritans Pit since William Yeo, a Presbyterian cleric in Cromwell's time, patrolled the town with a constable to ensure locals kept the Sabbath holy. When the monarchy was restored in 1660, Yeo lost his post, but he and other Puritans would meet secretly at night in the pit to worship.

Brixham

William of Orange, the Protestant Dutch prince invited by the English establishment in 1688 to take the throne at the expense of the Catholic James II, landed with his supporters at Brixham on the Devon coast of Torbay. William's party was led by a chaplain waving a Bible, proclaiming that the prince had come to England to save the Protestant religion. Significantly, the date of William's landing at Torbay was 5 November, eighty-three years to the day after an earlier James had survived a Catholic plot to destroy the monarchy. The Dutch prince took the throne as William III on 13 February 1689, James deemed to have abdicated by trying to flee the country the previous December.

→ William wins the Battle of Boyne, p. 299

Crediton

The Dartmoor village sports a number of memorials to Boniface, patron saint of Holland and Germany, who was born here *c.* 680 as Winfrith. He is known as the apostle of Germany thanks to his pioneering work laying down the foundations of Christendom in northern Europe.

Exeter

EXETER CATHEDRAL, Cathedral Close

A rare instance of 'murder in the cathedral' occurred in Exeter in 1283. The victim, Walter Lechlade, was knifed to death in the cathedral close as he walked to evening services. He was probably killed for being an associate of the bishop, Peter Quinel, who was engaged in a power struggle with the dean, John Pycot. Lechlade's family sued Pycot and nineteen of his associates. The case dragged on without solution for two years before the bishop asked King Edward I to intervene. Edward eventually sentenced five men to be executed and sent Quinel to a monastery.

The cathedral was one of the key English locations during the Reformation of the 1530s for it was here in autumn 1531 that an unknown rebel affixed papers to the door identifying the Pope as the Antichrist. It echoed the actions of the pioneering Protestant Martin Luther who famously posted his ninety-six theses on popish indulgences to the door of the church in Wittenberg on the eve of All Saints Day 1517.

A week after the Exeter incident a man heading to early Mass saw a boy fixing a piece of paper to a gate on South Street. The child was a pupil of a certain Thomas Bennet who ran a private school. Bennet was hauled in for questioning by the bishop and, having been found to hold Lutheran ideas, was burnt at the stake outside Exeter on 10 January 1532.

In 1539 during the dissolution of monasteries Simon Heynes, who had been imposed as dean on the cathedral, carried out new edicts outlawing pilgrimages by defacing Exeter's images of Thomas à Becket, the archbishop murdered in Canterbury Cathedral by Henry II's knights. He also obliterated references to Becket and the Pope in the prayer books. After his mentor, Thomas Cromwell, lost his position as Henry's chief minister in 1540, Heynes himself was removed from his post and imprisoned for heresy.

A decade later the Bishop of Exeter was Miles Coverdale. He was involved in producing one of the first Bibles published in English. Coverdale was preaching in the cathedral in July 1553 when the accession of Mary Tudor to the throne was announced. Given Mary's Catholic inclinations, Coverdale knew immediately that he would lose his post. He was, however, allowed to leave the country rather than be taken to the stake.

During the Civil War of the 1640s the city council took over the cathedral and decided to allow worship by two different denominations – Presbyterians and Congregationalists. So that both groups could use the building, a dividing wall was erected inside, with Presbyterians sitting in the quire and Congregationalists in the nave.

After landing in Devon to take the throne of England for the Protestant cause in 1688, William of Orange held court in the deanery before heading to London.

→ St Giles Cathedral, Edinburgh, p. 271

ST NICHOLAS, Fore Street

The church commissioners came to Exeter in 1539 to close down the priory at St Nicholas, but quickly adjourned for lunch, leaving a workman in charge. Meanwhile, a crowd of women had decided to vent their anger at the authorities' actions and had broken into St Nicholas. They chased the labourer into the church tower and the poor man had to resort to jumping out of a high window to escape.

Plymouth

The great naval city has strong associations with Nonconformist Christianity: it was the departure point for the Pilgrim Fathers who sailed for America in 1620 and it is now the spiritual home of the austere Plymouth Brethren.

The Pilgrim Fathers were separatists who first appeared in 1605 in Scrooby, Nottinghamshire, and soon merged with a similar group from Gainsborough. The sect rejected the authority of the Church and its hierarchy. Attempting to model their behaviour on the New Testament, the Pilgrim Fathers avoided contact with what they claimed was the 'impurity' of other churches.

Having been challenged by the authorities, they fled to Amsterdam. The group returned to England in 1612 but eight years later left for America. Their connection with Plymouth came about solely because they pulled into the harbour to repair one of their vessels.

When the emigrants arrived in the New World they named their landing place Plymouth Rock and founded the New Plymouth colony in what is now Massachusetts. Even though around half their number died in the first winter, more settlers joined them over the next decade. The name Pilgrim Fathers first appeared in eighteenth-century poetry, the pilgrim description coming from Hebrews 11:13 – Christians who were 'strangers and pilgrims on the earth'.

John Nelson Darby founded a group of conservative evangelical Christians in Dublin in 1827 who later became the Plymouth Brethren due to their preaching in Devon. Darby had been a Church of Ireland clergyman, but quit when his bishop insisted that converts should swear allegiance to the British Crown. A colleague, Francis Newman, described him thus: 'A fallen cheek, a bloodshot eye . . . a seldom shaven beard, a shabby suit of clothes and a generally neglected person, drew at first pity, with wonder to see such a figure in a drawing room.'

Darby began preaching in South Devon in 1830 and soon his group was being described as 'the brethren from Plymouth' owing to their custom of calling each other 'brother' – later shortened to Plymouth Brethren. Their aim was to break bread without having ordained ministers and they placed much emphasis on baptism and communion. They believed the churches had gone astray by becoming involved with the secular world.

Within a year the Plymouth Brethren had 1,500 members. Soon there were followers worldwide, but a split in the movement in 1848 saw them divide into the Open Brethren and the Exclusive Brethren. Each branch has since split into further subdivisions, usually over interpretations of baptism.

The houses of worship for all wings of the movement are simple and usually named 'Hebron', 'Shiloh' or 'Bethel'. There are no visible crosses, no set liturgy or central hierarchy. Followers do not 'join', and feel that non-believers present receive no spiritual benefit in being with them. The meeting rooms of the Exclusive Brethren have no windows. Both wings follow a strict code based on Bible teaching and like to keep themselves separate from non-believers, including other Christians, to protect themselves from a world they believe to be a place of wickedness ('Remove the wicked person from amongst yourselves,' they recite from 1 Corinthians 5:13). Members are forbidden to indulge in such worldly activities as watching television, listening to the radio, owning pets, voting, reading newspapers and fiction, and using computers or mobile phones.

When James Taylor Jnr took over the Exclusive Brethren in the 1950s he decreed that men should marry early, take care to be clean shaven, keep their hair short and refrain from wearing ties. Brethren could not eat with non-members, or even befriend them. The only safe places were meeting-rooms and their own houses. In 1970 Taylor was found in bed with a female follower. The movement split and some 8,000 members left.

The most famous figure to have emerged from the Plymouth Brethren is the Satanist dilettante-aesthete Aleister Crowley, once dubbed the 'wickedest man in the world' on account of his occult activities and licentiousness.

→ The Plymouth Exclusive Brethren in Aberdeen, p. 264

Sampford Courtenay

The Prayerbook Rebellion of 1549, the county's greatest act of sedition, was centred on this Dartmoor village. It erupted when the first Protestant king, Edward VI, who reigned from 1547–53, introduced a law decreeing that Mass had to be said in English rather than Latin.

Catholics and traditionalists everywhere took offence at this diktat from London, especially in Cornwall and Devon. In Sampford Courtenay the parishioners claimed the new liturgy was 'nothing but a Christmas game' as the prayer book asked men and women to file into the quire on different sides in order to receive the sacrament, which reminded locals of country dancing. They insisted the local priest keep to tradition, which he did. The authorities demand that West Country people obey the new rules led to an altercation outside the church that resulted in one of their number being killed with a pitchfork.

The traditionalists banded together and, spurred on by the war cry 'Kill all the gentlemen and we will have the Six Articles up again and ceremonies as they were in King Henry's time,' marched on several towns. At Crediton the reformers set barns on fire to obstruct the rebels. The traditionalists then turned their attention to Exeter. The inhabitants sent messages of support but would not open the city gates, which led to a siege. Defeat for the rebels came at the hands of Lord Russell's army of mercenaries, who marched west and confronted them at Fenny Bridges, near Exeter, that August. In the fighting 300 rebels were killed. Another battle soon followed at Clyst St Mary, which the authorities narrowly won after slaying around a thousand rebels. The third and final battle of the prayerbook took place at Sampford Courtenay, resulting in complete victory for the king's forces. Reprisals followed swiftly and many who had opposed the new laws were hanged.

GLOUCESTERSHIRE

Blockley

Joanna Southcott, the most notorious of the British false messiahs, spent much of the last ten years of her life in the early nineteenth century in the quiet Costwolds village of Blockley. Here she awaited the virgin birth of Shiloh, the child saviour identified in the Bible that would rule the nations 'with a rod of iron', whose imminent arrival was supposedly revealed to her by a spirit when she turned sixty-four in 1814.

While preparing for Shiloh, Southcott 'greatly rejoiced', as she noted in her memoirs, 'for I am as weary of the world as the world is of me'. But, she added mysteriously, 'I cannot enter into particulars of what was revealed to me as it was ordered to be sealed up in the presence of seven friends and put into the box that is not to be opened till my Great Trial, and then will be seen what was revealed to me every day.' Southcott died that year in London, childless, amid denunciations in the newspapers of her so-called powers. The box she left continues to be the subject of controversy (→ p. 80).

Bristol

Such was King John's hostility to the town's Jews in the early thirteenth century that he sentenced Abraham of Bristol, who refused to pay a tax of 10,000 marks, to have seven teeth extracted, one a day, unless he paid the levied amount.

James Nayler's arrival in Bristol in 1656, claiming to be the messiah, caused turmoil in the town. He was seated on a horse, accompanied by a group of fawning women singing hosannas, imitating Christ's entry into Jerusalem on Palm Sunday. Nayler was promptly arrested by the authorities, who sent him to London for trial on charges of blasphemy and of claiming divine status.

Nayler was one of the first Quakers, a group that believed in universal salvation, free will for all men, and that God's message came to people directly through personal inspiration. However, Bristol's Quakers swiftly dissociated themselves from him, and in London the Second Protectorate Parliament under Oliver Cromwell declared Nayler guilty of the blasphemy charges. Some MPs demanded he be stoned to death, but after Cromwell called for leniency the punishment was lightened: he was sentenced to be whipped through the streets, placed in the pillory, branded on the forehead with the letter 'B' for blasphemer and have his tongue pierced with a red-hot iron. Nayler was also sent back to Bristol, where he was made to repeat his ride in reverse, tied to a cart looking at the rear of his horse. He was then returned to London for a spell in solitary at Bridewell Prison. In September 1659 Parliament declared an amnesty for all Quaker prisoners and Nayler was released.

Around a hundred years later John Wesley, the founder of Methodism, met much opposition when he arrived in Bristol. 'The beasts of the people,' he later wrote, 'were stirred up almost in all places to knock these mad dogs on the head at once.' At first no magistrate would listen to his complaints, but on 1 April 1740 troublemakers filled the court and much of the street during a hearing over alleged disturbances of the peace. The mayor called on them to disperse and, when they refused to do so, ordered his officers to arrest the ringleaders. At the Quarter Sessions they insulted Wesley, but the mayor cut them short, saying: 'What Mr Wesley is is nothing to you. I will keep the peace; I will have no rioting in this city.' Wesley held his last conference in Bristol in 1790, the year before he died. More than 130 preachers attended but he was frail and feeble, and barely able to read the hymns.

→ Richard Brothers, Prince of the Hebrews, p. 75

WORLD'S OLDEST METHODIST CHAPEL, 36 The Horsefair

John Wesley, father of Methodism, founded what is the world's oldest Methodist chapel in 1739. It contains a double-decker pulpit and an octagonal lantern window (to reduce the amount liable in window tax) and was used as a schoolroom for the local poor. Above are rooms in which Welsey and other preachers lodged. After his death the Welsh Calvinist Methodists took over use of the building but in 1909 it returned to the mainstream Methodist Church.

Gloucester

John Hooper, the reforming Bishop of Gloucester, often called the 'father of Nonconformism', was burnt to death for heresy just outside the city walls on 9 February 1555. A decade earlier Hooper had spent much time in central Europe championing Swiss Protestantism, opposing not just the Catholics but the Lutherans as well.

Back in England in 1549 he was appointed Bishop of Gloucester, where he found to his astonishment that among the clergy fewer than half could list the Ten Commandments and that some could not even recite the Lord's Prayer in English. Hooper ran into trouble after denouncing the exuberance of Catholic prayer robes. It cost him a spell in London's Fleet Prison, after which he decided to conform to establishment practice.

When Mary Tudor, a diehard Catholic, became queen in 1553, Hooper was sent back to the Fleet on trumped-up charges of debt. He was relieved of his bishopric and executed by burning before a crowd of around 7,000. It was a slow lingering death: the fire didn't catch light quickly and Hooper's legs were burnt off as he cried for the flames to consume the rest of his body.

Little Sodbury

William Tyndale, the first person to publish the Bible in English, began his monumental work in the 1520s in his bedroom in the manor house at idyllic Little Sodbury. Here he was employed as chaplain and tutor to the owner, Sir John Walsh, a warrior who had been proclaimed Henry VIII's champion at the king's coronation in 1509.

Tyndale devoted nearly all his time to translating the Bible, giving up the chance of marriage and family life. In the early sixteenth century it was illegal under the 1408 Constitutions of Oxford to have an English translation of the Scriptures. The Bible was then available only in the original Hebrew and Greek, or the first Latin translations, and so only the intelligentsia could understand it. To Tyndale this was an elitist stance contrived 'to keep the world still in darkness, to the intent they might sit in the consciences of the people, through vain superstition and false doctrine, to satisfy their filthy lusts, their proud ambition, and insatiable covetousness, and to exalt their own honour . . . above God himself'.

Tyndale decided the word of God had to be made available to the public after hearing a local priest proclaim: 'We are better without God's laws than the Pope's.' He thundered back: 'I defy the Pope and all his laws. If God spare my life, ere many years, I will cause a boy that driveth a plough shall know more of the Scriptures than thou doest.' He began with translations of the writings of Erasmus, the Dutch scholar and humanist who had proposed the notion of a personal faith, of man faced directly with God rather than through the Church. This made him a controversial figure with the local Gloucestershire clergy, who charged him with heresy.

Forced out of Little Sodbury, Tyndale moved to London in 1523. There the bishop, Cuthbert Tunstall, was unimpressed with the idea of an English Bible. So was Thomas More, Henry VIII's chancellor, who denounced Tyndale as a 'beast' and a 'hell-hound in the kennel of the devil'. In May 1524 Tyndale left for Germany, where he arranged with a Cologne printer to publish the New Testament in English. Again the clergy were horrified and banned the work. The print shop was raided and the presses were stopped at Matthew 22.

Tyndale and his assistant, William Roy, fled along the Rhine to the German city of Worms. There they printed the first New Testament written entirely in English. Of the 3,000 copies produced three survive today. By January 1526 the first Tyndale

Bibles were being smuggled into England in bales of cloth and barrels of flour.

Cardinal Wolsey, Henry VIII's leading minister, was horrified. He had coveted the papacy and had once complained to Rome that the printing press had made it possible for 'ordinary men to read the Scriptures'. Wolsey hunted down Tyndale's 'heretical' translations throughout Cambridge and Oxford, and in London Bishop Tunstall burnt several copies outside St Paul's. Ironically, Tyndale's best customers were the king's men, who bought up every available copy just so they could burn them. Tyndale used the money to print even more.

Tyndale moved to Antwerp in 1530 after Wolsey's death. There he was befriended by Henry Philips, an Englishman who showed an interest in his work. But he didn't know that Philips was an agent of the new Bishop of London, John Stokesley. Tyndale was captured by officers sent by Holy Roman Emperor Charles V, who vehemently opposed the Reformation, and was imprisoned in Vilvoorde Castle near Brussels. On 6 October 1536, after 500 days in jail, where the Church authorities tried to reconvert him to Catholicism, Tyndale was strangled and burnt at the stake in the courtyard. His dying words were: 'Oh Lord, open the eyes of the King of England!'

Although Tyndale did not live to complete his translations, two followers, Miles Coverdale and John Rogers, took up his work. Coverdale's Bible, the first complete edition in English, appeared in October 1535. For the New Testament he used Tyndale's version, and for the Old Testament German and Latin texts as he was not familiar with Hebrew, thus losing much of the meaning. Coverdale's Bible was the first to be licensed by the English throne. John Rogers was the first Bible scholar to produce an English translation from the Old Testament Hebrew. It appeared in 1537.

→ The King James Bible, p. 59

Let there be light

William Tyndale's translations of the Scriptures formed the basis of the 1560 Geneva Bible and Britain's better-known King James Bible. Heavily influenced by Martin Luther's reformist ideas, Tyndale used words that signified the new shift in religious power from the establishment to the individual worshipper, so he talked of 'congregation' instead of 'church' and 'elder' for 'priest'.

Tyndale's Bible is also the earliest that the ordinary modern-day reader can easily understand. For instance, the phrase 'Nellen ge deman, daet ge ne syn fordemede' from an Anglo-Saxon translation makes no sense to someone without a grounding in ancient languages. John Wycliffe's fourteenth-century version of the same phrase – 'Nyle ze deme, that se be nat demyd' – makes little more sense. But when Tyndale renders the same as 'Iudge not, lest ye be yet iudged', everything is clear, even if the exact phraseology is no longer common.

But it was Tyndale's imagery that was most powerful, and some of his phrases are now among the most quoted in the English language. They include:

'In the begynnynge God created heune and erth' (Genesis 1:1)
'Let there be light' (Genesis 1:3),
'Am I my brother's keeper?' (Genesis 4:9),
'Let my people go' (Exodus 5:1),
'The truth shall make you free' (John 8:32),
'Eat, drink and be merry' (Luke 12:19)
'Signs of the times' (Matthew 16:3)
'Love thyne neighbour as thyself (Leviticus 19:18)
'Iudge not that ye be iudged' (Matthew 7:1)

Winchcombe

HAILES ABBEY, Salter's Lane

A now ruined abbey founded in 1246 by Richard, Earl of Cornwall, brother of Henry III, Hailes became a place of great pilgrimage in the Middle Ages as visitors flocked to see what was supposed to be a vial of Jesus Christ's blood, bought in Germany in 1270. With the money collected from the pilgrim's the abbey was rebuilt on a sumptuous scale and it prevailed until the 1530s' dissolution when Henry VIII's commissioners declared – with no scientific proof but great probability – that the blood was not that of the Lamb of God but more likely that of a lamb from the field, regularly renewed.

The buildings were converted into residences but later demolished. A small church that was part of the estate survives.

Hampshire

Hordle

Mary Ann Girling, a self-proclaimed messiah from East Anglia, attempted to lead a group of celibate followers – the Children of God – into the Promised Land in 1859 but got no further than Hordle in Hampshire's New Forest.

Girling had received her first vision the previous Christmas Day when Jesus Christ, with nail marks on his hands and feet, appeared in her Ipswich bedroom. 'My flesh was consumed upon my bones, bloody sweat pressed through the pores of my skin, and I became as helpless as an infant,' she later explained. Claiming to be the 'woman clothed with the sun', as foretold in the Book of Revelation, Girling left her husband and children and journeyed to London. In the capital she fell in with the so-called

Peculiar People of Plumstead, preaching excitedly before crowds of several thousand from a railway arch in Walworth Road, which led to the nickname 'the Jumpers of Walworth'.

Perturbed by the vanities of London, Girling left for Hampshire with more than 150 dancing, shaking acolytes whose hysterical chanting and fainting fits brought them a new name – 'the Convulsionists'. Opponents accused Girling of hypnotism and witchcraft (in an earlier age she would probably have been burnt), but she attracted prominent followers, including a local judge, Andrew Peterson, who built a folly, Peterson's Tower, in her honour in the New Forest. One of Girling's tenets was that as the new messiah she could not die, but die she did – supposedly – in 1886.

→ The Peculiar People of Plumstead, p. 64

Winchester

The Saxon capital of England was the setting in 1072 of the Accord of Winchester with which William I granted the Archbishop of Canterbury primacy over of the Archbishop of York.

WINCHESTER CATHEDRAL, The Close

One of the most powerful medieval bishoprics, Winchester attained religious significance in the ninth century as the last resting place of St Swithun, whose bones could supposedly heal the sick. Pilgrims duly flocked to the cathedral to buy relics.

Winchester had the only bishop left in England in 1205 after Pope Innocent III excommunicated King John, following a row over the appointment of a cardinal. Yet the bishops of Winchester later became some of the richest clerics in Europe, controlling one third of the country's wealth by the time of the mid-sixteenth-century Reformation.

At the death of the Catholic queen, Mary Tudor, in 1558 the Bishop of Winchester complained that 'the wolves be coming out of Geneva and other places of Germany and have sent their books before, full of pestilent doctrines, blasphemy and heresy to infect the people' – in other words, that the Protestants with their Bibles were gearing up to take over Christianity.'

The cathedral is now home to the twelfth-century Winchester Bible, said to be the finest of its time. It was written in Latin by a single scribe and illuminated in gold and lapis lazuli.

Somerset

Glastonbury

There is on the confines of western Britain a certain royal island, called in the ancient speech Glastonia, marked out by broad boundaries, girt round with waters rich in fish and with still-flowing rivers, fitted for many uses of human indigence, and dedicated to the most sacred of deities.

St Augustine, *c.* AD 600.

Glastonbury is the capital of 'alternative' Britain, home of New Age thinking and maverick non-establishment Christianity and its vibrant counter-culture fills the town throughout the year, especially during the annual rock festival which brings tens of thousands of visitors every summer. Yet the tiny town has a unique place in British religious history.

According to a well-known myth, some time around the year AD 30 Joseph of Arimathea, a merchant from the Holy Land and great-uncle of Jesus Christ, journeyed across the Mediterranean after Jesus' crucifixion with the Holy Grail, the vessel used by Jesus and the Apostles at the Last Supper, and preached the first Christian teachings heard in England here.

The myths surrounding Glastonbury were first written down in the early twelfth century by William of Malmesbury in his *On the Antiquity of the Church of Glastonbury*. He claimed that the Apostle Philip sent Joseph of Arimathaea to western Europe with the gospel and a relic of the Holy Blood. Joseph allegedly landed in Wales, and made his way across the Bristol Channel and through the marshy ground of the Somerset Levels to what was then the Isle of Avalon, a name still used by writers and musicians when wanting to depict Glastonbury romantically. At Wearyall Hill, a local landmark, Joseph and his companions rested, and at the foot of the nearby tor built Britain's first church.

The search for the Grail, the most famous long-running quest in world religion after that for the Hebrews' biblical Ark of the Covenant, dates back to the twelfth century when Robert de Boron, a French poet, originated the idea that Joseph brought the Holy Grail to England after using the vessel from the Last Supper to catch the last drops of blood from Jesus' body on the cross. Some thirty monks from Glastonbury Abbey headed into the tunnels underneath the town looking for the Grail but only three emerged, one rendered dumb, the other two mad. (The tunnels are now sealed off.) Others have looked for springs that are believed to run red with the blood of Christ, although sceptics have pointed out that the red tinge is more likely due to the iron contents of the water, as in the canal at Worsley, Greater Manchester.

By the late medieval period the Glastonbury legends were in full swing. The revered historian William Camden, writing in 1609, called Glastonbury 'the First Land of God, the First Land of Saints in *England*, the Tomb of Saints, the Mother of Saints'. In 1652 Elias Ashmole, the leading Freemason and intellectual, related the story of the magus John Dee and his colleague, Edward

Kelley, who, around a century earlier, had discovered 'a very large quantity of the Elixir in some part of the ruins of Glastonbury Abbey'. The Glastonbury legends were reinvigorated in the eighteenth century by a sudden fashion for the Druids, whom many looked upon as proto-Christians rather than pagans, and again in the late twentieth century following the founding of the festival.

Yet there is no evidence to support any of the Glastonbury myths. No proof has been found that Joseph of Arimathea came to Glastonbury even though his arms, a green cross raguly with blood drops, can be seen in a number of local places such as in the sixteenth-century stained glass of St John's church on the High Street and in stone outside the abbey's St Patrick's chapel. No one can verify that here Joseph's staff turned into a hawthorn bush (the Holy Thorn of Glastonbury) which thrives and flowers every Christmas and Easter, and no one has found the Holy Grail.

GLASTONBURY ABBEY, Magdalene Street

Once one of the wealthiest religious establishments in the country but now merely ruins, Glastonbury Abbey was built in 670–78 on the site where Joseph of Arimathea, who had administered at Christ's crucifixion, supposedly established the first church in Britain *c.* AD 37. In another claim typical of the problem of separating myth from reality at Glastonbury, here allegedly are buried the bones of King Arthur, the chivalrous sixth-century monarch – who may not even have existed. More prosaically, two Saxon kings, the tenth-century Edmund and Edmund Ironside from the early eleventh century, *are* buried here.

Then there's the legend of the abbey's last steward, popularly known as Jack Horner. The nursery rhyme 'Little Jack Horner' (Little Jack Horner/Sat in the corner/Eating a Christmas pie/He put in his thumb/And pulled out a plum/And said 'What a good boy am I!') was written about Horner, who had been sent to Henry VIII with the deeds of a number of valuable properties hidden in a large pie to foil thieves. The story is spoiled by the fact that the steward's name was Thomas, not Jack, and dates no earlier than the eighteenth century.

During the Reformation Glastonbury was one of the last three abbeys to fall, holding out until 1539. The assets were then handed to Edward Seymour, Duke of Somerset, and the rubble used as building material. Blessed John Thorne, the abbey treasurer when the house was dissolved, hid the riches from the king's forces and paid for it with his life – he was dragged through the streets by horses before being hanged, drawn, and quartered on the nearby tor on 1 December 1539.

The Church of England bought the site in 1907.

→York Minster, p. 208

GLASTONBURY THORN, Wearyall Hill

A staff that may have belonged to Jesus Christ was struck into the ground on this hill by Joseph of Arimathea, according to Glastonbury legend, and immediately flowered into what has become known as the Glastonbury Thorn. The tree supposedly blooms on Christmas night even though such hawthorns usually flower only in the spring. Cuttings from the thorn are sent to the queen each Christmas. To dispel the religious superstition surrounding the Glastonbury Thorn, Oliver Cromwell's soldiers cut down the bush in 1650. Supporters had, however, hidden away sufficient cuttings to allow it to be replanted.

GLASTONBURY TOR

Richard Whiting, the last abbot of Glastonbury, was hanged alongside two of his monks on the tor for practising earth and fertility rites on 1 December 1539. Local historians have accused Henry VIII of devising a blasphemous act that echoed the crucifixion of Christ on Calvary.

ISLE BREWERS

The tiny village near Taunton was the death place of Joseph Wolff, an early nineteenth-century Jewish-born Christian missionary. In 1828 Wolff walked 600 miles across central Asia, and according to the legends that surround him was bastinadoed by Kurds in Iraq, horsewhipped by Wahabites in Abyssinia, valued for sale at 25 shillings in a slave market, and stripped by Afghans, which left him having to enter Kabul naked. Asked to become a Muslim, Wolff defiantly refused.

During his travels in the Yemen, Wolff spent six days with the Rechabites who, he explained, 'drink no wine, plant no vineyards, sow no seed and live in tents. With them were the children of Israel of the tribe of Dan who expect, in common with the children of Rechab, the speedy arrival of the Messiah in the clouds of heaven.' Among the Christian Arabs of Yemen Wolff found a book, *Seera*, which stated that Christ would return in 1840, but maintained he was 'not dissuaded by the inability of the Messiah to return that year'.

In England Wolff married Louisa Decima, a vicar's daughter, signing himself in the register as 'Apostle of Our Lord Jesus Christ for Palestine, Persia, Bokhara, and Balkh'. He moved to Somerset in 1745 and became vicar at Isle Brewers towards the end of his extraordinary life.

→ The incorrigible vicar of Stiffkey, p. 118

South Petherton

When Thomas Coke was dismissed from his post as South Petherton curate on Easter Sunday 1777 for hosting Methodist-style open-air meetings, his parishioners celebrated by ringing the church bells and breaking open a hogshead of cider. Coke had met John Wesley, the founder of Methodism, a year earlier and become a close assistant. Wesley called Coke 'the flea' as he was always jumping around on his missions, and in 1784 appointed him superintendent. Coke became the first Methodist bishop before leaving for America to carry out pioneering work to establish the new creed.

Spaxton

The Abode of Love, or Agapemone, was a maverick religious community established in Spaxton by Henry James Prince in 1849. Prince was an Anglican minister who, in 1843, three years after his ordination, became convinced that he was the prophet Elijah reincarnated and that he had divine powers. Gathering disciples to his Somerset set-up, he told them: 'Look on me. I am one in the flesh with Christ. By me, and in me, God has redeemed all flesh from death, and brought the bodies of breathing men into the resurrection state.'

Prince was married but took a virgin bride from the community while preaching the notion of celibacy to the less holy. His chosen was one Sister Zoe, sixteen years old, whom he impregnated and who was then cast out of the community for being the devil's offspring. Prince died in 1899, which surprised those supporters who thought him immortal, although they did bury him standing up to smooth through an easier resurrection. By then the collection of houses and cottages that comprised the Abode of Love was enclosed by a 12-foot-high wall guarded by baying bloodhounds.

With Prince departed from the corporeal world, a messianic successor emerged, the Revd John Hugh Smyth-Pigott. A charming Dubliner, he built an extravagant temple, the Ark of the Covenant, in Lower Clapton, London, and took over at Spaxton, where the community now comprised around one hundred women and only a handful of men. The Church of England defrocked Smyth-Pigott, but he retorted: 'I am God. It does not matter what they do.' He became increasingly unpopular outside the Spaxton community and on one occasion a member of the cult mistaken for him was beaten, tarred and feathered. Following Smyth-Pigott's death in 1927, membership declined, although the Abode of Love stumbled on until the 1960s.

The main Abode of Love house near Barford Road has since been renovated into flats.

→ The Brotherhood Church of Stapeleton, p. 204

Wells

WELLS CATHEDRAL, Cathedral Green

Cardinal Wolsey, early sixteenth-century Archbishop of York, made his son, Thomas Wynter, Dean of Wells Cathedral as well as Provost of Beverley, Archdeacon of York, Archdeacon of Richmond, Chancellor of Salisbury, Prebendary of Wells, York, Salisbury, Lincoln, and Southwell, and rector of Rudby in Yorkshire and of St Matthew's, Ipswich – while the boy was still at school. Wolsey, as a Catholic churchman in those pre-Reformation days in England, was not of course supposed to have a son.

At that time the Bishop of Wells was William Knight who was also secretary to Henry VIII. It was Knight whom Henry sent to Pope Clement VII seeking the annulment of his marriage to Catherine of Aragon on the grounds that the papal bull which had sanctioned it after Catherine's first husband, Arthur, Henry's brother, died was granted unfairly. Knight had difficulty getting to the Pope, for at that time he was the prisoner of Catherine's nephew, Holy Roman Emperor Charles V.

In 1988 choirboys from the cathedral were at the centre of a row for singing on the soundtrack of the controversial Martin Scorsese film *The Last Temptation of Christ.* Not only did some Christian groups deem the film blasphemous, even though an equal number saw it as kindling a reaffirmation of faith, but the recording had been made in the cathedral's Chapter House. George Carey, then Bishop of Bath and Wells, who later became Archbishop of Canterbury, predictably called for Christians to boycott the film.

→ St Giles Cathedral, Edinburgh, p. 262

Wiltshire

Remarkable ancient relics dating back to the time of Christ were unearthed in Wiltshire during the 1530s Reformation when Thomas Cromwell began closing the religious houses. For instance, at Monk Farleign the clerics sent Cromwell the *vincula* (girdle) of St Peter and Mary Magdalen's comb, while those at Maiden Bradley priory found 'two flowers wrapped in white and black sarcenet that on Christmas eve, in the hour in which Christ was born, will spring and burgeon and bear blossoms' plus a 'bag of relics [containing] part of God's supper on the Lord's table and part of the stone [of the manger] in which was born Jesus in Bethlehem'. The relics are believed to have been fakes.

Amesbury

STONEHENGE, A344

The nature of what is one of the world's most inspiring and mysterious ancient sights continues to fascinate historians and members of the public. Stonehenge could have been built as long ago as 1500 BC, the stones having been transported some hundred miles from Pembrokeshire, for reasons unknown. It may have been a calendar given that its axis aligns with sunrise on the longest day of the year in mid-June, when it attracts attention from pagans and Druids. Or it may have had some kind of religious purpose involving sacrifices, for ancient pig bones have been found on the site.

Avebury

One of Britain's most dramatic-looking stone circles was probably a pagan sun temple and spiritual centre used between 2600 and 1600 BC, which makes it older than the better-known Stonehenge. Unlike at Stonehenge, access to the Avebury stones is possible, and the stones are still used by local pagans especially around the time of the summer solstice. Yet it is lucky they have survived at all. In the Middle Ages locals, determined to stamp out paganism, knocked the stones down and buried them. They were rediscovered by archaeologist Alexander Keiller in the 1930s.

CHAPTER 8

SCOTLAND

Religion in Scotland has long been coloured by the turmoil surrounding the Reformation of the 1530s, the Jacobite rebellions of the mid-eighteenth century and by the creation of a multitude of intriguingly obscure sects. There is the Free Church of Scotland, commonly known as the 'Wee Frees'. They shouldn't be confused with the Free Presbyterian Church of Scotland, which claims to be the spiritual descendant of the Scottish Reformation, and is known colloquially as the 'Wee Wee Frees'. Then there is the United Free Church of Scotland which was formed in 1900 from the United Presbyterian Church of Scotland . . . If it's all too difficult to follow, escape is provided by the island of Iona, a major pilgrimage site and burial place for the kings of Scotland, Ireland and Norway. In recent years Iona has been a leading centre in the revival of Christian Scottish spirituality.

At least the level of violence that has cursed religion in Scotland has diminished. For instance, when Charles I tried to impose the English prayer book on Scotland in the 1630s there was considerable trouble. A riot broke out in St Giles Cathedral and a stool was thrown by a woman who shouted at the dean: 'Thou false thief, wilt thou say Mass at my ear?' as others in the congregation cried out: 'The Mass! The Mass! Popery! Popery! Down with the Pope! Down with him!'

Nowadays simple excommunication usually suffices, as it did in 1989 when Lord MacKay, Lord Chancellor of Britain, was expelled from the Wee Frees for attending a Roman Catholic Mass after the funeral of a friend.

Key events

1128 **King David I founds Holyroodhouse as a monastery after seeing a cross between the antlers of a stag he is hunting.**

1296 **Edward I of England seizes the Stone of Scone, allegedly a biblical relic, from the Scots for Westminster Abbey. Four Scottish students steal it back on Christmas Day 1950. Prime Minister John Major returns it officially in 1996.**

1561 **Mary, Queen of Scots, breaks the law by attending Mass in the Palace of Holyroodhouse in August 1561.**

1618 **To the horror of the Protestants, James I draws up the Five Articles of Perth to force the Scots to worship in the English manner. Twenty years later the General Assembly of the Kirk throws the Articles out.**

1637 **A riot at St Giles Cathedral, Edinburgh, greets Charles I's plan to impose the English Book of Common Prayer on the Scots.**

1639 **Charles I's attempt to impose the English prayer book on Scotland leads to the Bishops' Wars.**

1679 **The Battle of Bothwell Bridge in Lanarkshire, caused by Charles II's insistence on having the Church run centrally by bishops, ends with the arrest of 1,200 prisoners, some of whom were hanged, some transported overseas.**

1688 **Edinburgh students, excited by news of the Glorious Revolution dance around the Mercat Cross in Edinburgh shouting: 'No Pope, No Papists.'**

1843 **The Church of Scotland splits into two factions in the Great Disruption: on one side are the Moderates, on the other the Evangelicals.**

1929 **Part reunification of the Kirk is resisted by a small group of Evangelicals in the Highlands and Islands – the ultra-conservative Free Church of Scotland, or Wee Frees.**

Aberdeen

The ascetic fundamentalist Protestant sect the Plymouth Exclusive Brethren were torn apart in July 1970 after their leader, James Taylor Jnr, already an alcoholic, committed adultery, witnessed by a number of followers, in an Aberdeen house. Members felt they could no longer tolerate his behaviour. Surprisingly, the husband of the woman with whom Taylor lay explained that the leader's actions were 'quite suitable behaviour' as his wife had been 'ministering' to Taylor, who was a 'pure man'.

There were also allegations that Taylor was exerting too tight a rein over his flock, taking the instructions in the Book of Leviticus about dealing with lepers too literally by banning members suspected of 'sin' from meetings and contact with other Brethren. One member was even prevented from living with his wife and children for fifteen years.

The Aberdeen Brethren withdrew their support for Taylor and reported him to the sect's New York headquarters. The American office refused to investigate the allegations, for fear of antagonising Taylor's supporters in the various Exclusive Brethren communities. Many left the organisation but the matter was resolved that October when Taylor died. By then the Aberdeen dissidents had become the Strange-Walker Brethren, named after their new leaders.

→ The Plymouth Brethren, p. 241

Berwick

The bitter dispute over Charles I's decision to impose the English prayer book on Scotland in the 1630s led to the Bishops' Wars, in which the border town of Berwick – then in Scotland, now in England – played a significant role.

In spring 1639 King Charles assembled a ragtail army of 20,000 men in the north-east of England to invade Scotland. He received word that he could expect no help from his allies in Ireland and that he should delay his campaign. Indeed, at Berwick his badly prepared, disease-ridden, underfed troops came up against a better trained force under Alexander Leslie.

Realising that his campaign was falling apart, the king decided to accept the Scots' proposals for negotiations. Both sides agreed to disband their armies, and the king agreed to settle all disputed questions through Parliament or a General Assembly. The Bishops' War was cancelled after what was called 'the Pacification of Berwick'. It was the war that never happened.

An assembly in Edinburgh then declared that churchmen could not hold civil office and that the appointment of bishops was against God's laws. Charles was now placed in an impossible position. How could he rule as a constitutional monarch in one kingdom (Scotland) and as an absolute monarch in the other (England)? He returned to London, but immediately began planning a new campaign against the Scots.

Rather than waiting for Charles to attack first, his Scottish opponents (the Covenanters) staged a pre-emptive strike by crossing the border on 17 August 1640. The Scots swept into Newcastle, halting the supply of coal to London. But this, the Second Bishops' War, also fizzled out. The peace negotiations took place in Ripon that October although few were willing to take the king at his word. The Scots were allowed to keep their new northern territory, and with the signing of the Treaty of London in August 1641 Charles agreed to accept decisions taken by the Edinburgh Parliament and the Scots army withdrew from northern England. Nevertheless relations between the king and Parliament deteriorated so badly that the 1640s were dominated by the English Civil War which ended with Charles losing his head and the monarchy being (temporarily) abolished.

→ The Battle of the Boyne, p. 299

Edinburgh

EDINBURGH CASTLE, Johnston Terrace

The archly romantic castle is home to the Stone of Scone around which has been weaved one of the most unusual legends in British history. The block of stone is supposedly Jacob's pillow, the headrest the patriarch used in Genesis 28: 'And Jacob rose up early in the morning, and took the stone that he had put for his pillows, and set it up for a pillar, and poured oil upon the top of it.'

According to Kabbalist legend the stone contains the sapphire on which is written all knowledge: the knowledge that was, the knowledge that is, the knowledge that will be. It was brought to the British Isles in biblical times by the prophet Jeremiah, and later used at the coronation of Irish and Scottish kings. In 1296 Edward I of England seized the Stone of Scone and took it to Westminster Abbey.

On Christmas Day 1950 four Scottish students stole the stone and broke it in two looking for the golden sapphire (→ p. 263). After it was repaired in Glasgow, they finally left it on the altar of Arbroath Abbey. The stone was sent back to Westminster but then returned to the Scots in 1996 by Prime Minister John Major.

GREYFRIARS KIRK, Greyfriars Place

A group of Scottish Presbyterians (believers in an independent church) signed the National Covenant in the churchyard in 1638 outlining their opposition to a state-sponsored Church hierarchy and interference by the Stuart kings (based in London) in the Scottish Church, instead supporting a local Church run by elders. The Covenanters opposed the way that Charles I, who was then on the throne, saw himself as the spiritual head of the Church, and maintained that only Jesus Christ could be spiritual head of a Christian Church.

The Covenanters' uncompromising views resulted in much bloodshed in what came to be known as the Fifty Years' Struggle. During that time ministers who sympathised with their views were forced out of their congregations and had to preach at 'conventicles' in barns, something that was soon punishable by death. When Charles II took the throne after an eleven-year break from the monarchy following Charles I's execution, the reprisals were more severe. This spilled over into the Battle of Bothwell Bridge in Lanarkshire on 22 June 1679, caused by the king's insistence on introducing episcopacy – a Church run centrally by bishops. Around 1,200 prisoners were taken, 400 of whom were sent to Greyfriars. Here they were jailed for the winter on bread and water rations. They faced either execution or transportation overseas unless they renounced their independent views. Of those 250 men lucky enough to escape the gallows for the colonies nearly all drowned when their boat was wrecked off the Orkney Islands.

→ Charles I and the Bishops' War, p. 265

MERCAT CROSS, Royal Mile

In their excitement at hearing news of the 1688 Glorious Revolution Edinburgh students began dancing around the Mercat Cross, Edinburgh's traditional site for important proclamations, shouting: 'No Pope, No Papists.' They burnt an effigy of the pontiff at the cross on Christmas Day 1689. It was from here that Charles Edward Stuart, the Young Pretender, proclaimed – unsuccessfully it turned out – the (Catholic) Stuarts as rightful heirs to the British throne at the expense of the (Protestant) Hanoverians in 1745.

PALACE OF HOLYROODHOUSE, Horse Wynd

The ancient palace at the eastern end of the Royal Mile was home to the Scottish monarchs before the union of the crowns in 1603 and was central to the romance surrounding Mary, Queen of Scots, the Catholic alternative to Elizabeth I as England's monarch in the late sixteenth century.

Holyrood was founded as a monastery by the Scottish king David I in 1128 after he was attacked by a stag while hunting in the grounds. David supposedly saw a cross (or rood) between its antlers, reminiscent of the True Cross on which Jesus was crucified, part of which was supposedly in the possession of his mother, Queen Margaret. That night he had a dream in which a voice told him to build an Augustinian monastery on the spot where he had seen the stag. The monastery later became Holyrood Palace, the name an anglicisation of the Scots *Haly Ruid* (Holy Cross), the ruins of which remain in the grounds.

After Mary, Queen of Scots, broke the law by having Mass celebrated in the palace in August 1561, John Knox, Scotland's leading Protestant, complained from the pulpit of Edinburgh's main church, St Giles. The queen summoned Knox and accused him of inciting rebellion. He proposed a compromise as long as her subjects found her rule agreeable, he was willing to accept her governance – like the Christian pioneer Paul had done under the emperor Nero.

The most dramatic interview between Mary and Knox took place here on 24 June 1563. This time the queen summoned him after hearing that he had been preaching against her proposed marriage to the son of the King of Spain. Mary burst into tears, crying: 'What have ye to do with my marriage? What are ye within this commonwealth?' Knox replied: 'A subject born within the same, Madam,' and continued, 'in God's presence I speak: I never delighted in the weeping of any of God's creatures; yea I can scarcely well abide the tears of my own boys whom my own hand corrects, much less can I rejoice in your Majesty's weeping'. Mary sent him from the room.

The murder of David Rizzio, Mary's private secretary, by a group of noblemen took place in the palace's northern turret room on 9 March 1566. The noblemen had been hired by Mary's husband, Lord Darnley, who was jealous of Rizzio because rumours had swept Europe that the pregnant queen was having an adulterous affair with the Italian-born official. Although this was unlikely given his overt homosexuality, on that March day rebels overpowered the royal guards, burst into the supper chamber where Rizzio was with the queen, and demanded he be handed over. Mary refused, and the Italian hid behind the queen, who tried to protect him, but was herself threatened at gun point. Their hysterical screams were heard by locals, and several hundred men ran to the palace. With a gun at her back, the queen sent them away. Rizzio was then stabbed fifty-seven times and thrown down a staircase. He was buried two hours later in Holyrood cemetery.

The pregnant Mary escaped later that night by climbing out of the palace windows on knotted sheets and fled the city on horseback. She returned to Edinburgh triumphantly a few days later where with 8,000 troops who drove the rebels away, and honoured her late friend with a lavish funeral. Tourists are shown

Rizzio's alleged bloodstains on the floor of the palace room where he was killed.

In the grounds of the palace is Holyrood Abbey, where Charles I held his Scottish coronation in 1633. The king antagonised the Scots by bringing with him as adviser William Laud, the quasi-Catholic Archbishop of Canterbury. The service featured candles, crucifixes and genuflecting bishops. With ministers wearing surplices and the presbyteries threatened with dissolution, feelings ran high and the word 'popery' was on everyone's lips. Soon the Scots were yearning for the once unpopular policies of his father, James I, who had at least adopted a position of compromise between the Presbyterians (those who wanted rule by Church courts and a simple Puritan form of worship) and Episcopalians (those who liked being part of a Church with bishops and a hierarchy).

Charles II rebuilt the complex in the 1670s. His brother, the unfortunate James, Duke of York, took refuge here during the debates about his suitability to rule Britain as James II. (He was a Catholic and therefore unacceptable to most English people.) In 1689, after the accession of his successor, William of Orange, an anti-papist mob sacked the palace's Jesuit seminary and threw heaps of beads, crucifixes and pictures into the street outside, which they then set fire to.

→ Durham Cathedral, p. 195

PARLIAMENT HOUSE, Royal Mile

The Scottish Parliament building witnessed innumerable religious debates in the late medieval period. In 1525 the Scottish Parliament banned Lutheran, i. e. Protestant, books from the country and the preaching of Lutheran ideas. Rome even sent a papal envoy to the Scottish court to urge the king (James V) to stand firm in defence of the Church. It was mostly in vain. Protestant ideas were soon circulating, and Patrick Hamilton, abbot of Ferne, was the main instigator. He was arrested, tried for heresy, and executed in 1528. Nevertheless Scotland soon turned Protestant.

Parliament met here in August 1560 to discuss religious issues at the height of the turmoil in Scotland over the Reformation. John Knox and five other ministers were called upon to draw up a new confession of faith. A week later Parliament abolished the jurisdiction of the Pope, condemned all policies opposed to the reformed faith, and forbade the celebration of Mass. Knox and his followers were told to reform the Church through a Book of Discipline. From now on the Kirk would be run on democratic lines. Congregations could choose their own pastor, whom they could not then fire, and each parish would be self-supporting. One figure who refused to obey the order about Mass was Mary, Queen of Scots, who celebrated it at Holyrood on 24 August 1561.

The Scottish Parliament was abolished with the Act of Union of 1707, although it has recently been reinstated.

→ Houses of Parliament, Westminster, p. 81

ST GILES'S CATHEDRAL, Royal Mile

A riot in 1637 marked Charles I's plan to impose the English Book of Common Prayer on the Scots alongside the full liturgy and structure of the Church of England. On the morning of Sunday 23 July, the day the king had chosen for the introduction of the new prayer book, crowds gathered at St Giles wondering what would happen. When the dean entered, wearing a white robe instead of the black one in which the Scottish clergy usually preached, tension rose. As the dean began the service he was drowned out by the noise of protest. Missiles were thrown, including a stool (now safely stored in the National Museum of Scotland) hurled by a Jenny Geddes, who shouted: 'Thou false thief, wilt thou say Mass at my ear?', while others in the congregation began to cry out: 'The Mass! The Mass! Popery! Popery! Down with the Pope! Down with him!'

Some women rushed at the dean and tore the white surplice from his shoulders. Members of the Privy Council fled to Holyroodhouse, where they barricaded themselves to evade the mob. Back in St Giles the Bishop of Brechin conducted the service with a pair of loaded pistols next to him but his protestations against the violence were not enough to calm the crowd. Eventually, soldiers threw out the rioters, and outside the church the mob continued jeering and banging on the doors. The bishop escaped with his life only by being escorted out of St Giles by a guard of soldiers.

Thousands of Scots signed a petition, the National Covenant, in favour of religious freedom. King Charles was unimpressed and called for the petitioners to be dispersed and punished. In February 1638 he issued a proclamation, read in public in Edinburgh, ordering the nobles who were resisting the prayer book to submit to his will. The conflict turned to war – the Bishops' Wars – in 1639. Charles eventually lost and was forced to withdraw the Prayer book.

→ The Bishops' Wars, p. 265

Iona

Christianity arrived in Scotland when St Columba and twelve companions landed on the Hebridean isle of Iona in the year 563. Columba sought penitence for the guilt he felt at starting a war in Ireland, and founded an abbey at a site that lay on the border between the Christian Scots and Pagan Picts. The monastery developed into one of Europe's greatest libraries. The island became a major pilgrimage site and the burial place for the kings of Scotland, Ireland and Norway. In recent years it has been a leading centre of the revival in proto-Christian Scottish spirituality.

Irvine

Elspeth Buchan, a Scottish woman in her forties, declared herself in 1783 to be the 'woman clothed with the sun' of the biblical Book of Revelation and claimed immortality. In this Ayrshire town she founded a group she called the Buchanites, who, according to local rumour, were soon taking part in orgies in the woods with a 'community of wives'. The town authorities expelled the Buchanites from Irvine, as did those running various other Scottish towns they tried to take refuge in, which forced them to head for Templand Hill in Dumfriesshire, where in July 1786 they built a platform on which they stood wailing and singing awaiting transfer to heaven . . . in vain.

The famous Scottish poet Robert Burns, dismissed them for promoting a 'strange jumble of enthusiastic jargon . . . [Buchan] pretends to give them the Holy Ghost by breathing on them, which she does with postures & practices that are scandalously indecent, they have likewise disposed of all life, carrying on a great farce of pretended devotion in barns, & woods, where they lodge and lye all together'. Elspeth Buchan died in 1791, thereby at a stroke ruining her claims of immortality.

→ The Peculiar People of Plumstead, p. 64

Perth

The Five Articles of Perth were a set of commands drawn up by James I in 1618 to force the Scots to worship in the English manner. They ordered kneeling during communion, private baptism, private communion for the sick or infirm, confirmation by a bishop and the observance of Holy Days such as Christmas, Good Friday, Easter, Ascension and Whit Sunday. The Scottish

Parliament ratified the Articles in 1621 despite vehement opposition from Protestants who regarded them as an attempt to make the Scottish Church more Catholic. In 1638 the General Assembly of the Kirk threw the Articles out.

The Battle of Sheriffmuir was an attempt by the Earl of Mar in 1715 to take Perth for the Catholic Jacobites and eventually wrest the British throne from the Protestant Hanoverians. Although the Jacobites had considerably more men, the battle was inconclusive. Nevertheless both sides claimed victory, as Robert Burns noted in his song named after the battle. Regardless of who really won the Jacobites failed to take the throne for James Stuart, son of the deposed James II.

→ Was James Stuart royal at all? p. 95

ST JOHN THE BAPTIST

Declared an outlaw in Dundee during the fierce battles over early Protestantism, John Knox, the leading reformer in sixteenth-century Scotland, fled in 1559 to Perth, a walled town that could be defended from a siege. Here Knox preached a furious sermon against idolatry which led to a riot when a mob stormed the church. In the fracas the building was destroyed and the mob then left to storm two local friaries which they looted for gold and silver. After that St John's ceased to be a Catholic church.

Roslin

ROSSLYN CHAPEL, Chapel Loan

Since the publication of the Dan Brown fantasy *The Da Vinci Code* in 2003 tens of thousands of curious visitors have come to the fifteenth-century chapel, located seven miles from Edinburgh, to look for secret messages on the chapel walls regarding the Holy

Grail, the cup Jesus drank from at the Last Supper. Rosslyn's connections with the Grail stem from its role as a place of worship for the long defunct Knights Templar, medieval warrior monks who protected those making pilgrimages to the Holy Land, and who may have inherited a number of biblical treasures before they were (officially) disbanded by the Pope in 1312. The chapel's Apprentice Pillar has drawings of Joseph of Arimathea, who may have been Jesus' uncle, holding the Grail, and some devotees even believe that the Grail itself lies within the masonry. Metal detectors have indicated that an object of the right size is inside, but the Earl of Rosslyn who owns the chapel refuses to allow the pillar to be X-rayed.

→ Canonbury Tower, p. 8

St Andrews

Protestant zealots smashed the churches of St Andrews in 1560, stripping the altars, destroying the icons and whitewashing the walls in an attack on Catholic excess. The iconoclasts were annoyed at the treatment meted out to George Wishart, a Protestant preacher who in 1546 had been imprisoned in the dungeon of St Andrews Castle and accused of heresy. At his trial Wishart refused to accept that confession was a sacrament (a rite in which God is present) and rejected the idea that the infinite God could be 'comprehended in one place between the priest's hands'. He announced that the true Church was where the Word of God was faithfully preached, and was burnt at the stake for his pains. A few weeks later Wishart's friends sneaked into the castle, sought out the cardinal who had condemned Wishart, killed him and hung his body from the battlements.

Sanquhar

The Revd Richard Cameron, accompanied by twenty armed men, marched into this Dumfries market town on 22 June 1680 and fixed to the village cross a declaration disowning Charles II, who was too Catholic for their liking, as king. After singing the Psalms of David they read a speech called the 'Sanquhar Declaration':

. . . *We, being under the standard of our Lord Jesus Christ, Captain of Salvation, do declare a war with such a tyrant and usurper [Charles II], and all the men of his practices, as enemies to our Lord Jesus Christ, and His cause and covenants; and against all such as have strengthened him, sided with, or anywise acknowledged him in his tyranny, civil or ecclesiastic; yea, against all such as shall strengthen, side with, or anywise acknowledge any other in like usurpation and tyranny . . . Also we disown the Duke of York, that professed Papist, as repugnant to our principles and vows to the Most High God.*

It was in effect a declaration of war and paved the way for public opposition to the Stuarts in the Glorious Revolution of the late seventeenth century that certified Protestant ascendancy.

CHAPTER 9

WALES

The principality has always always enjoyed a reputation for Nonconformism, manifested in the ubiquitous 'chapel'. This independent stance stems mostly from Wales's geographical location. Being separated from England by major physical boundaries, if not sea, its inhabitants have zealously defended its language and culture from foreign influence.

The Welsh regarded the Church of England as a body unconcerned with Welsh needs and too closely associated with the landed gentry. A strong tradition of preaching in Wales saw eighteenth-century figures such as William Williams, Daniel Rowland, and Howell Harris spread the gospel from town to town at excited gatherings, to the alarm of the establishment. The early nineteenth century was the key period of expansion for Welsh Nonconformism, with one chapel built every eight days. Later generations mused that since the established church represented only a minority of the Welsh, it shouldn't enjoy the power of the state and take tithe payments from the masses. Hence it was no surprise when in 1914 the Anglican Church in Wales separated from the Church of England.

Key events

1530s **Rowland Lee, Bishop of Coventry and Lichfield, carries out a particularly bloodthirsty attack on Welsh rebels, hanging some 500 men.**

1649 **John Miles founds Wales's first Baptist congregation at Ilston, Gower. Many such chapels are soon built across south Wales.**

1740 **The mob murders Methodist preacher William Seward in Hay-on-Wye. He is the sect's first martyr.**

1881 **Thanks to pressure from the chapels the Sunday Closing Act is passed outlawing pubs in Wales from opening on Sundays.**

1914 **The Welsh Church Act sees the Anglican Church in Wales separate from the Church of England.**

1920 **The Welsh church is at last allowed to elect its own bishops.**

Carmarthen

Robert Ferrar, Bishop of St David's, was burnt at the stake in Carmarthen on 30 March 1555 at the height of the anti-Protestant executions, dying, he claimed, as a 'true bearer of the cross of Christ'. Appointed during the Protestant Edward VI's reign, Ferrar fell out of favour after the accession of the Catholic queen, Mary Tudor. He was indicted on fifty-six counts, including 'abuse of authority' and 'maintenance of superstition contrary to the King's ordinances and injunctions'. During his ordeal Ferrar never moved except to hold up his burnt hands – that was until one of the prosecuting officers hit him on the head with his staff, killing him.

→ Mary Tudor burns the Protestants, p. 19

Hay-on-Wye

William Seward, a mid-eighteenth-century preacher, became the Methodists' first martyr when he was murdered by a mob in the border village of Hay on 22 October 1740. Seward had just returned from a tour of America, but encountered more hostile crowds in South Wales. 'Before he died,' claimed the Methodist historian Elmer T. Clark, 'he prayed for his murderer and begged that no attempt should be made to punish him.'

Llandaff

After a hearing before the Bishop of Llandaff in 1555, Rawlins White, a fisherman, was charged with heresy, which eventually led to his execution. White's crime had been to meet secretly with friends to read the Bible during the years of Catholic fundamentalism that marked the reign of Mary Tudor. The bishop told White that if he repented of his crimes against God, the authorities would show him mercy. If not, the law would be applied most rigorously.

As White considered himself to be a Christian and believed in the Scriptures, he felt he had done no wrong and asked his captors to show him which part of the Bible condemned his actions. They were not persuaded by this argument and put him in Cardiff jail until the warrant for his execution in London arrived.

On being brought out of prison White was shocked to find he was to be escorted by a group of soldiers. 'What meaneth this? Soldiers are not needed. By God's grace I will not run away. With all my heart I give Him thanks that I am considered worthy to bear all this for His name's sake.' He went to the stake with carefree spirit, fell down upon his knees, and recited the words: 'Earth unto earth, and dust unto dust; thou art my mother, and unto thee I shall return.'

Llandysul

The west Wales village was the birthplace of one of the most important preachers and religious pioneers in Welsh history: Christmas Evans (1766–1835). Evans not only had an unforgettable name, he had an unforgettable appearance, having lost an eye in a fight. He became a Baptist minister and missionary, and helped lead a revival in religious feeling that gave rise to an enormous chapel-building programme in Wales, from village to village. One new chapel was built every eight days towards the end of the eighteenth century, their combined seating capacity exceeding the principality's population, according to some irreverent commentators. Because of Wales's traditional independent streak, it is the chapel form of worship in small congregations rather than the hierarchical Anglican model that has stayed strong.

Wrexham

Richard Gwyn, a teacher, was hanged, drawn and quartered in Wrexham's Beast Market on 15 October 1584 for high treason (being a Catholic). Three years earlier he had been taken to a local church, carried around on the shoulders of six men and put in shackles by the pulpit. Gwyn was then placed in the stocks and taunted by an Anglican priest who explained how the keys of the Church were given as much to him as they had been to St Peter. Gwyn replied: 'But when Peter received the keys to the Kingdom of Heaven, the keys you received were obviously those of the beer cellar.' He was fined £280 for refusing to attend Anglican services but refused to pay. This led to a spell in prison and torture during which he never lost his faith.

Just before he was executed, Gwyn addressed the crowd. 'I have been a jesting fellow, and if I have offended any that way, or by my songs, I beseech them for God's sake to forgive me.' The hangman then kindly pulled on Gwyn's leg irons to relieve his ordeal and hasten his death. But he was still conscious as he was disembowelled, expiring only when his head was cut off. Gwyn's last words were in Welsh 'Iesu, trugarha wrthyf' (Jesus, have mercy on me). He was beatified in 1929 and canonised in 1970.

CHAPTER 10

NORTHERN IRELAND

The history of Northern Ireland is one of religious violence. Indeed the sole purpose of the British state in 1920 in creating the province was to secure a Protestant majority in Ulster, whose borders roughly coincide with Northern Ireland's.

That Protestant majority was not the result of religious choice but of colonisation. Although Ireland has long enjoyed a Catholic majority, Ulster was settled early in the seventeenth century by immigrant Scottish Presbyterians promoted by James I, and the province has since proclaimed a Protestant identity that clashes with the religious views of the rest of Ireland.

Hopes that the new Northern Ireland of the twentiethth century would be a land of peace and progress were naïve. Before long there was sectarian conflict in which nearly 500 people died. Even after the violence abated an undercurrent of tension remained. Protestants feared that the Catholic community would eventually outnumber and outmanoeuvre them, while the Catholics in the North continually complained that they were being discriminated against over jobs and housing, and would continue being so while living in a Protestant statelet.

The worst sectarian and religious violence took place at the end of the twentieth century in what is usually referred to as 'the Troubles' – three decades of mostly Catholic nationalist agitation against the Protestant establishment with army occupation from England, often spilling over into assassination and terrorism.

Various political measures enacted since the resignation of Margaret Thatcher as prime minister in 1990 have seen a decline in violence, if not a solution to the long-standing religious antagonism.

Key events

445 **St Patrick converts Ireland to Christianity in Armagh, the site now covered by St Patrick's Cathedral.**

1688–9 **In the Siege of Derry local Protestants prevent Catholics from breaching the city walls. It goes down as one of the most dramatic conflicts in British history.**

1795 **Protestant rebels kill thirty Catholics in Loughall at the Battle of the Diamond. The victors form the Orange Order in celebration.**

1922 **Northern Ireland exercises its right under the Anglo-Irish Treaty to opt out of the new Irish dominion and remain in the United Kingdom to protect the contrived Protestant majority within its borders.**

1934 **Lord Craigavon, Northern Ireland's first prime minister, tells the province: 'We are a Protestant parliament and a Protestant state. I am an Orangeman first and a member of this parliament afterwards.'**

1966 **The Troubles that have blackened Ulster history over the last forty-plus years are sparked off on Belfast's Shankill Road by the start of the Loyalist UVF (Ulster Volunteer Force)**

paramilitary group's campaign of intimidation against local Catholics.

1969 The British government sends the army into Ulster to protect the civil rights of the beleaguered Catholic population.

1969 The Cupar Street Peace Line separating the Catholic and Protestant communities is built in Belfast of iron, brick and steel with walls up to 25 foot high.

1969 Religious violence once again breaks out in Londonderry, this time in the Battle of the Bogside.

2007 In a shock U-turn the fundamentalist Protestant preacher and politician the Revd Ian Paisley agrees to go into government with the leading nationalist Martin McGuinness of Sinn Fein. Paisley is vehemently opposed at his own Martyrs Memorial Church in Belfast.

Armagh

ST PATRICK'S CATHEDRAL, **Cathedral Close**

The Church of Ireland cathedral is named after the patron saint of Ireland who converted the inhabitants to Christianity and built a church on this site in 445. The entire Patrick story is, however, based on unsustainable myth, created to make an insignificant missionary appear divine so that he could compete with pagan gods. The legend is ruined by the way the saint is always shown dressed in the clothes of a seventeenth-century bishop, vestments he could never have worn, and dates back to a twelfth-century monk called Jocelyn. He wrote a biography of Patrick in 1185 in which he invented the claim that the saint had rid Ireland of snakes even though two centuries before Patrick came to the country the Roman writer Solinus noted the absence of snakes on the island.

The Vikings raided Armagh ten times between 832 and 943, and the church was almost destroyed by lightning in 995, remaining a ruin until 1125. The warlord Shane 'the Proud' O' Neill burnt down the cathedral in 1556 'lest the English should again lodge in it'. It has since been rebuilt.

Belfast

No city in the British Isles has been as torn apart by religious conflict as Belfast, where life during the twentieth century was marred by eternal conflict between Protestant forces loyal to the British throne and the mostly Catholic nationalists aiming for that political impossibility, a united (socialist) Ireland.

Nineteenth-century industrialisation made Belfast a major city. Catholics settled in the west, parts of the north and the market area to the south, while Protestants took the east. The partition of Ireland by the British government in 1920–21 worsened conflict between the two main strains of Christianity. Often the authorities were to blame for increasing tension. Lord Craigavon, Northern Ireland's first prime minister, fanned the flames of religious unrest in 1934 when he announced: 'We are a Protestant parliament and a Protestant state. I am an Orangeman (→ p. 283) first and a member of this parliament afterwards.'

Violence erupted when an Orange (Protestant) Parade marched through a Catholic area in 1935. A fifteen-year-old girl was shot on her way from Mass, Catholics were attacked as they came home from work, and a Catholic publican was gunned down. Catholics were expelled from the shipyards and mills. In all some 2,000 Catholics were burnt out of their homes. The

Protestant Bishop of Down urged Orangemen to ignore 'old feuds, triumphs and humiliations', but the Orange Grand Master retorted: 'Are we to forget that the aim of these people is to establish an all-Ireland Roman Catholic state, in which Protestantism will be crushed out of existence?' – a response typical of the continuing imbroglio.

Conflict intensified in Belfast in the late 1960s in what became known as the Troubles. When the Troubles began some Catholics (with the help of the nationalists' terrorist wing, the IRA) burnt their own homes rather than let someone else burn them down. When the nationalists protested against being denied their civil rights, the mainly Protestant Royal Ulster Constabulary launched a clampdown that led to a state of attrition which stopped just short of outright civil war and lasted for the rest of the century.

Although the British government sent the army into Ulster in 1969 to protect the beleaguered Catholic population, those very forces soon came to be seen as the enemy, and were targeted accordingly. Even in 1985, a relatively quiet year, there were 54 assassinations, 148 bombings, 237 shootings, 916 woundings, 522 arrests on terrorism charges, 31 kneecappings and 3.3 tons of explosives and weapons were seized. And that in a country with a population of just around 1.5 million people.

Trouble ebbs and flows. While in the twenty-first century relations have improved, shops on the Shankill Road still pay protection money to Protestant paramilitary groups. As long as Northern Ireland and the Republic of Ireland retain their extreme religious stances the prospect of a return to hostilities always looms.

CUPAR STREET

The religious divisions in Belfast have geographical boundaries. There are some thirty peace lines – borders between Protestants and Catholics – in Belfast. Of these, one of the most famous is by

Cupar Street, a frontier between the two factions since 1969, with barriers of iron, brick and steel, and walls up to 25 foot high. To the south is the Falls Road, a working-class Catholic district of two-storey nineteenth-century houses, built for linen-mill workers. It is an area plagued by lawbreaking, where most homes have been burgled and the post office is regularly robbed. To the north is the Protestant neighbourhood around Shankill Road, where the houses are roomier and more spaced out.

→ The Battle of Bogside, p. 292

FALLS ROAD

One of the most infamous residential areas in the world, Falls Road has been bedevilled by near incessant violence fuelled by religious bigotry since the Troubles began in the late 1960s. When British troops first appeared on the Catholic Falls Road after the riots of August 1969 they were welcomed by Catholics living in fear of Protestant attacks. But because of the imposed curfews and army raids for IRA weapons, it wasn't long before the Catholics felt intimidated by the army, which it saw as the embodiment of their Protestant tormentors.

→ The Gordon Riots, p. 4

MARTYRS MEMORIAL CHURCH, Ravenhill Road

Ian Paisley, the most infamous religious (and political) figure in Northern Ireland since the Second World War, has been minister at the Martyrs Memorial Church since 1969, chief place of worship for the religious group he founded, the Free Presbyterian Church, which now has around sixty congregations.

In his heyday Paisley preached here three times a week. A typical speech would have him thunder:

Oh God, save Ulster from popery!
Oh God, save Ulster from apostasy!
Oh God, save Ulster from going into an Irish Republic.

Paisley has long denied fuelling sectarian hatred. 'I dislike the Roman Catholic religion, I make no secret of that. But I've never had any spite against individual Roman Catholics.' He 'found Christ', as he told the *Sunday Tribune* in 2007, when in 1932 at the age of six he heard his mother preaching in his father's church about the lost sheep. In his teens Paisley would rise at 4 a. m. to read the Bible, and still reads the Scriptures all the way through three times a year. 'It can't be rushed, it has to be meditated upon. It's a great book for challenging a man. It cracks open every egg and puts the knife through all hypocrisy,' he also told the *Sunday Tribune.*

In the 1960s Paisley campaigned against Northern Ireland's Prime Minister Terence O'Neill holding talks with the Irish Republic's Taoiseach, Sean Lemass. Throughout the Troubles he refused to have any contact with the Irish government. Even as late as July 2006 Paisley insisted that loyalists and republicans would share government only 'over his dead body'. Which is why it came as such a shock when he eventually agreed to go into government with the leading nationalist Martin McGuinness of Sinn Fein.

After this remarkable U-turn, hardliners in the Church threatened to oppose Paisley's re-election as Moderator. In September 2007 outside the Martyrs Memorial opponents handed out leaflets condemning his decision. 'Ian Paisley's own words stand as a condemnation to him. He is guilty of all that he accused others of being guilty of. There's only one thing left for Ian Paisley to do: repent.'

The following Sunday Paisley told the Martyrs Memorial congregation that he had agreed to stand down because his church was facing a 'very real crisis. While I am no longer going to carry the weight which I have carried for over fifty-six years as moderator of our presbytery, I have news for you. I will be here and I am praying to God that I will be able to preach right to the end of my days.'

→ Riots at St Giles Cathedral, Edinburgh, p. 262

ST MATTHEW'S, Bryson Street

An eight-hour gun battle between loyalists and nationalists took place at this Catholic church on 27 June 1970. It began when loyalists raided the nearby Catholic Short Strand area, convincing locals that they were going to be burnt out of their homes. Without any troops to protect them, Catholics took up sniper positions in the grounds of the church, defending the building in what turned out to be the biggest conflict of the Troubles to date.

Seven people were killed during the shootout: two Catholics, five Protestants.

In the following week around 500 Catholic workers at the Harland and Wolff shipyard were forced out of their jobs, and riots spread throughout Belfast as troops searched the Falls Road area to recover paramilitary weapons. That July Home Secretary Reggie Maudling visited the province. As his flight took off, he infamously exclaimed: 'For God's sake bring me a large Scotch. What a bloody awful country!'

SHANKILL ROAD

The best-known Protestant stronghold in Belfast, lined with chilling loyalist murals which are now about to be painted over, was where the late twentieth-century Troubles began in May 1966. It was then that the Loyalist UVF (Ulster Volunteer Force) Protestant paramilitary group embarked on a campaign of intimidation against local Catholics. They painted sectarian graffiti on houses and threw a petrol bomb through the window of one property, killing a 77-year-old Protestant woman. The UVF then issued a statement:

From this day, we declare war against the IRA and its splinter groups. Known IRA men will be executed mercilessly and without hesitation. Less extreme measures will be taken against anyone sheltering or helping them, but if they persist in giving them aid, then more extreme methods will be adopted . . . we solemnly warn the authorities to make no more speeches of appeasement. We are heavily armed Protestants dedicated to this cause.

A UVF group calling themselves the Shankill Butchers began to carry out late-night abductions, torture and murders of random Catholics. Although many of the gang's rank and file members were caught and received some of the lengthiest prison sentences in British legal history, the Butchers' leader, Lenny Murphy, evaded prosecution until November 1982, when he was murdered by the IRA, probably acting in unison with loyalist paramilitaries who saw him as an uncontrollable threat.

Carrickfergus

On the shore of Belfast Lough, about eight miles from the capital, is Carrickfergus, once Ulster's main port. It was here that the Dutchman William of Orange, the new Protestant British king, invited by the London establishment to replace the Catholic James II, stepped ashore on 14 June 1690 to quell Irish support for James. William was received with much acclaim and set off to wage war with the ousted monarch, which culminated at the Battle of the Boyne. The Dutch prince triumphed there, as enshrined since in Protestant mythology. Ironically, many of William's soldiers were Catholic and he had no lasting interest in Irish politics, simply using the war in Ireland as a means to achieve his wider ambitions.

Chapter 10

Derry/Londonderry

The Ulster city with the strangely anglicised name was the setting for one of Ulster's bitterest conflicts, the 1688–9 Siege of Derry, when local Protestants prevented Catholics from breaching the city walls.

Westminster had long targeted the city, one of the biggest in Ulster, and one of the few major places in the British Isles it didn't control. After several partly successful putsches, the early seventeenth-century king, James I, devised a new strategy. With the help of the London trades guilds, he sent English and Scottish migrants, mostly Protestant and loyal to the throne, to colonise the area. The success of the mission saw the city name prefixed with that of the English capital.

The new Londonderry was given a modern layout and solid walls. Indeed, it was the last city in the British Isles to be encircled with defensive walls, fortifications which, rare for Europe, have never been breached – though not for want of trying. When the Catholic king of Britain, James II, was in danger of losing the throne in the 1680s because of his religious views, his viceroy in Ireland, Richard Talbot, wanted to ensure that all major locations were held by garrisons loyal to the king. Derry had one of the few wavering garrisons in Ireland, and so in the autumn of 1688 James ordered the Earl of Antrim to replace it with a more reliable force.

The elderly earl wanted recruits who were six feet tall, but it cost him much time to find them. Eventually he and around 1,200 men, the Redshanks, marched on the city and its mostly Protestant population. The Bishop of Londonderry urged the inhabitants to submit, but he was outvoted. Thirteen apprentice boys seized the city keys and on 7 December 1688, amid cries of 'No Surrender', raised the bridge and locked the gates in defiance of the oncoming army. This earned them a permanent place in Irish politico-religious mythology as the Apprentice Boys, symbol of Protestant fortitude against Catholic imperialism.

James fled Britain at the end of December but, hoping to win back the throne, arrived in Ireland in April. He expected an easy victory over William, who was preoccupied with war against France, and soon only Londonderry and Enniskillen had not fallen to James's Jacobites. But when his forces tried to regain the city the local people stayed firm. The Siege of Derry lasted 105 days, during which the inhabitants were reduced to eating rats, cats and candle grease. By the time the city was relieved by ships bringing much needed supplies of food, around 9,000 people had died.

Nearly 300 years later Derry was rent asunder by another religiously inspired bout of violence – the Battle of the Bogside. It took place in August 1969 after the Protestant Royal Ulster Constabulary attempted to disperse nationalists demonstrating against the annual loyalist (Protestant) Apprentice Boys' parade along the city walls.

The riot sparked widespread mayhem throughout Northern Ireland which indirectly led to the Troubles that marred the last decades of the twentieth century. The annual Apprentice Boys' march is often beset by clashes between loyalists and nationalists (mostly Catholics) who now enjoy a 70/30 percentage majority in the city.

Loughall

THE BATTLE OF THE DIAMOND

Attacks by Protestant settlers from Scotland on Ulster Catholics at the end of the eighteenth century culminated on 21 September 1795 in what became known as the Battle of the Diamond. The battle was named after the crossroads at Loughall where the Protestant Peep O'Day Boys (so named because they would usually attack at the break of day) killed about thirty Catholics.

The victorious Protestants celebrated by daubing copious graffiti on surrounding properties threatening 'To hell or Connaught' – hell supposedly being preferable to inhospitable Connaught in western Ireland. They would then destroy the houses.

The Orange Order

Celebrations held in a Loughall inn following the 1795 Battle of the Diamond resulted in the victorious Protestants forming the Orange Order, one of the world's most infamous religious clubs. Its orange is that of William of Orange, the Protestant Dutch prince who became king of England in 1688 when James II was forced out, and its aims are to promote 'Biblical Protestantism' and the principles of the Reformation.

Fired up by propaganda warning that the Catholics were plotting against them, the Orangemen went on the rampage after the Battle of the Diamond, forcing as many as 7,000 Catholics from their homes in the so-called Armagh Outrages.

Lord Gosford, Governor of Armagh, was not enthusiastic about the new group. 'It is no secret that a persecution is now raging in this country . . . the only crime is . . . profession of the Roman Catholic faith. Lawless banditti have constituted themselves judges . . .' Yet the government soon began to give tacit backing to the Orange Order. As Thomas Knox, British military commander in Ulster, explained in 1796: 'We must to a certain degree uphold them, for with all their licentiousness, on them we must rely for the preservation of our lives and properties should critical times occur.'

In 1823 the Unlawful Oaths Bill outlawed societies like the Orange Order. It was quickly dissolved, but soon reconstituted. Two years later another bill banned unlawful associations and compelled the Orangemen to dissolve their association once again. When Westminster passed Catholic Emancipation in 1829 the Orange Order reappeared, more militant and strident than ever. By the end of the century it was again in decline, but received a fillip from the moves for Home Rule – that the Irish should be allowed to run Ireland – for that convinced some Protestants that they would soon be at the mercy of a Catholic majority.

The Orange Order continued to prosper throughout the late twentieth-century Troubles, mostly as a Protestant fraternal society, more sectarian than the Masons, almost as outlandishly dressed with their umbrellas and bowlers, and highly visible around the time of their annual marches which culminate in the 12 July celebrations of the Battle of the Boyne (→ p. 299). There are Orange lodges in British cities with a history of sizeable Catholic immigrant populations such as Glasgow, Liverpool and Manchester.

Portadown

GARVAGHY ROAD

Although Portadown is mostly Protestant, the area around the Garvaghy Road is Catholic and a regular target for the fundamentalist Protestant Orange Order. In 1996 during the July marching season the order staged a sit-down in the road, insisting it was their right to march here. Locals insisted that with equal vehemence that it was their right not to be subjected to intimidating marches. This impasse reoccurs regularly and usually leads to violence between the Orangemen and the police, itself Protestant-run, in the nearby fields.

• Local road signs, with some degree of sarcasm, read: 'No Talking. No Walking.'

CHAPTER 11

THE REPUBLIC OF IRELAND

The borders given to the new republic created by Westminster in 1922 were chosen with the certainty that they would encompass a Catholic majority, something which shows no sign of changing. Since the free state's founding there has been negligible religious and political violence in this part of Ireland, especially when compared with the North (see above), but this simply masks the bloody centuries of conflict in the greater part of Ireland that have accompanied attempts by the British forces to forcibly carry out Westminster's wishes, resulting in what the nineteenth-century historian Thomas Carlyle called 'a scene of distracted controversies, plunderings, excommunications, treacheries, conflagrations, of universal misery and blood and bluster'.

Key events

432 **St Patrick converts King Aengus to Christianity at the Rock of Cashel.**

1641 **The Catholic-led Irish Rebellion spreads across the country until it is brutally suppressed by Oliver Cromwell.**

1690 **William III's forces beat off the challenge of the outgoing British king, James II, at the Battle of the Boyne.**

1703 **The Popery Act 1703 rules that when a Catholic dies his estate must be divided equally among his sons unless the eldest converts to Protestantism.**

1829 **Catholic emancipation is achieved following pressure from Daniel O'Connell's Catholic Association.**

1879 **Fifteen people see a vision of the Virgin Mary, St Joseph and St John the Evangelist at their parish church in Knock – now known as the Marian Shrine.**

1919 **Seventy-three Irish MPs representing the mostly Catholic Sinn Fein party refuse to take their seats in Westminster and set up their own Irish Parliament.**

1919–21 **The Irish War of Independence ends with the South forming the mostly Catholic Irish Free State – the Republic of Ireland from 1948.**

Cashel

ROCK OF CASHEL, Rock Road

A collection of medieval buildings, the traditional seat of the kings of Munster, it is where St Patrick is believed to have converted King Aengus to Christianity in 432. During the conversion the devil supposedly flew over Ireland, took a bite of the Slieve Bloom mountains, and spat it out to form the rock.

Chapter 11

County Clare

With the Reformation of the 1530s, the British clamped down on Catholicism in Ireland. Early in the seventeenth century James I seized land in Ulster from Catholics and handed it to incoming Protestants from Britain. The evicted Catholics struggled to survive in the surrounding hills. Catholics were barred from holding public office and serving in the army, and were fined for failing to attend Protestant services. Revolt spread across Ireland, which boiled over into the Irish Rebellion of 1641, brutally suppressed by the Lord Protector, Oliver Cromwell, in the 1650s.

Under Cromwell Catholic clergy were expelled from the country so worship took place in secrecy. With the restoration of the monarchy in 1660 many of the most extreme laws were rescinded. However, the Popery Act 1703 that followed on from the Protestant Glorious Revolution ruled that when a Catholic died his estate had to be divided equally among his sons – unless the eldest converted to Protestantism, in which case he could inherit all the land. This was aimed at reducing the size and influence of Catholic estates. And Protestants couldn't convert to Catholicism without forfeiting all their property.

The calls for civil rights for Catholics grew in the late eighteenth century despite the collapse of the (Catholic) Stuarts' attempts to regain the British throne. With few concrete improvements in place by the early nineteenth century, in 1823. Daniel O'Connell, a barrister, set up the Catholic Association, a pressure group to counteract discrimination against Catholics. Members paid a 'Catholic rent' of a penny a month, collected after Mass on Sunday. Two years later the society was declared illegal, such was its popularity. O'Connell won the County Clare seat at the British general election of 1828 but was unable to take it as Catholics were not allowed to sit in Parliament at the time. The following year the British government conceded defeat and granted Catholic emancipation.

→Anti-Catholic laws passed at Westminster, p. 301

Drogheda

One of the largest towns in Ireland, Drogheda was the setting for two major incidents of Irish history. In 1649 it was here that Oliver Cromwell first began imposing his Draconian anti-Catholic measures. Just over fifty years later it was the setting for the Battle of the Boyne at which the deposed Catholic king of Britain, James II, lost a decisive battle to win back the throne.

After ridding Britain of the unpopular King Charles I, who was executed in January 1649, Oliver Cromwell became Lord Lieutenant and commander of the forces in Ireland. He arrived in Dublin in August 1649 with 9,000 men, aiming to capture royalist towns still loyal to the monarchy. Tempering his blood lust, he ordered his soldiers not to 'abuse, rob and pillage, and execute cruelties upon the Country People'. But he was also considering ways of exacting reprisals on the Catholics for massacring some 5,000 Ulster Protestants in 1641. For a decade Catholics had been enjoying freedom, but back in London sensationalist newspaper reports were alarming Protestants with stories of how papists were 'deflowering many of the women, then cruelly murdering them and pulling them about the street by the haire of the head and dashing their children's brains out'.

In September 1649 Cromwell marched on Drogheda. He sent a summons to the governor in which he outlined how 'to the end effusion of blood may be prevented, [but] I thought fit to summon you to deliver the same into my hands to their use. If this be refused you will have no cause to blame me.' When

Governor Ashton failed to respond, Cromwell's troops broke through and destroyed the steeple of St Mary's church. They then massacred people indiscriminately – all in the name of beating down Catholicism. As the Marquis of Ormonde, army commander-in-chief in Ireland, wrote to Lord Byron: 'Cromwell exceeded himself more than anything I ever heard of in breaking faith and bloody inhumanity; the cruelties exercised there for five days after the town was taken would make as many several pictures of inhumanity as are to be found in the Book of Martyrs.'

Cromwell's own soldiers railed against killing prisoners who had surrendered, but England's new ruler later explained that 'It was set upon some of our hearts, that a great thing should be done, not by power or might, but by the spirit of God . . . and therefore it is good that God alone have all the glory.' Once Drogheda fell, nearby towns such as Dundalk and Newry soon surrendered. By 1650 much of Ireland had been subdued, and perhaps as much as 15 per cent of the population killed or exiled. Anyone who had been involved in the anti-Protestant 1641 rebellion was executed, while thousands were transported to the Caribbean as slaves. No Catholics were allowed to live in towns and their land was confiscated. The religion was banned and its priests hounded. Cromwell returned to England triumphant.

A generation later, on 1 July 1690, the Battle of the Boyne took place at a fordable bend in the river, four miles west of Drogheda. On one side were forces loyal to the deposed British king, James II, forced out for his Catholic views. On the other was the army fighting for the Protestant cause led by William of Orange, James's nephew and son-in-law.

The two camps took their place on the banks of the river. James had made an alliance with Louis XIV of France and believed that he could make a decisive strike against William by winning here, but his army of mostly new recruits could not deal with William's forces, which were 10,000 men stronger. The deposed king rode off to Dublin to warn the city of William's arrival. He then left for

France, which he reached before the end of the month. William entered Dublin on 6 July and gave thanks for victory at Christ Church Cathedral. However, the Protestants managed to gain control only in the north-east, which Scottish raiders had earlier colonised and almost driven out Catholicism.

With Ireland as a whole remaining mostly Catholic, the Westminster Parliament took their revenge by continuing to clamp down on the religion. For instance, in 1719 the House ruled that all unregistered priests caught in Ireland were to be branded on the cheek with a red-hot iron. The privy council increased this to mutilation, but when the bill was sent back to Parliament for approval the original clause was restored. Fortunately – for the priests – it never became law.

The Battle of the Boyne was later commandeered by Protestant myth-makers, in particular the Orange Order, as iconic. They consider the waters of the Boyne holy and use them to make toasts. Memorials to the battle can be found dotted throughout Protestant Ulster. For instance in Ballywalter, Newtonards, a triumphal arch features in its central panel William of Orange on his white horse. Two side panels depict the red hand of Ulster on a white background, and the phrases NO SURRENDER and REMEMBER 1690. Above are two flags: the Union Jack and the Drumcree flag of crown, Orange sash and the words HOLY BIBLE. More prominent is the legend at the bottom: DRUMCREE . . . HERE WE STAND, WE CAN DO NO OTHER . . . CIVIL AND RELIGIOUS LIBERTY.

The Battle of the Boyne myth-makers tend to skirt over the complicated details: that the Pope backed William, not James, as part of his conflict with France, and that the papacy only later changed its policy to support James against William, by which time it was too late.

→ The Orange Order, p. 293

ST PETER, West Street

This late eighteenth-century Catholic church contains the shrine of St Oliver Plunkett, the last Catholic martyr to be executed in England, who was hanged, drawn and quartered in July 1681. Catholicism had been banned in Ireland following Oliver Cromwell's invasion of 1649–53 so Plunkett fled to Rome and in 1669 was appointed Archbishop of Armagh in exile. He returned to Ireland and set about restoring the Catholic Church, but when anti-Catholic feeling increased in 1673 Plunkett went into hiding. He was arrested in 1679, taken to Dublin Castle and eventually found guilty of high treason 'for promoting the Catholic faith'.

Dublin

ADAM AND EVE, Merchant's Quay

This Franciscan friary takes its unusual name from a nearby pub, called the Adam and Eve, where the Franciscans held Mass in secret in the seventeenth century, gaining entrance by posing as drinkers and speaking the password: 'I am going to the Adam and Eve.'

It was here that the Spanish priest-catcher John Garxia stayed in 1717 posing as a priest, all the while looking out for signs of what was then illegal papist activity. Priest-catching was a lucrative but reviled business. Those willing to take the risk of being the most unpopular person in town could net a handsome £50 for seizing a priest and the outlandish figure of £150 for capturing a bishop or archbishop. But there was a price to pay if rumbled, and it was common to see a mob several hundred strong tearing down the road in pursuit of the priest-catcher.

A series of anti-Catholic laws passed at Westminster were enacted to stamp out Catholicism in Ireland (unsuccessfully). A few priests were allowed to say Mass, but were not replaced when they died. Any unregistered priest who entered the country could face the death penalty. It took until 1829 for Catholic emancipation to be achieved.

ST PATRICK'S CATHEDRAL, St Patrick's Close

The largest church in the country belongs to the Church of Ireland rather than to the Roman Catholics, and its chancellor in the early seventeenth century was James Ussher. He was an indefatigable scholar who calculated the entire chronology of life on earth right back to Creation itself, which he set in the evening of 22 October 4004 BC. Ussher was a vociferous Protestant who backed efforts to make Guy Fawkes's Day – 5 November – a religious festival, and once declared that 'The religion of the Papists is superstitious and idolatrous, their faith and doctrine, erroneous and heretical; their Church, in respect of both apostatical.'

Knock

MARIAN SHRINE, Church of St John the Baptist

Fifteen people saw a vision of the Virgin Mary, St Joseph and St John the Evangelist at their parish church in Knock on 21 August 1879. First was Mary McLoughlin, housekeeper to the local archdeacon, who recalled that 'on passing by the chapel, at a little distance from it, I saw a wonderful number of strange figures or appearances at the gable; one like the Blessed Virgin Mary, and one like St Joseph; another a bishop; I saw an altar.' McLoughlin returned to the church with a friend half an hour later to lock up. They both saw the vision and went to fetch others. The witnesses stood in the rain for a couple of hours reciting the rosary.

For Catholic nationalists the apparition was a godsend, and they named the shrine 'Our Lady of Knock, Queen of Ireland' at the expense of Queen Victoria. Rome later declared the sightings to be trustworthy and the Pope, John Paul II, made a pilgrimage to Knock in 1979. He was followed by Mother Teresa in 1993. More than 1.5 million pilgrims now visit the shrine every year.

Nearby is Croagh Patrick, said to be Ireland's holy mountain, where St Patrick banished Ireland's snakes. Each year on the last Sunday in July (Reek Sunday) pilgrims climb Croagh Patrick, mostly barefoot.

Waterford

Ireland's oldest city vociferously participated in the rejoicing throughout much of Ireland that greeted the death of Elizabeth I in 1603, more on religious than personal grounds. In Waterford crowds prevented the authorities from proclaiming James as king – in Munster they chose the Habsburg archduchess, Isabella, queen, instead – and were sent into raptures by a sermon from the local vicar who likened the late queen to Jezebel from the Old Testament, whose body was thrown to the dogs.

But the people were urged to think again when Lord Mountjoy, Lord Deputy of Ireland, arrived with an army of 14,000 men to ratify James's accession. Locals cheekily sent along the same vicar who had insulted the late monarch to negotiate terms. The city surrendered on 3 May, its churches were quickly converted to Protestant chapels and their Catholic vestments, icons and crosses were removed. But the chapels stubbornly remained half-emty, and it wasn't long before the authorities had to resort to dragging people into them, such was the unpopularity of the new religion forced on the people of Ireland.

John Wesley, founder of Methodism, tried to reach Waterford in 1750, but the ferryman, fearful of the gathered mob, refused to land. Wesley returned two years later to preach but was drowned out by another noisy crowd. In 1763 he tried again. A preacher, Samuel Wood, later recorded the incident:

I shall never forget the feelings excited within me when I was hardly five years old, in April, 1773, when I saw that venerable servant of God, the Rev. John Wesley, shamefully treated by a rude and desperate mob while he was preaching in the Bowling Green, Waterford. I felt all my blood rushing into my face. I stood at the table upon which Mr. Wesley was standing; and while I heard the shouting of the crowd, and saw the dead animals and cabbage stalks flying around his hoary head, I was filled with pity and horror.

INDEX